FLYING INTO HELL

FLYING INTO HELL

THE BOMBER COMMAND OFFENSIVE
AS SEEN THROUGH THE EXPERIENCES
OF TWENTY CREWS

MEL ROLFE

GRUB STREET · LONDON

First published in hardback by
Grub Street
4 Rainham Close
London SW11 6SS

Copyright © 2001 Grub Street, London
Text copyright © Mel Rolfe

Copyright this edition © 2004

Reprinted 2004, 2005

British Library Cataloguing in Publication Data
Rolfe, Mel
  Flying into hell
  1. Great Britain. Royal Air Force, Bomber Command. 2. World
  War, 1939-1945. 3. World War. 1939-1945 – Aerial operations, British
  I. Title
  940.5´44941
ISBN 1 904010 89 X

Typeset by Pearl Graphics, Hemel Hempstead

Printed and bound in Great Britain by
Biddles Ltd, King's Lynn, Norfolk

DEDICATION

Flying Into Hell is dedicated to the aircrews who feature in this book, and the many thousands
of others who flew to hell in Bomber Command to save Britain from the tyranny of Hitler.
Those who came back to rebuild their lives were the lucky ones. Over 55,500 were killed.
This book is also dedicated to the ground crews, who worked hard, often in rain and freezing
conditions at dark dispersals, to keep the bombers in the air.

ACKNOWLEDGEMENTS

My grateful thanks go to the men who willingly gave their time to talk modestly and patiently
to me about their careers in Bomber Command, together with the following who all
contributed, in different ways, to my research: Reg Cleaver, the late Bernard Dolby, Bill
Dufty, Mike Ellis, the late Don Hanslow DFM, John Hoeg, Victor Jordan, Les King DFM,
Sheelagh and Roger Lewis, Fred Marsh, Christine Morris, Gerry Payne, Stephanie Roll, John
Slee, Charles Stansfield, Brian Wilson and the *Grantham Journal*.

Considerable thanks are due to my dear wife, Jessie, who has again stoically suffered my
mood changes as I have careered across the country talking to veteran aircrew, trying to
recapture how they lived so long ago. Without her support not an interview would have been
carried out, nor a single word written. By acting as my unpaid and uncomplaining sub-editor,
Jessie has kept me on course to the completion of another book.

CONTENTS

INTRODUCTION

The amazing resilience of the human spirit has never been displayed more strikingly or gallantly than by the men who flew with Bomber Command. Their aircraft were packed with high-explosive bombs, incendiaries, ammunition and thousands of gallons of high-octane fuel, all of which combined to convert them into flying coffins.

RAF fighters saw off Goering's Luftwaffe intruders during The Battle of Britain night after night between June 1940 and the early summer of 1941, but it was our bombers which packed the killer punch. Many of the men who fought and won the bomber war for Britain from September 1939 until May 1945 were little more than boys. Some, seeking adventure, had come straight from school and had known no other life. They all wanted to do their bit: to bomb to smithereens the brutal Nazis' gigantic war machine, making sure that Germany would never start another war.

CHAPTER ONE

FIELDS OF CONVENIENCE

Early in the Second World War there was no fixed length of time for a tour in Bomber Command. Newly-qualified aircrews arriving in high spirits at operational squadrons, soon realised they were expected to carry on flying either until the war ended, or they were dead. This was an unhealthy situation, not dissimilar to the Great War when young men were liberally used as cannon fodder, being urged from the trenches as inadequate battering rams against the shells of the German guns. Even so, aircrews were not too dismayed. They were young, believing themselves to be immortal. It was only the other fellows who would be killed.

Former bomber pilot Hedley Hazelden says: 'The open-ended tour obviously didn't encourage one a great deal, but we very soon got used to it. Although after leaving on my first trip and getting involved with the enemy guns, I thought it would be curtains for me and was rather surprised when I got back. By later experience it was not a tough op, but to me as a beginner it was.'

Twenty-five-year-old Hazelden was based at Waddington, flying twin-engine Hampdens with 44 Squadron, co-pilot to Sergeant Jimmy Kneil, a Devonian, when they were briefed to attack Antwerp on 17 September 1940.

Hazelden recalls that first sortie:

'There was a lot of gunfire, which I'd never seen before, and I made an error while going across the North Sea by laying off the wind the wrong way. I fortunately realised the mistake after about half-an-hour and was able to correct it, so we did make the target, but we must have done rather an odd track across the sea.

'Radar was in its infancy. We hadn't anything in the way of radar in the aircraft. Navigation was all dead reckoning. We had a magnetic compass, but no radio compass and none of the radio aids which became commonplace later on. I did all the navigating then, when we got to the target, I moved round to the bomb sight, advised the skipper how to steer on to it and, eventually, released the bombs.

'Navigation was very much a matter of what we called eye-balling, being able to see where you were going. Clear moonlit nights were our busy times. If you couldn't see you could probably navigate into the area of the target, using compass and calculations, for dead reckoning. But if the target was covered by cloud you might have to abort because you wouldn't know where you were dropping the bombs.

'We bombed the docks at Antwerp from 8,000ft and I was highly delighted when we got back. Coming under fire for the first time you have the feeling that anybody on the ground who pointed a gun into the air couldn't miss you. In fact, of course, he could, and most of the time he did. There's an awful lot of sky and we later realised it took a bit of doing to direct a gun to hit a moving aircraft.

'During my first tour few German fighters seemed to be in action. I saw one once when he took a shot at me, which missed, after crossing the Belgian coast on the way home from a raid.'

The Handley Page Hampden was known aptly as 'The Flying Suitcase'. It was cramped, uncomfortable and unheated. Maximum width in the fuselage was three feet, reducing to a few inches, room enough only for the crew to sit down. Fair-haired Hazelden, a broad powerfully-built six footer, weighing nearly fifteen stones, reached his position by crawling under the pilot's seat into the nose. He had a table on which he could spread his navigator's maps. There was also a machine gun which he could use if they were attacked. He did not lack jobs to keep himself occupied. The bomber also carried two gunners, one of whom had the additional responsibility of wireless operator. The rear gunner sat underneath in 'the tin', with a pair of Vickers gas-operated guns. The Hampden was powered by two 980hp Pegasus XVIII engines.

In 1940 bombers did not fly in streams: this came later. For now, they flew as individuals. Given details of the target and concentrations of flak to avoid, they worked out their route and took off, without the inconvenience of a set time to arrive over the target.

In the month after Antwerp their targets included Boulogne, Mannheim, Bordeaux, Lorient, Essen, and Berlin, from which they returned with engine trouble. On 16 October, still flying with Kneil, Sergeant Hazelden was in Hampden P2142 carrying four 500lb bombs to drop on an oil plant at Leuna, near Leipzig.

They found the target which they bombed and turned for home, running into bad weather across Holland and flying blind over the North Sea. They groped their way back to the vicinity of Waddington, using a low-frequency r/t. They had bearings which indicated they were roughly in line with the airfield, but did not know how far out they were. They twice tried to get down by a ZZ landing, being talked down by a ground radio operator, but were unable to see anything and pulled away each time.

Hazelden, who had moved back to a position on the spar behind the pilot, peered into the darkness as Kneil, flying on instruments, made a third approach.

He says: 'I was looking over his shoulder when I suddenly saw a flashing light ahead and above us. I hit Jimmy on the shoulder and cried: "Full power and climb!" Which he did, yelling: "What the bloody hell's that?" It was the

Waddington water tower which had a flashing beacon on top. We just cleared it.

'We called up control, which in those days virtually had no power over us other than to advise, but as we couldn't see to land they said the best thing was to go to Bircham Newton, which is north-east of King's Lynn. They hoped the weather was better there, but obviously hadn't spoken to them because when we called up Bircham Newton they said emphatically: "You can't land here, we've got fog. Go to Mildenhall." So we turned south. By now I was back in the nose, turning up maps to find exactly where Mildenhall was and giving Jimmy a course to steer to get there.

'Five minutes after setting our new course we suddenly flew out of cloud into clear moonlight. It was the first time we could clearly see the ground since we were over Germany. By this time we were nearly out of fuel. We'd been up for nine hours, which was about the limit for a Hampden. The port engine began spluttering and we appeared to have a little fire under it. The engine died and the fire went out, but it was clear we would not reach Mildenhall.

'Jimmy said: "What shall we do? Shall we bale out?" I'd moved behind him again.

"How high are we?"

'He said we were at 800ft, losing height, and I replied: "That's a bit low, can't you do a belly landing?"'

Kneil saw a field and aimed for it, throttling back on the fuel-starved starboard engine. The field came up to meet them rather rapidly. It was then they saw the only tree for miles around. The port wing smashed crunchingly into its top branches. The impact flipped them on to the starboard wing and they hit the deck with a frightful clatter at around 90mph. Desperately hanging on they hurtled along the ground on the aircraft's belly, leaped a water-filled twelve-foot dyke and creaked to a standstill in the middle of a field of sugar beet, near the village of Ramsey St Mary's. It was about 3am. They had been airborne 9hr 15min. No one was hurt and there was no fire.

The rear gunner's landing position was sitting on the floor of the wireless operator's compartment with his feet virtually dangling in the seat which he had just vacated. Seconds after Sergeant Thorne clambered out of his turret it was torn off when the Hampden struck the dyke. Thorne's legs hung outside the aircraft as he contemplated his lucky escape. Kneil and Hazelden got their breath and set off for help, leaving Thorne and wireless operator Sergeant Yates to look after the wreck.

The field was soaked with the previous night's heavy rain and it was slow hard work dragging through the muddy field. They set off towards a light in a distant cottage until reaching another dyke at the edge of the field. Neither fancied a cold swim so they walked beside it until finding somewhere to cross.

Hazelden recalls the moment they arrived at the cottage and stared up at the lighted upstairs window:

'We knocked at the door, but there was no answer, so we threw gravel up at the bedroom window. The window opened, a head popped out and we said we were RAF pilots who had crashed. Could he help us?

'In October 1940 the whole of Britain was expecting a German invasion and we turned up here in the middle of the night wearing flying gear. He was a member of the Local Defence Volunteers, the forerunner of the Home Guard, and seemed a bit nervous. The LDV had been hastily put together in local groups who were armed with pitchforks or whatever they could lay their hands on.

'He opened the front door and we could see he had pulled on his britches but was in his socks. He was also holding a museum piece of a gun, which looked like a small blunderbuss. He was terrified, obviously thinking we were Germans.

'I said: "If you think we're Germans you can't keep us here, we're your prisoners. You'll have to take us to the police." The penny was gradually dropping when I added: "Put your boots on and we'll walk in front and you tell us where to go."

'While he was pulling on his boots I reached down and drew a packet of Players out of the shin pocket of my flying suit. When he saw them he thought we must be English and relaxed a little. I gave him a cigarette and that was that. He left the gun behind and took us to the farmer's house where there was a telephone. We rang up Waddington which arranged for us to be picked up by transport from the nearest RAF base, Upwood, a training station near Huntingdon.'

The four men, who had not eaten since 3pm the previous day, were given breakfast in the sergeants' mess. It was here they encountered the station warrant officer, who was responsible for discipline. Immaculate, in crisply-pressed uniform, and gleaming black boots, clutching his swagger stick, he bore imperiously down upon them with an angry bellow of disbelief, babbling loudly about them being incorrectly dressed in the mess and threatening to kick them out.

Kneil said mildly: 'We have just crashed in a field nearby. We were brought here and only have the kit we are wearing. We've nothing else to change into.'

Exit an embarrassed SWO who was probably deeply offended by the impertinent intrusion of war which had led to so much indiscipline and sloppy behaviour among the lower ranks. Waddington sent an Anson to pick them up and carry on with the war.

Hazelden again: 'I flew Hampdens until the end of my first tour, having completed forty-three operations. It was around this time that they decided to limit the number of ops for a first tour. I suppose some men were breaking down with stress-related problems and it was realised you could not press people too far. I didn't feel stressed, I didn't know what the bloody word was, but if chaps did not feel like going on it was regarded as a lack of moral fibre.

'I very nearly, quite inadvertently, got accused of LMF in November 1940 when I had a bit of diarrhoea. I went to station sick quarters and asked for something to keep me going on that night's op. They kept me in overnight and it was obvious they thought I was going yellow. I'd just been given a new skipper and was questioned whether I didn't like him. As far as I was concerned he was quite capable, I had never given it a thought. But I had given it a thought that I didn't want to be shitting myself during the op. The incident was forgotten and the same month I was made captain. I was commissioned at the end of 1940.'

In December Hazelden became involved in a top-level plan to discover the heights at which German bombers came in over England during the Battle of Britain.

He says: 'Our defences needed more information about these raids. They had radar now which told them when the raid was coming. They could see the aircraft forming over the French coast and heading this way. Several squadrons in 5 Group, including Waddington, Scampton and Hemswell took part, all with Hampdens. An unladen Hampden could climb fairly high and had several hours' endurance. Bomber Command planned to have an aircraft on each 500ft level from about 15,000ft up to as far as we could go, which was around 22,000ft. We took off, got to our allotted altitude and circled over Oxford, which was roughly the centre of the country, because although we knew the raid was coming we did not know which target it was going to attack. The op was aborted because by the time they knew where the raid was, at Plymouth, we were too far away.

'On 11 December we climbed to 21,000ft in an aircraft which had been stripped down. The raid was on Birmingham where anti-aircraft guns had been silenced because we were there as well as the Germans. We patrolled over Birmingham and saw the Germans give the city a hell of a pasting. I saw sticks of German bombs going down and exploding, but there was nothing we could do about it. I had a shot at one aircraft and he fired back, but there was no damage to either of us.

'It was the highest I had been in a Hampden which was unheated and in December, bitterly cold. When I landed at Waddington I had frost-bitten fingers. I couldn't do anything with my hands. The doc who always met us when we landed took me out into the field. He rubbed my hands in the snow to thaw them out and I got away with it. Now, at eighty-five, I'm getting arthritis so, perhaps, I can blame that on him.'

On March 20 1941, Hazelden was skipper of Hampden X3137 which was sent on a gardening trip to St Nazaire. The mines were dropped satisfactorily but aircrews had been warned at Waddington that the weather might have deteriorated by their return. In fact it was an overheating starboard engine which persuaded Hazelden not to press on for Lincolnshire.

'On the way back we came over the airfield at Boscombe Down, the experimental station, where I was trained as a test pilot in 1943 and spent four years there. They had a special lighting system laid out on the grass field. It was a nice bright flare path, everything was all clear and I decided it was better to land there. Nobody would tell us not to. Besides, I didn't want to run into trouble with this misbehaving engine which might lead to a prang. I discovered later that these lights were a bit misleading. I had done around 560 flying hours, quite experienced for the time, but there was an awful lot I didn't know. Not having been to the airfield before I didn't know that it was shaped a bit like a saucer. The lights appeared as pools of light on top of a layer of ground mist, which was about seventy-feet thick. Viewed from circuit height at 2,000ft it all looked clear and level.

'I came in, made the approach, all of which seemed perfectly straightforward. I went over the lights, throttled back, held off and we stalled on top of the fog that made me think we were down. We went down and down and down, still going forward, but you've lost lift and virtually lost control. The idea of landing with a tail-wheel aircraft was that, assuming you could see what you were doing, you came in and held off, aiming to stall with the wheels as close to the ground as you could judge it. If you could arrange for the wheels to touch and the stall to occur, that's the perfect landing. But I had got the stall too soon because I had landed on top of the fog. Because of the saucer effect we were probably a lot closer to the ground at the beginning of the run, but as I went along the lights, thinking I was approaching the deck, the ground was getting lower and lower under the fog. The further you went the deeper it got. I thought I was doing the right thing until it happened.

'I reckon we dropped in from about fifty feet. It wrecked the aeroplane, shoving the undercart up through the wings. We slid forward and stopped. I used the radio to tell the station where we were, but it took them half-an-hour to find us because the fog was so thick. The only injury was to me: I'd bitten my lip which made shaving difficult for a while.'

Hazelden was brought up at Riverhead, near Sevenoaks, Kent. A bright boy, he matriculated at fourteen, worked as an insurance clerk for six years in the City of London, and began learning to fly at the end of 1938. He was known for his blunt speaking and intolerance of fools.

After his first tour Hazelden spent six months instructing on Hampdens at 14 Operational Training Unit, Cottesmore, where he had been trained. On 15 October 1941 he went to Finningley, Lincolnshire, for a conversion course on the Manchester, the twin-engine forerunner of the Lancaster. He was then posted to 83 Squadron at Scampton.

'The Manchesters were under powered,' says Hazelden. 'The Rolls-Royce Vulture engines were supposed to give them 1845hp, which they might have managed with a bit of a push, but it wasn't enough. We couldn't fly any higher in them fully loaded than the Hampdens, about 8,000 to 10,000ft.'

On the night of 8/9 April 1942 Flight Lieutenant Hazelden, recently married, flew to attack Hamburg in Manchester L7484. His co-pilot was Wing Commander Crighton-Biggie, who had been based at Air Ministry and was seeking operational experience before commanding a squadron. Crighton-Biggie's job was made a little difficult as the Manchester did not have a seat for a co-pilot and so he was mainly occupied with the duties of a flight engineer at the instrument panel which was mounted on the starboard side of the aircraft behind Hazelden. He had a long bench, known as the organ seat, on which he could move forward or aft to monitor the engine instrument panel.

They had dropped six 1,000lb bombs on Hamburg and were at 9,000ft over the Heligoland Bight when Hazelden, with a sense of relief, lit a cigarette.

He says: 'We used to have a cigarette in those days on the way home. While inhaling I looked over my shoulder and saw an instrument with its needle flicking about. I said: "What's that doing?"

'CB said: "I'm not sure, I've been watching it for three or four minutes. It's the rad temperature gauge."

'I could see the starboard engine by turning round. Its exhaust, which came over the top of the wing, was beginning to throw out sparks. "Christ!" I said, "that engine's catching fire."

'He looked out and said: "You're right."

'We decided the only thing to do was feather the propellor and stop the engine. There were two feathering buttons low on the dashboard which went right across in front of me. I had to reach across to my right to get to them. So they didn't get knocked inadvertently in the dark cockpit there was a cover over each button. Everything was done by feel. When a feathering button was pressed it held itself in as the hydraulics in the engine turned the blades to the fully-feathered position and the engine stopped.

'I reached across and felt what I thought was the cover over the port button, moved across to the next one and pressed it. I was looking over my shoulder all the time and watched the prop run down and stop. There was no sign of fire. Now, of course, I had asymmetric power so I had to do a little bit of trimming. The first thing I noticed was that it didn't seem to be much out of trim.'

Over the intercom, at the very moment Hazelden realised the bomber had become curiously quiet, came the hoarse voice of the wireless operator, Sergeant C. J. Taylor: 'Christ! They've both stopped.'

Hazelden remained calm. He had no reason to believe anything was wrong with the port engine and wondered why it had stopped.

He says: 'We were now acting like a glider and going downhill. The procedure for starting an engine was the reverse of feathering it, except that the button had to be held in manually until the engine starts to turn and pick up when you must release the button. But if you release it too soon the engine does not get sufficiently unfeathered to start controlling again. It just goes idling round at the speed where you let go the button. So you must press it again. Now when you press it a second time it feathers again. The danger of keeping your thumb on it too long is that you might go all the way through to fine pitch and overspeed the engine. That will break up the engine, so you must be a little circumspect when you let go. It took me three goes. I took my thumb off too soon on a couple of occasions and on the third time I kept it on a bit longer, got the power back on the port engine and trimmed out. We'd lost half our height, down to 4,500ft, heading back across the North Sea.

'There had been a chance that the engine would not restart. If that had happened we would have finished up in the drink, not a happy prospect. We might not have been dead when we got there but we would have been soon afterwards.

'It turned out it was my fault. CB had felt his way round from the other side of the aeroplane, touched the first button, knew it was the one for feathering the starboard engine and pressed it. I had inadvertently pressed the button to feather the port engine.

'Running parallel to the German coast at 4,000ft I broke radio silence. I thought if I was going into the drink somebody needs to know where I am, even if it's the Germans. I got a string of fixes from British airfields so we knew how we were progressing and they knew where we were if we went into the sea. So would the Germans, of course, but fortunately we didn't go in. It took a while to find the best speed to fly at to avoid losing height, and that turned out to be 137 knots.

'We didn't take the chance of going all the way to Scampton, landing instead at Horsham St Faith, which is now the civil airfield at Norwich. It was a good landing but when I endeavoured to turn round and taxi on to the perimeter track I got a wheel off the runway and we got bogged down. We were pulled out by a ground crew with a tractor. We had been in the air 5hr 20min, including 1hr 30 min on one engine.'

Due to engine unreliability Manchesters were withdrawn in the early summer of 1942 and converted into the Lancaster with four Rolls-Royce Merlin engines.

Hedley Hazelden's skill and reliability as a pilot was recognised with a Distinguished Flying Cross and Bar.

His last brush with death came after the war. On 30 August 1958, a test pilot with Handley Page, he was to demonstrate the merits of the Herald 44-seat airliner for photographers on the way to the Farnborough Air Show. Hazelden's deputy, Johnny Allam, was flying a Victor and the photographers were in a Hastings. Inside the Herald, which had twin turbo-prop Rolls-Royce RDA7 engines, were seven engineers, and Hazelden's wife, Esma.

Hazelden recalls: 'We did a series of pictures with the Herald close to the Hastings and the Victor on the outside. It was a bit difficult for the Victor to keep down to my speed, he wanted to go a lot faster. To change over I got out of the way while Johnny tucked himself in and I was prepared to go under him. It was then, flying at 6,500ft over Surrey, that my turbine flew apart and set the starboard engine on fire.

'I turned away so I didn't have to worry about what the others were doing. I'd still got the port engine which was working normally, but the fire on the starboard side soon caused considerable shaking and difficulty in controlling the aircraft.

'The first radio call I got was from the captain of the Hastings, asking me to get in position on the port side of the Victor. I said: "I'm on fire." That was all. Everything went quiet because there were a lot of aeroplanes on this frequency.

'Then Farnborough came on and said: "Choc Ice One. Farnborough. Check." They didn't know whether I had crashed or was still in contact.

'I called back in a very shaky voice because the aeroplane was beginning to shudder: "Farnborough. Choc Ice One. I'm crashing."

'Just after that the Herald rolled heavily to the starboard side and I thought this was where we were going to go in. I thought I was dead, but instinctively tried to pull the wing up. It came up and I was still in business. The field I had been looking at was now getting close and I could see what the difficulties were, but had no time to look for anywhere else.

'We passed over Eashing village, near Godalming, at 150ft with flames streaming out from the burning wing to fuselage length behind the aircraft. There were some electric cables on wooden poles running across the middle of the field. At the far end was a wood. It would be touch and go. I aimed to get as near to the poles as I could, where there was least sag in the wires. As I was on final approach I realised someone had left a bit of farm machinery in the way. So I had to move over to starboard and that took me over the top of an eighty-foot oak tree. I had to get over the oak then down and under the wires, a life or death situation. I succeeded, we landed and the aircraft slid to a standstill. No one was hurt. We all got out pretty quickly.'

CHAPTER TWO

ESCAPE OVER BERLIN

One month after the long war had ended, four young men met for the first time since their bomber had been shot down eighteen months before. Their emotions were mixed because they had escaped over the burning city of Berlin from an exploding Halifax in which their three crewmates died. They were still getting to grips with the unreality of peace at a time when it seemed impossible to detach their bruised minds from the grim actuality of war. It was not possible to measure the amount of luck needed for men to survive after their bomber had plunged earthwards, wreathed in flames, and blown up while their companions, a few feet away, were propelled into extinction during a shattering fraction of a second. How good luck favoured one man, having deserted another remains a shuddering mystery to all those who are left over fifty years later. Some men, of course, created their own luck.

The sun shone but a cool wind sneaked in from the North Sea as the men removed their caps and walked into St Barnabas' Church, at Linthorpe, Middlesbrough, where bomb aimer Flight Lieutenant Laurie Underwood was getting married. Underwood had enjoyed a run of good fortune on eleven operations which was threatened shortly before takeoff on the twelfth, by a startling premonition which, without doubt, saved his life.

The air bomber and his three companions, faintly surprised to be still alive, but longing to be absorbed quickly back into civvy street, had eagerly ditched the traditional stag night, taking their girlfriends to a dance at Coatham Hotel, Redcar. Underwood and Beryl Pooley, a chemist's assistant, had become engaged at a time when aircrews were being ruthlessly annihilated by German night fighters and flak. Many other young lovers were afraid of pledging themselves to each other during the war, but these two believed their engagement would act as another lucky charm to add to the bomb aimer's maroon and blue scarf, knitted for him by Beryl to wear on every trip.

The first hint that their immortality could not be guaranteed was brutally rammed home when the crew returned from leave to discover their skipper, Flying Officer 'Viv' Vivian, had been killed. Vivian had reported early to their new posting at 1663 HCU, Rufforth, Yorkshire, the day after his wedding, and was forced to fly as second dickey on an operation to Nuremburg which ended in disaster on the night of 10 August 1943.

Underwood, from Stockton-on-Tees, recalls: 'My crewmates and I flew with different pilots for several operational trips with 102 Squadron on Halifaxes from Pocklington. On some flights we all went together, but we often filled in individually for people who had been killed, gone sick, or were not flying again. Some aircrews preferred to be settled with a regular crew, but it didn't make life difficult for me. There was normally intercom silence when we were on a trip and each of us was an expert in our own field. You had your own job to do and it was not necessary to be all that close to the other guys on the aircraft.'

Navigator Flight Sergeant Reg Wilson was more critical of a system which left a crew headless, fair game to be scattered among the squadron after they had twice lost their pilot.

He says: 'We each flew as a spare bod with chaps we may not have met before. None of us knew how we would react to each other. There was no time to create the team spirit which was so essential when our lives were at stake.'

They flew several times with A Flight commander Squadron Leader Peter Harvey. Harvey, who had been with them at Rufforth as a flight lieutenant and was skipper on their first three bombing operations, was awarded a DFC later that year.

A slim friendly man, who had already completed a tour flying Wellingtons in the Middle East, Harvey had earned the early respect of his crew, but this wavered at the heavy conversion unit when their Halifax unexpectedly turned upside-down near Rufforth on fighter affiliation. It wavered even more on their first sortie which involved gardening – mine laying – in the Baltic on 2 October 1943. It was nearly dark when they took off at 6pm in Halifax II HX151 F-Freddie.

Pilot Officer Underwood had looked forward to being operational at last and says:

'We thought mining in the Baltic would be a doddle. None of us, including the skipper, anticipated any problems. I was lying on my stomach in the nose, well over the North Sea, watching out for the enemy coast when the pilot called me up on the intercom and asked me to take over the controls while he used the Elsen toilet at the back of the aircraft.'

There was a stunned silence as Underwood cautiously considered the question, wondering if it could be serious, while the rest of the crew thought: 'What the hell is going on?' They had not encountered this curious command during training. It could be equated to a senior surgeon asking a hospital filing clerk to take over during a critical stage of a delicate heart operation.

Underwood again: 'I told him I wasn't a failed pilot, as many bomb aimers were. I had never handled an aircraft, nor even sat at the controls. I said: "Are you sure?"'

Another pause while Harvey considered the priorities: whether he should empty his bladder before coming in sight of the enemy coast, or bottle it up for several hours, screwing up his concentration and risk wetting himself. On the whole the pilot preferred to keep his trousers dry and believed his bomb aimer who was, after all, a commissioned officer, a man of proven intelligence and ability, could surely be trusted to keep a Halifax pointing towards the target for a few minutes while he went for a piss. His blind faith in Underwood, who had not even driven a car, was flattering. The most complicated machine Underwood had been in sole charge of in his twenty-one years was a bicycle.

'Never mind, take over, bomb aimer, it'll only take me a minute,' Harvey said, emphatically, and Underwood climbed up to the cockpit as the pilot vacated his seat. Harvey flapped his hands vaguely at the controls and complicated banks of dimly-lit gauges and instruments and yelled: 'Hold it steady,' before abruptly vanishing into the dark interior of the fuselage.

The skipper's perfunctory attempt at compressing a pilot's course into five seconds not surprisingly drew a few sharp intakes of breath from all parts of the aircraft. The deepest and most incredulous sigh came from the aggrieved navigator, Reg Wilson, twenty, a meticulous and precise man, who always spent considerable time carefully preparing his flight plan and now saw his neat calculations being pissed carelessly into the Elsen. Harvey was an experienced pilot: why didn't the silly bugger have a slash before getting into the aircraft? He stared anxiously at his chart, which was illuminated by a feeble light, as a knot of worry took over his thoughts.

While the others were praying their skipper would not inflict a terrible injury on himself stumbling to and from the portable chemical bog in the dark, leaving them with a mine-packed Halifax and no one who could fly it, Underwood, unexpectedly promoted to second pilot, unpaid, was having fun.

'I wasn't nervous. I thought this was fine, I'm flying a bomber, wow! I held the control column, enjoying the experience. The navigator wasn't all that happy after a while and he had a little mumble about it as, not surprisingly, I was unable to keep the correct course, speed or height. We drifted off course at around 16,000ft and managed to lose the bomber stream. Quite soon we were alone in the sky and as the skipper returned after five minutes or so, he yelled his thanks, patted me on the shoulder and took over. He didn't seem at all disturbed. When I got back to my position I saw the Danish coast and a lot of German searchlights reaching up for us. There were no other bombers around for them to take an interest in. We went straight into their flak.'

A German gunner soon got their range. There was a mighty whooof! and the bomber recoiled like a dog kicked by an enraged bull as a shell smashed into the Halifax's belly, ripping off the H2S cupola beneath the aircraft and damaging the bomb doors. Harvey called up each member of the crew, asking: 'Are you okay?' Everyone was uninjured although the mid-upper gunner Sergeant Alex McCarroll's voice sounded taut and anxious. He was not hurt but a lump of flak had whizzed past, uncomfortably close to his chin, shattering the perspex turret. The navigator reported that they no longer had the benefit of H2S or Gee.

They flew on, out of the flak, crossing Denmark at 10,000ft to the Baltic, where they reduced height as the navigator, using direct reckoning, guided them to the map reference point they had been given at briefing, off the island of Samsö.

They were at 8,000ft over a German shipping lane east of Denmark when Underwood, believing the bomb doors had been opened, activated the bomb release triggers. Nothing happened. He tried again, but the two 1,500lb magnetic mines stubbornly remained aboard and he reported a ticklish situation to the pilot. It was clear the bomb doors had been damaged, but impossible to tell how seriously. Harvey tersely ordered them to be released manually so the mines could drop out but the bomb doors, although partly open, had been jammed by the German shell. The pilot turned for home with a furrowed brow and everyone had his own horrible vision of the released mines, great steel cylinders, packed with high explosives, squatting heavily on the bomb doors, waiting for an opportunity to blow them out of the sky.

Homeward bound Wilson, needing to use the Elsen, negotiated the dark fuselage with a torch, climbed over the main spar then nearly fell through a great hole in the floor on the other side. Unable to go any further, he urinated through it.

Tension mounted as they drew nearer to Pocklington and most wished they could skip the next few minutes and somehow be whisked off safely to the warm debriefing room. The hydraulics had gone; if they overshot the runway they would be unable to go round again. The Halifax slid uncomfortably towards the ground. They touched down at 12.52am. There was an awesome shriek as the deformed bomb doors flew open and a great thump as a mine hit the deck and lumbered after them along the runway. It did not explode. The Halifax taxied to dispersal, leaving the armourers the unenviable task of retrieving the mine.

As they climbed shakily from the aircraft the second mine, badly dented by flak, partly wrapped up in its parachute, could be seen trapped inside the bomb bay.

Alex McCarroll could not forget how close he came to death on that first sortie and never flew again. He was reduced in rank to lowly aircraftman and posted to Elvington eight miles away.

By 20 January 1944 there were only three of Vivian's original crew still flying together. One was Laurie Underwood. He had passed the exam to go to the local grammar school, but his parents could not afford the uniform. At fifteen he left secondary school to be a cost clerk with South Durham Iron and Steel Company in Stockton. Stockily built, standing an inch under six feet, he joined the RAF's accounting branch in May 1939, later remustering to aircrew. Rarely seen at Pocklington if the crew was not needed for flying, Underwood's fiancée lived at Middlesbrough and he spent all his spare time with her.

Reg Wilson, twenty, from Goodmayes, Essex, was commissioned on 1 December 1943, becoming a pilot officer. He had been a junior clerk with Unilever based at Blackfriars, London, before joining up.

Sergeant Johnny Bushell, the rear gunner, twenty, had worked in a small family newspaper shop with his mother and aunts in Bedford. He was a jolly chap with a hearty laugh. Turning turtle with Harvey near Rufforth was the catalyst that saved his life. Bushell says:

'My parachute was kept on a bracket just inside the fuselage, but if I needed to get out in a hurry I would never have got to it. After that trip I always carried the 'chute in the turret, tucked in behind my back.'

Wilson, also moved to think more seriously about survival, now put his parachute on over the target.

They flew two more sorties with Harvey and six others with four different pilots before teaming up on 29 December with Flying Officer George 'Grif' Griffiths who, like Harvey, had completed his first tour in the Middle East. Griffiths, who had been decorated with a DFM, was popular with his new crew who felt comfortable with him in the driver's seat.

On 20 January 1944, 102 Squadron sent sixteen Halifaxes to bomb Berlin. One was piloted by Griffiths. Underwood recalls the previous day when he had asked the bombing leader if anything was on that night:

'He said: "You can put your Middlesbrough suit on." So I hitch-hiked to York railway station and spent the night with Beryl dancing to Jack Marwood and his Band at the Maison de Danse in Stockton. I returned to Pocklington in the early hours of next morning to learn we were flying that night. After the briefing I had a premonition that I would not be coming back, at least not for some time.'

Sceptics believed there was little difference in premonitions and lucky charms, all of them being a load of bollocks. Premonitions however, were more difficult to fathom. A rabbit's foot or a scarf usually remained lucky only until the wearer was killed or badly injured. They could almost be equated to a child's security blanket for these young men were only grown-up children and while a few, at first, were more children than adults, those who survived the traumas of flying in Bomber Command often became older and wiser than their parents.

Premonitions were darker, more mysterious, briefly transporting some fliers into a strange world where their future was laid out like a book, which sometimes read like a horror story.

Underwood was superstitious, like many wartime aircrews, but he had never believed in premonitions until his head was bombarded by thoughts which seemed to have been carried to him by a supernatural force. Troubled, he sat down in the billet and wrote a letter to his fiancée.

'I said I'd had a premonition and wouldn't be coming back for a long time. It was not a serious letter, nor even one showing concern, just a matter of fact. I would be back eventually, not to worry and please would she wait for me? Obviously, I couldn't say where our target was. I thought about saying something to my crewmates, but knew that was not right. I also thought about shaking hands with the ground crew as we got on board and knew I couldn't do that either. I said nothing to anyone except to Beryl in her letter which I left with a chap who was not flying that night with the instructions for him to post it if I didn't come back.'

The premonition left him with an odd tingling feeling, as if he was the only man on the aircraft who was in possession of some privileged or hush-hush information. His decision to quietly clip on his parachute for the first time at the start of a bombing trip, saved his life. Often a man felt for his parachute when it was too late. Parachutes saved lives but they became clumsy contraptions when moving about and working inside the cramped aircraft.

With regulars Griffiths, Wilson, Underwood and Bushell was co-pilot Sergeant K. F. Stanbridge, twenty-two, who was flying as second dickey for experience. The wireless operator was twenty-four-year-old Flight Sergeant E. A. Church. Sergeant I. Bremner was flight engineer. They had a French Canadian in the mid-upper turret, Warrant Officer G. G. Dupueis, twenty-four, who was carrying his lucky rabbit's foot. Without telling any of them, the superstitious Dupueis had volunteered for a relatively safe thirteenth sortie, dropping leaflets, with another crew. This was his fourteenth op.

Griffiths lifted Halifax FLW337 into the darkening sky at 4.45pm and 102 Squadron's sixteen bombers began climbing for the rendezvous. A total 769 aircraft – 495 Lancasters, 264 Halifaxes and ten Mosquitoes – were despatched to Berlin. Thirty-five aircraft were lost, including five from 102 Squadron, which lost another two crashing in England. It was the squadron's most disastrous operation of the war. The following night the squadron lost four more in the first major raid on Magdeburg.

Their route took them over the top of the Zuider Zee to a point sixty miles north of Berlin when they turned south.

Underwood stretched out comfortably on his stomach in the nose and tried to relax even though he was virtually certain something unpleasant would happen. He remembered a previous raid on Berlin a few weeks before when the city was in flames as they arrived at 18,000ft. A few hundred yards away to starboard and a little ahead he had seen another Halifax coned. Searchlights had clamped on to the corkscrewing bomber but flak surged up until the bomber burst into flames. As it went spiralling down someone muttered: 'That poor bastard's bought it.' Some watched the doomed aircraft until it was a scorching pinprick of light and disappeared, carrying its crew to oblivion.

Tonight they ground steadily and untroubled straight and steady for the bombing run. Underwood thought he was a daft sod believing in premonitions and after cheerfully calling out: 'Bombs away, Skipper!' continuing over Berlin before turning for home, he was convinced it was all cobblers and imagined having a good laugh about it with Beryl.

Seconds later at exactly 8pm the aircraft was rocked by a tremendous explosion and the starboard outer engine burst into flames. The fire spread rapidly to the starboard inner, took hold of the fuselage and reached the port wing.

Underwood recalls the moment when premonition and fact came together like a great clash of cymbals and rolling of drums:

'Berlin was still burning below. The raid was still on above, the searchlights were busy and Grif, with the controls floppy in his hands, said: "Prepare to abandon". The escape hatch was in the nose near the navigator's work table. Reg stood up and quickly folded his table. He had his parachute on. He tried to open the hatch, but it jammed. Church, the wireless operator, joined Reg and I stamping on the hatch. It loosened and fell out. As flames streamed fiercely across the Halifax the pilot, who knew he was losing control, cried: "Abandon aircraft!"

'The drill was that the bomb aimer should follow the navigator out, followed by the wireless operator. Reg sat down, took off his helmet and oxygen mask, removed the intercom lead, and boof! he's out. I followed him into the cold sky'.

Time whether they lived or died was already ticking away and had been measured in milliseconds after the aircraft had been hit. Underwood slipped away, tucked up, with his hand on the D-ring, but passed out due to lack of oxygen before he finished counting to ten.

'When I came to I felt a hanging sensation and was terrified I was caught up on the burning aircraft. I looked up, saw my open parachute billowing above me and no sign of the Halifax. Berlin was burning below and bombs rained down. Anti-aircraft shells whooshed past and I saw tracer bullets hosepiping above. Despite all this deadly activity I was calmly and gently floating downwards, remembering I needed to break my fall by flexing my knees.

'I realised my premonition had come true and if everything else went according to plan I would be unharmed and would one day get safely home to Beryl.

'There was no need to flex my knees because I landed in a wood on the outskirts of Berlin. My 'chute enveloped a huge tree and I was held firmly twenty-five feet from the ground. Some 200 yards away on the edge of the wood was a German gun battery, which was too close for comfort, I could hear their guttural commands. I swung from side to side, grabbed a substantial branch, released my parachute which remained entangled above me and climbed down the tree trunk.'

When Underwood disappeared through the escape hatch Church edged forward to follow him. He was too late. The bomber suddenly fell out of the sky and he was pinned helplessly to the side of the fuselage by G-force, unable to drag himself a few inches to safety.

Bushell, his parachute clipped on, swung his turret round, slid open the doors and was met by a rush of air as he struggled to throw himself out backwards before an explosion sent him whirling into the sky.

He says: 'I hit the ground in seconds, landing in a park near a searchlight battery. I had heard of no airmen walking out of Berlin and was dead scared. I watched the searchlight, gathering courage to give myself up, watching the guards change. When I walked across I found they were all in my age group and shook hands with me. They gave me a meal and, later, a bed.'

Griffiths, trapped in his seat, thought his number was up. Before the aircraft started spiralling Stanbridge, the sprog pilot, passed the skipper his parachute.

Desperate to survive, but gripped in the jaws of G-force and unable to raise a finger to help himself, Griffiths watched the altimeter rapidly unwinding until it went through 7,000ft. He remembers nothing more until he regained consciousness outside the aircraft a few hundred feet above the ground. He had been blasted, like a human shell, through the disintegrating airframe of the exploding Halifax.

He says: 'We flew lower than the Lancasters and I believed at the time and for several years afterwards that one had dropped a bomb through my wing. Stanbridge saved my life because he handed me my parachute. Waking up in free fall, I reached up, pulled the ripcord, felt the canopy open and within a few seconds hit the ground.'

He landed safely, with the wreckage of his Halifax falling around him about seven miles south-east of the target. Any luck that was available had gone his way. Stanbridge, Church, Bremner and Dupueis were all killed.

The aircraft had not been 'bombed' by a Lancaster. The kill was claimed by Messerschmitt Bf-110 pilot Hauptmann Leopold Fellerer, holder of the Knight's Cross, who had shot down five British bombers that night and would notch up forty-one victims by the end of the war.

There were patches of snow on the ground as Underwood started walking. He says:

'I got out of Berlin and walked down a village street. A door opened and three drunken Germans started walking towards me. It seemed they expected me to say something. I flapped my hand and said: "Aagh!" in a loud exclamation of contempt and kept walking. They went in another direction. I avoided an armed guard under a bridge and walked all night. When it started to get light I climbed into the top of a barn, pulled hay over me, crashed out and slept the whole day. It was becoming dusk as I woke. Famished, I ate the chocolate from my emergency rations, setting off when it was dark. I saw a bicycle beside a house in a village and had my hands on it when a door opened and a German civilian came out. I can still remember the outraged expression on his face. I ran like hell and he soon gave up the chase.

'I had a compass and could read the stars. I was walking to Switzerland, which seemed a million miles away. I headed south beside an autobahn, seeing little traffic. A German Army lorry stopped, ostensibly to give me a lift. The driver spoke but I don't know what he said. He then exclaimed: "Ja, Engländer." He took out his revolver and motioned me to get into the cab.'

Underwood was put into a cell and given a bowl of turnip soup at an Army barracks. Three officers later took him to an underground shelter at Spandau where he was briefly reunited with Johnny Bushell who had a blood-stained bandage round his head.

While Wilson and Bushell ended up in Stalag IVb at Muhlberg,

Underwood and Griffiths were sent to Stalag Luft III, Sagan, where they were interrogated by senior RAF officers to make sure they were not German stooges. The prisoners here were working hard towards a mass escape. Each escape tunnel had been given a code name: Tom had been discovered before Underwood and Griffiths arrived. Dick was abandoned after the Germans cut down a wood to build another compound at the very spot where the tunnel was planned to emerge. The tunnel called Harry, now proceeding at full steam, was well organised.

Some 200 POWs acted as sentries throughout the camp, logging the whereabouts of every ferret – German guard – to avoid nasty surprises. Underwood, a lookout, positioned at the end of a washroom block, opened and closed a window to warn of ferrets approaching the camp theatre. A lot of soil from Harry was dumped in the undiscovered tunnel, Dick, the entrance of which was inside the theatre.

Underwood did not want to waste time as a prisoner and, helped by the Red Cross, he studied for the Royal Society of Arts book keeping and accountancy course. He took a supervised examination and got a first class pass. He also studied German.

A mass escape through Harry was fixed for the night of 24 March 1944. The plan to release 200 prisoners foundered when the tunnel – over 350ft long – ended short of the woods, and seventy-six escaped into the German countryside. Fifty were murdered by the Gestapo on direct orders of Adolf Hitler. Three got to England, the others were sent to prisons or concentration camps after what became known as The Great Escape.

George Griffiths was best man and Johnny Bushell and Reg Wilson were groomsmen at Underwood's wedding on 6 June 1945. They did not meet again until 20 January 1994, the fiftieth anniversary of their escape from the burning Halifax. With the three wives – Bushell had never married – at a Peterborough hotel, dinner was served at 8pm, the time the four men had been attacked over Berlin.

Griffiths rang his former bomb aimer every year after the war at 8pm on 20 January until he died in June 1998. He always said: 'Happy anniversary, Laurie, we've survived another year.'

CHAPTER THREE

WAITING TO LIVE OR DIE

The Blenheim fighter was a solitary speck crawling across an otherwise empty sky above the Essex countryside on a clear day in 1940. Weeks before the Battle of Britain, the twin-engine aircraft, based at North Weald, was on a training exercise. Crammed into it were the pilot, Sergeant John Jones and three observers, Sergeants Stan Hauxwell, Hester and Jarvis. The trip was routine, becoming dull, and nineteen-year-old Hauxwell, who since early childhood had dreamed of being a fighter pilot, thought it should be livened up.

He said: 'Come on, John, show us some aerobatics.'

Jones, a year older, who normally flew by the book, surprised them all by turning into a slow roll. As the Bristol Blenheim creaked on to its back a shower of accumulated muck from the floor: dirt, dried grass, bits of plywood marked 'instrument panel', and a redundant oxygen pipe, cascaded upon them. Obviously, this was a new experience for the aircraft. Hauxwell, from Harrogate, one of two men without a proper seat, clung grimly to the spar to avoid being propelled out of the top hatch. The fighter, still inverted, began screaming towards the ground. The cries of youthful exuberance turned into gabbles of horror when it was clear something was seriously wrong.

Hauxwell recalls: 'John must have forgotten that you pulled the stick back to climb, but only when you're the right way up. When you're upside-down the aircraft goes into a dive. We were going like the clappers, probably at nearly 300mph, towards the small island of West Mersea. I thought we should never have started this and could see John's white face. Suddenly there was a scream from the back: "Christ! The tail's coming off." The aircraft was shuddering and John twice eased the pull out from the dive to stop the vibration, but we didn't come out of it until we were 100ft off the ground.'

This was the closest the four frightened youngsters would ever get to dropping in as casual visitors to West Mersea and even Hauxwell's relish for excitement had taken a severe battering. As the airframe and the crew stopped shaking and they turned sedately towards North Weald he noticed a pasteboard notice beside him which made interesting reading: 'This aircraft has a cracked stern frame. For God's sake treat it gently.' It was signed by Squadron Leader J. R. Hallings-Pott, commanding officer of 25 Squadron. Hauxwell waited until they had landed before quietly conveying this unsettling information to the pilot.

Back in 1940 Hauxwell, and Jones, of Boroughbridge, Yorkshire, saw a long dark sinister cigar shape creeping down the Thames Estuary, looking very much like an uninvited U-boat. Unable to raise their sector controller on the duff r/t neither knowing what to do, they watched the submarine surface and roared down behind it with the pilot's thumb on the firing button. A microsecond away from sinking their first U-boat it sent the colours of the day soaring skywards and hasty signals were flashed from Aldis lamps. It was British.

Their duties, which mainly involved escorting daylight convoys through the North Sea, did not always go according to plan. Once Hauxwell and pilot Sergeant Dickie Smith were disturbed by a terrifying shriek as the starboard propellor ripped itself off, spun through the air and disappeared. It landed in the back garden of an Essex semi, later to be reported exclusively by the *Daily Mirror* as a secret German weapon, with a picture of a perplexed housewife, her washing on a line stretched across the lawn, and the Blenheim prop embedded deeply into the ground.

Hauxwell, a slim 5ft 9in, with penetrating brown eyes, hair as black as wet coal, and a handsome twirling moustache, had been designing model fighter aircraft from the age of twelve. His plans focused only on becoming a fighter pilot. When he joined the RAF in April 1939, after training as a civil engineer, he had been told no more fighter pilots were needed at that time, but if he trained as an observer he could go later on a pilots' course. His faith in the integrity of the RAF was later shot to pieces when, at the end of his tour in Fighter Command, he and several other observers from North Weald, were suddenly drafted into bombers. It was the last thing he wanted.

Sent to 12 Operational Training Unit, Benson, Oxfordshire, his luck later picked up. On 22 July 1940 his name was crossed off the authorisation book because he was collecting a telegram from the sergeants' mess, and checking his reconnaissance photographs at the armoury when a detail was called for a cross-country training flight. The Fairey Battle he should have been flying in struck high-tension cables near North Stoke, hit the ground and blew up. There were no survivors. Hauxwell numbly followed his commanding officer's advice to go into Wallingford that night and get drunk.

That September, stationed at 10 OTU Abingdon, Oxfordshire, flying Whitleys, his RAF career was rudely interrupted when the steering went at 70mph on his Singer Le Mans. The sports car did a clumsy somersault, two inelegant rolls and slid like a manic vegetable slicer along the road on its side with him trapped underneath. He sustained a fractured skull, internal injuries and three compound fractures of the right arm, and was in hospital until the end of the year before being moved into a convalescent home. He returned impatiently to Abingdon and was dismayed to discover he had been posted absent without leave. Paper pushing did not reach an art form in the wartime RAF.

In April 1942 Hauxwell, sometimes known as 'Hawkeye', joined 78 Squadron, which flew from Croft, near Darlington, having just converted to Halifaxes from Whitleys. Two months later the squadron moved to Middleton St George, and would soon be commanded by Wing Commander Willie Tait.

Hauxwell recalls the gifted bomber pilot, who in two years would be in charge of 617 Squadron:

'He was slim, taller than me, with dark straight hair, brushed back. He walked on his toes like a spring-heeled jack. A tough disciplinarian, if anyone fell down on the job the roof caved in. He once decided that as there were no ops on we could go for a cross-country run. You can imagine how popular this was among chaps who rarely stirred from a settee in the mess. He led us out of the camp and as we struggled down a lane we met our gallant leader sitting on the grass verge. He grinned and said: "Press on, chaps, I'm knackered."

'I had always flown as second pilot on takeoff and landing, but he didn't need me. He said: "No, you get back behind the main spar with the rest." Willie reckoned he didn't need a crew and could fly the aeroplane by himself and that is probably true.'

Hauxwell flew most often with Flight Sergeant John McCalla Tait, a twenty-one-year-old Irishman, who was not related to the CO, nor did he share his flying skills. The youngster, who was known variously as Mick or Harry, intended returning to Queen's University, Belfast, after the war as a medical student. He was not the best pilot in the world, having once set his compass for north instead of south after setting off to bomb the Channel ports, but he was an affable companion. A short man, no more than 5ft 3in, he always raised his seat to its highest position before taking off, propped up by a fat cushion which was whipped away by Hauxwell as soon as they left the ground and the seat was immediately lowered. Hauxwell says:

'Mick looked out during takeoff, at other times he was happy to drop down and stay there, concentrating on his instruments. He never liked looking out. We were once heading towards the Baltic when there was a terrible rattling on the port side of the fuselage. Fred Lemon, the flight engineer, and I leaped to Mick's side, looked out and yelled to him: "Freeze! Keep straight ahead, hold it steady." We'd been struck by the trailing aerial of a Lancaster that went over us so close we could see the filth and mud splashes on its bomb doors.'

Hauxwell was perched on top of a Halifax at Middleton St George in the summer of 1942, cleaning the astrodome ready for ops that night when he heard men shouting. 'Pull out! pull out!' He looked up at the port side of a diving Halifax which had collided with a little Oxford trainer. The bomber smashed a great hole in the ground just outside the perimeter, near a farmhouse. In the rear turret the four Brownings, which had melted in the great heat, looked like bananas. Both crews were killed.

Mick Tait once brought a 4,000lb Cookie back trapped in the buckled rear bomb doors. They did not know it was there. The entire station and the surrounding countryside would have known if they had had a rough landing.

When Mick Tait developed glandular fever in August his crew flew as odd bods with other pilots, but he was back in February 1943 when they were briefed one night to drop two 1,500lb mines off the Frisians, a long chain of islands in the North Sea, which stretch along the coasts of Holland, Germany and Denmark. They were now based at Linton-on-Ouse, Yorkshire.

Pilot Officer Ray Keen, a Tynesider, was wireless operator. Their bomb aimer was former school teacher Sergeant Johnny Johnston, from Vancouver, Canada. Quietly-spoken Sergeant Fred Lemon, an ex-groundcrew fitter was flight engineer. Sergeant Dickie Huleatt, the rear gunner, from Liverpool, was, at twenty, the baby of the crew. He was blond with blue eyes and topped six feet.

Although Sergeant Andrew Wilson was officially the mid-upper gunner, he did not have any guns. The nose and upper turrets had been removed to help boost the Halifax Mk II's poor performance. Wilson's position was an uncomfortable one, lying prone in the rear fuselage looking through a perspex blister in the floor to warn of night fighters. The blister was removed when H2S was fitted.

Wilson, twenty-six, of Paisley, had a secret which he shared with few people. Not wanting his wife, Gert, to worry about him when he was away from home Wilson had not told her he was flying in operational bombers. She believed he had a safe job on the ground. The young couple had a six-month-old son, Brian.

They headed north at around 6,000ft, slipping down as they roared up the North Sea, turning to starboard until they were at 100ft drawing close to the Frisians. Hauxwell remembers the night well:

'You knew the state of the tide and where the tide line should be on the island. We had to go low across the island turn round and come back out again. It was a timed run on a certain heading from the tide line. You count the seconds, press the bomb tit and the mines drop in position into the sea. It should have been as simple as that, but not this night. After turning into the island searchlights came up at us from both sides and light flak started.

'None of us was brave but when the action started we got angry not scared. Mick had been taught to get under light flak so we went down and hammered across that island at around thirty feet. The mines were still aboard and there were up to six guns firing at us. There was an enormous bang when a cannon shell smashed in where the front turret would have been. The nose turrets had been taken out of our Halifaxes and the shell burst through the alloy skin, the original fairing, blowing me against the steps. Part of it ripped open the top of my helmet. Mick's hand was scratched and Johnny was unhurt down in the nose after being hit by bits of shrapnel. My Gee set was wrecked and the nose cap of the shell disappeared into the back of the instrument panel. The de-icer tank was pierced and I was drenched by the Glycol mixture, which ran down my face.

'When we were out of range of the guns we dropped the mines smartish. We didn't know where they'd gone. We'd been told at briefing that they were top secret and we were a bit worried, hoping they'd gone into the drink and would not fall into enemy hands. The big problem was: what do we do now? We had to turn round and realised there was no way we could get home without going into enemy territory. We would be asking for it at this height, going into Holland. There was only one thing to do.

'We swallowed hard, got some height, stuck the nose down, piled on the speed and went back to cross the island. The searchlights came on and the flak started, but they were lousy shots. I remember, as clear as day, seeing the German gunners desperately trying to traverse their guns. I was standing beside Mick as he turned and went down at them, he was bloody angry. We were saved by the searchlights, illuminating the sea.

'I shouted: "Mick! Christ, the sea! Pull up!" He pulled back on the stick. All aircraft squash and aircraft like the Halifax squash more than most. The nose will come up, but the rest will keep going down before it finally rises. He got the nose up just in time, but we squashed. You are squashing down on the air. The back end, very low, was still going down. Suddenly there was a hell of a bang and for the first time in my life I knew I was going to die.

'I did not experience fear as the bomb doors struck the sea, just an immense feeling of regret. No one would know what had happened.'

The big bomber bounced and hung dripping, a few inches above the icy sea. The pilot feverishly delivered every scrap of power available to the four bellowing engines which clawed desperately at the air.

Hauxwell again: 'Nobody said anything. I just stood there and listened. "Woh! woh! woh! woh!" The four Merlins were still churning away. "Vroom! vroom!" Slowly, we began climbing. I said: "Thank God for that," and we disappeared into the darkness. Everything was running okay. If the nose had been down there would have been the most ginormous crash. Nobody would have survived that. We might have had people killed by the flak. That didn't happen either. We were incredibly lucky.'

The pilot, breathing easier, sinking more deeply into his seat, said: 'Where the hell are we?'

Hauxwell returned to his devastated position. His precious instruments had all gone and the de-icing fluid had melted the paint on the chart table. The chart, stuck fast, had become part of the table. The gyrocompass had died, but Hauxwell gave Tait a heading, and kept his fingers crossed. The Halifax ploughed alone through the night at 2,000ft and Hauxwell, at the pilot's side, kept the Pole star on the starboard wingtip. The reprieved crew were in lighter mood but their navigator was torn by doubts and when, some time later, he saw searchlights on the port beam and flak going up he thought: 'God, what have I done?'

'I thought we'd gone into Germany and run into a raid on the Ruhr. I said nothing. Everybody was happy and I'd made this terrible mistake. Then I saw a reflection on water ahead, the penny dropped and Johnny, the bomb aimer, called out in the nose: "Stan, it's Flamborough Head, dead ahead".

'You'll never know what relief that was. It was Hull we could see getting a pasting. We roared over Flamborough Head and Johnny said: "There's a flashing pundit ahead".

'I said: "What's it flashing?"

'He said: "Driffield."

'I said: "Fine, just as I expected." Lucky devil. Then there was Linton, blinking away. It was a sheer fluke, nothing else. Back at base the ground crew found seaweed trapped in the bomb doors.'

Getting towards the end of his tour Hauxwell's request to be transferred to a Mosquito squadron was turned down. Instead, he was elated to know he could go on a pilot's course.

On 25 March Hauxwell went to Canadian pilot Ed Spencer's end-of-tour party in the sergeants' mess. Hauxwell was enjoying himself until he caught his hand on a broken chair and drove a long splinter into his thumb. This had the spoilsport effect of immediately sobering him up. He got to bed around midnight, joining the others next morning for a lecture from a PFF officer about bombing flares. They were told not to bomb the first TIs, but wait until the others went down to make sure they were on the target.

Hauxwell was still suffering from the amount of booze he had taken on board the previous night and decided to clear his head by walking round the perimeter of the misty airfield. He got back for lunch and was told there had been a Tannoy message for him. Then he learned there was an op that night, forgot about the message, and no one bothered to seek him out again.

Months later he learned the message was to tell him he was being commissioned and was to go on immediate leave. Without Hauxwell Mick Tait would have been assigned a spare navigator, if one was available. If not, the crew would have been stood down that night.

Instead of returning home to Harrogate, bursting with news about his commission, Hauxwell was with the others in the briefing room, learning their target for that night was Duisburg.

This was the navigator's fifth visit to Duisburg, an industrial city and river port standing near the junction of the Rhine and Ruhr. It marked the end of his first tour.

They took off in Halifax W-7931 J-Jig. There was a second dickey that night, Sergeant James Wilson, a twenty-one-year-old New Zealander, from Auckland. He was no relation to the mid-upper gunner.

Hauxwell says: 'Duisburg was a relatively short trip and there was around 14,000ft of solid cloud over Germany. We were bombing on sky markers and there shouldn't have been an enemy fighter leaving the ground that night. It was the fighters we were scared of, they were much worse than the flak. We never thought much about that except when we were coned and that was a nasty experience.

'We made the first turning point over Holland. The damned Gee wasn't working and I got the flight engineer to take star shots for me. We went a bit off track, but were going along quite nicely. We saw the flares going down over Duisburg and remembered what had been said that morning.'

The shuddering bang came before they turned on to the bombing run and after the Halifax lurched miserably the flight engineer reported, anxiously: 'Number four's gone, Skipper.'

Hauxwell remembers thinking: 'That's no bloody loss because the generator driving the Gee set was on number four and that hasn't worked all night. We can press on with three.'

Then he looked out at the starboard wing and realised the outer engine had literally gone, dropping out while ripping away at least fifteen feet of the starboard wing.

The wing remaining was in flames and the news got worse as engineer Fred Lemon snapped: 'Christ, the inner's gone as well.'

Hauxwell recalls the terrifying seconds as the grim reality of the situation struck them all.

'I was beside the skipper and yelled: "Mick, can you do anything? Anything?" I'd flung my helmet down and grabbed the big red handle of the jettison toggle on the starboard side of the dashboard. We had to get rid of the bloody bombs. Mick had full left rudder on and the wheel hard over as far as it could go, full aileron, in an attempt to bring the starboard wing up. I'd have propped the wing up myself if I could have got out there to it. Christ! My last trip, they couldn't do this to me.

'Mick flung his hand down to me in despair and cried: "It's no good, Stan, I can't hold her, I can't hold her. Get out! get out!"

'I didn't jettison the bombs, it was time to leave. I yelled at the second pilot to bale out, but he stood there immobile. I had no time to bugger about with him. This was last ditch stuff. Whether he was hanging on to help Mick I shall never know.

'I shot down the steps quicker than a rat through a pipe, flung the nav table up and everything with it to get to the escape hatch. Then I behaved like a prat. Being service minded you always follow the instructions which were: pull the hatch out then throw it through the hole. Why can't you leave it in the fuselage? It's not doing any harm. Who cares? The sodding plane's on its way down. But no, I have to throw it out and the bloody thing catches and jams in the hole. It wouldn't move, so I jumped on it. Luckily I was hanging on to something as I did because my feet went out, the rest of me nearly followed and I had no parachute pack on.

'We were at around 19,000ft and starting to roll. Ray was sitting at the hatch thinking about it. Time was short and I had to kick him out. I followed and Johnny came straight after me.'

Fred Lemon dropped out of the rear escape hatch where the gunners, Dickie Huleatt, and Andrew Wilson, had awaited their turn.

Huleatt yelled: 'Come on, get out! get out, Wilson.'

Wilson stood back for the crew's baby. 'No, you go.' The young rear gunner jumped through the hatch into the swirling clouds.

Hauxwell heard the Halifax hit the deck at 10pm before he landed near the village of Doetinchem.

'I heard the whoomph, saw flames and it was all over. I learned later that three had died: Mick Tait and the two Wilsons. Mick and James were found in the wreckage on the borders of the villages of Gaanderen and Pinnedijk, near Varsseveld in eastern Holland. Andrew Wilson, the gunner, had landed some distance away, with the silk of his opened parachute strewn around his body. I believe Andrew either jumped too late or his 'chute was faulty.

'Mick had actually got the aircraft the right way up when it went in, he was damned unlucky. He might almost have got away with it. They went into a field close to a farm but hit some buildings. If they'd missed the farm buildings a wood was waiting just ahead.'

Mick Tait knew his crew were leaving one by one. When he thought they had all gone he would think of saving himself, but perhaps a problem developed in the cockpit. Tait was probably helped by James Wilson, the second pilot, to get the Halifax level and they would have had a flash of hope when they blundered out of the cloud below 3,000ft and peered through the murk for a makeshift landing strip. If they hit a field just right they might live to fly again.

Hauxwell again: 'We told our story at interrogation when we got home, but no one took any notice. The least they could have done was award a posthumous decoration to Mick who sacrificed his life by staying at the controls to let us get out.

'The most tragic thing of all came in a letter from Mick's mother to my mother after we'd been shot down. Mick's father was a ship's captain in the Merchant Navy. A fortnight after Mick was killed his father's ship went down in the Atlantic. A tragic waste and Mick was an only child.'

Ray Keen broke his ankle when landing and was picked up by Germans who took him to the crash site where he saw the gouged-out trail which led to the smouldering wreckage of the bomber and the rubble of the outbuildings. Keen knew the two 1,000lb bombs still aboard had been fitted with delayed action fuses. He did not want to tell the Germans, but was worried one might go off and take him with it. Hauxwell heard one bomb explode as he was walking through the fields. The other went off the following morning.

After trudging through heavy rain Hauxwell lay up in a wood. The weather became so filthy he decided to move by day.

He says: 'It was not a good idea. I had removed all identification from my clothes but people picking potatoes in a field knew I was from a bomber crew and wished me good luck. I got to a village where an old man spoke English well, having spent time in America. The villagers sent me to a farm where they fed me. The farmer's wife was English.

'The sun was shining when I left and a man came up to me on a bicycle, saying he was the Mayor of Doetinchem. He told me I had been seen by a Nazi sympathiser leaving the farm. He said: "If you return to the farm, give yourself up and let them hand you over to the Germans they'll be all right. Otherwise they will be shot".

'There were children on that farm, I couldn't go on. I went back to the farm and they contacted the Dutch police, great guys. In the police chief's private quarters his son played the Dutch and British national anthems on the piano, an emotional experience. They passed me on to the Germans at the last possible moment.'

The raid on Duisburg was a failure. Bomber Command's report on the attack says five of the nine Mosquito markers returned early and the Germans sent up decoy flares. Searchlights were unable to penetrate the 10/10ths cloud but were used to illuminate the cloud base, possibly to assist night fighters.

Stan Hauxwell, who was gazetted by the RAF as a pilot officer shot down, believed killed, in action, discovered at Dulag Luft, the German's interrogation centre near Frankfurt, that the enemy knew rather more about him than he expected. He was startled when his interrogator, Major Brandt, mentioned the road accident in which he had been badly injured, and asked if his broken arm had healed satisfactorily. Brandt, who spoke perfect English, also knew of wireless operator Ray Keen's skirmish with death earlier in the war after his Anson had crashed. Keen, with several broken bones, spent an uncomfortable night with his crew on a Welsh mountainside. It was Brandt who told Hauxwell that three of his crewmates had been killed.

Hauxwell, held in several POW camps, was frequently thrown into the cooler for stealing German property to help make conditions more comfortable in his hut.

One morning in 1944, Hauxwell's laager officer, former paratrooper Leutnant Cuiser, a pleasant young man, told the navigator in an unusually grim tone of voice: 'Mr Hauxwell, you are accused of sabotage, sedition and destruction of Reich property and are to be court-martialled.'

The news stunned Hauxwell until the German snapped to attention and said, smiling: 'Sir, I apologise; my little joke. You are now my superior officer. We have heard, via the Red Cross, that your promotion to flight lieutenant has come through. You are now Hauptmann Hauxwell.'

CHAPTER FOUR

BACK FROM THE DEAD

Ron Emeny returned to a French village exactly three years after being shot down and was shown the site of his grave. The former gunner and his ex-WAAF wife, Jessie, were taken in the sunshine to an enormous grape vine which was growing against the end wall of a small farmhouse. Luce Carminac, veteran of the Maquis, pointed cheerfully at the foot of the great gnarled bole of the ancient vine and said:

'That is where we planned to bury you. The British would have received your identity disc after the war.' The little man smiled, eyes twinkling. 'But you did not die.'

That day Emeny also met people who had helped him in May 1944 after he had baled out of a blazing Lancaster. The terrible burns to his face were examined by a doctor who believed the gunner did not have long to live. He was left to die alone in the graveyard of La Selle sur la Bied.

In the spring of 1944 Sergeant 'Curly' Emeny, from Bow, London, who had been an apprentice motor-cycle engineer, was based with 207 Squadron at Spilsby, Lincolnshire. He was twenty, tall, stick-thin, weighing no more than nine stones, but bursting with life. In company with most young men flying in Bomber Command, he considered himself indestructible, with no plans to be lowered into an early grave.

His skipper was Flight Sergeant Les 'Lizzie' Lissette, a tough powerfully-built man, from Napier, New Zealand, where he had been a teamster with four horses hauling logs out of the mountains. When Emeny joined the crew at Castle Donnington, twenty-six-year-old Lissette picked up the skinny gunner's three kitbags and suitcase at the sergeants' mess and trotted off to their billet as if they were no more than loaves of bread.

Emeny, recalling the pilot, says:

'Lizzie was quiet, very deep and a thinker. He never did anything without thinking about it. He was calm, nothing ever threw him. He joined the Royal New Zealand Air Force as an engine fitter, then wanted to become aircrew and go overseas. He was a great all-round bloke, a good skipper. He had an old grocer's bicycle with a sturdy metal basket over the front wheel. Before we went flying, he piled parachutes and kit into it and rode out to dispersal.

His girlfriend was a nurse on a hospital ship which was bombed off Crete. I believe she was lost but he never said a lot about it.'

Flight Sergeant Jack Pittwood, from Warley, Birmingham, the grammar school-educated navigator, was a tall streak of nineteen, who was never more relaxed and cheerful than during a long night on a winning streak playing poker in the mess.

Wireless operator Sergeant Phil King, eighteen, whose home was near New Street railway station, Birmingham, had trained to be a printer in his father's business before joining the RAF. Quiet, unassuming, he wrote every day to his girlfriend, Mavis, who he married after the war.

Sergeant Laurie Wesley was much admired by his crewmates for his ability to shave swiftly every day, using a cut-throat razor, without losing blood. Emeny once watched, awed, at Wesley wielding the wicked razor on a speeding swaying train. Perhaps the practised sensitivity of his fingers had something to do with the accuracy of his bomb aiming. From West Bromwich, he had worked in management for the Midland Red Bus Company.

Ex-boy apprentice Sergeant Nick Stockford, twenty, from Chipping Norton, Oxfordshire, was an engine fitter at a training school in South Africa before a call went out for flight engineers, and he remustered.

Sergeant Ron Ellis, the twenty-six-year-old rear gunner, was a boy apprentice engine fitter before the war. He turned to gunnery before heavy bombers needed flight engineers, a job which would have been more suitable for him. From Doncaster, he was married to Kathleen. They had a daughter, also Kathleen.

Spilsby airfield, home to 207 Squadron from September 1943, stood on 630 acres in the fens less than five miles from the North Sea, quite handy for sending aircraft to bomb Germany, but it was vulnerable to attacks by intruding enemy fighters. In winter Spilsby was bleak, the flat land swept by howling winds with frozen teeth which made the war seem even more cruel and relentless.

On 3 May eighteen Lancaster crews of 207 Squadron were briefed to attack a German military camp which was near the village of Mailly-le-Camp in south-east France. The total force sent that bright moonlit night was 346 Lancasters and sixteen Mosquitoes.

At the Spilsby briefing crews were told their target was two German Panzer divisions which had returned wearily from Russia to be refitted. They were to bomb from 8,000ft, for accuracy, to hit tanks and buildings. Opposition was expected to be fierce.

Lissette was at the controls of Lancaster ND556 which lifted off from Spilsby with a 4,000lb Cookie and eight 500lb high-explosive bombs. An early minor calamity sent a tremor rippling through the nose after Wesley lost a can of orange juice through the flare 'chute.

Ron Emeny, in his mid-upper turret, saw several of the forty-two Lancasters lost that night go down in flames as they droned across France which was thick with darting German fighters. Over the target the carefully-planned raid turned into a shambles after the Marker Leader, Wing Commander Leonard Cheshire, ordered the Main Force in to bomb. The Main Force Controller, Wing Commander L. C. Deane, could not relay Cheshire's instructions because his transmitter had been incorrectly tuned and his VHF radio set was being drowned by an American forces broadcast.

Lissette was among hundreds of Lancasters who were left helplessly orbiting a yellow spot flare to the north of the target, near Châlons-sur-Marne, for several minutes while many were picked off by German fighters, like wildfowlers firing at tethered ducks. When the markers had sorted out the confusion the raid was surprisingly accurate. The damage was extensive, 218 German soldiers were killed and 156 injured, 102 vehicles, including thirty-seven tanks destroyed and many buildings hit.

Emeny recalls the night that turned sour:

'Some of us bombed at 5,000ft because when, at last, we were called in everybody made a dive for the target. It was like the Charge of the Light Brigade to get in and out quickly. We received slight hits by flak on the bombing run and felt the blast from our own Cookie when it hit the target area.

'Our rear gunner, Ron Ellis, spotted a Junkers-88 dead astern and the skipper did a banking search to starboard. I saw a Focke-Wulf-190 sitting about 500ft below us, gave orders to corkscrew and we escaped. Resuming course Ron reported another FW-190 coming in from the starboard quarter and we began to corkscrew starboard. As we went down there was a terrific explosion and the port outer engine burst into flames. The wing panels between the engine and the fuselage blew off with another explosion and I could see down through the wing to the ground below where the target was in flames. Next the dinghy came half out of its stowage in the starboard wing, started to inflate then ripped itself loose and flew out into space like a giant hoop-la ring past the tail fin. All this time we were taking evasive action and the skipper cried: "Prepare to abandon aircraft."

'The rear gunner was in a bad way because the failure of the port outer meant his turret was unserviceable and the hand rotation had been shot away. The engineer used the extinguishers, and the bomb aimer reported the flames in the engine were out. The engine was feathered and we continued on our way home.

'Soon afterwards I saw a fighter coming in from the starboard quarter and again gave orders to corkscrew. I returned fire from my turret and the fighter broke off the attack.'

Enemy fighters poured ecstatically across the sky snapping hungrily at the retreating bombers. A tremendous burst of cannon fire ripped into the belly of Lissette's Lancaster. One shell tore through the perspex of Emeny's turret. The navigator reported that bullets had come through the floor and hammered into his chart table, and the wireless operator said shells had smashed into the radio equipment.

They were still heading west when Ellis yelled: 'Corkscrew port!' and as they went down the Lancaster shuddered from another burst of fire in the tail and the rear gunner cried: 'I've had it!' as Emeny got the fighter in his sights and it broke away.

As Emeny fired his Brownings he felt a tremendous heat surging around his legs and yelled at the wireless operator to check the fuselage. King bellowed: 'The whole arse end's on fire.'

Lissette calmly replied: 'Bale out! bale out!' It was about 11.45pm.

'As I was getting ready to leave the turret,' says Emeny, 'I saw an FW-190 closing in on the port quarter, about fifty yards away. It was not firing at us, but I gave him a short burst and saw my tracers strike between the cockpit and wing root. The fighter pulled up sharply and as he stalled I gave him another burst in his belly and he fell out of the stall and went straight down.'

Emeny climbed down from his turret into a fearful mass of flames. The gunner's long-term future was made even more problematical when he discovered his parachute had disappeared from its clip on the side of the fuselage. Probably thrown off by repeated corkscrewing. He plunged into the funnel of fire, heading aft. His hair and eyebrows were burned off in seconds and as he pressed onwards he could feel the flames eating into the right-hand side of his face and ear.

He says: 'The aircraft was being thrown all over the bloody place. I suppose Lizzie was having a job keeping it under control. My progress was slow because of the flames and being flung around. By the step down at the bomb bay the two round perspex inspection windows were broken and flames were coming through like blow torches. I found my parachute by the rear door and put it on. Then I saw the rear gunner waving to me. On the floor was a dead man's handle to operate if the turret is immobilised, but that works on hydraulics from the engines and was u/s. I began crawling towards him through the flames, but he waved me away. I couldn't see his parachute. I don't know if he'd been hurt, but I think he knew that he'd had it.

'I plugged into the intercom at the rear door and said: "I'm going." Lizzie replied brusquely: "Hurry up! sod off!" I opened the door and took my helmet off. All I could see were flames leaping yards beyond the door. The aircraft began going down more steeply. I gulped, jumped, and believe I went clear over the tail plane. As I did so the aircraft lurched and went into a steeper dive. It was enveloped in flames and I saw it hit the ground with a terrible explosion and I was left thinking: "What the bloody hell am I doing here?"'

Emeny had felt little discomfort from his burns until his face hit the cold air when pain struck like a lashing whip and the burned flesh around his eyes sealed them shut after he glimpsed two other parachutes spinning from the burning aircraft. His parachute canopy had caught fire, letting him down more quickly than was advisable and shortly before he hit the ground hard he heard the wireless operator, Phil King, shouting his name.

King set off alone, while the navigator, Jack Pittwood, stayed with the badly-burned gunner, whose tattered clothes looked as if they had been stolen from a Guy Fawkes, rescued from a bonfire. They stuffed their parachutes up the chimney breast in the ruins of a house and began walking.

Pittwood told Emeny the port wing had broken off after he jumped out and the Lancaster had gone straight down, curtains for Lizzie Lissette and Ron Ellis. Pittwood also watched Emeny land and said a shower of sparks went up when he hit the ground.

They had landed in a field near Montargis, south of Paris and walked several miles before hiding in the hayloft of a small farm. The farmer gave them bread and wine but Emeny, his lips burned, was unable to eat. That night, with Emeny's face turning septic, they set off to find a doctor. They walked until daybreak, reaching the village of La Selle sur le Bied. Emeny, reeling in agony from his burns, could go no further. In the churchyard they found a family burial chamber which was like a tiny windowless stone house. They crept inside. Emeny was now delirious, wanting only to escape the excruciating pain that bludgeoned every other thought and desire from his head.

He says: 'I curled up inside on the floor. I could only see when I used my fingers to prise open the swollen flesh around my eyes. I wanted to scratch my face but, of course, I couldn't. It got to the stage when I was banging my head against the side of the wall and shouting. I made a lot of noise and told Jack to bugger off, but he wouldn't leave me.

'Allotments stretched beyond the wall around the graveyard. At 6am, when I was sounding off, an old man and his wife were digging their patch. They fetched their son, Bernard Biguet, a member of the local Maquis. Then Dr Trouveney came with a schoolteacher, a young woman in her middle twenties, who spoke good English.'

Emeny was now slipping in and out of consciousness as the doctor and teacher exchanged anxious glances.

'They left me lying in the crypt all day. That night I heard the teacher cry out in astonishment: "Mon Dieu, he's still alive".

'They carried me through the village and put us in a comfortable barn. We were given food but all I could eat were raw eggs sucked out of the shells. Dr Trouveney gave me an injection and dressed my wounds and we slept until midnight when we were wakened and told the Germans were coming. Arrangements had been made for me to be taken to a doctor who lived twelve kilometres away. Dr Robert Salmon, a specialist from a big Paris hospital had taken over his late father's practice in Chateau Renard. He knew about burns. Jack was taken to a safe house by the Maquis.'

Three villainous-looking young Frenchmen arrived with Emeny's transport: a bicycle. The gunner was lifted on to the saddle and his feet were guided to the pedals. Barely conscious, his eyes tightly shut, he was encouraged to pedal slowly into the night. One man stood at his side, keeping him upright. Another was behind, pushing. The third patrolled a few yards in front, watching for Germans. Progress was laborious. The remnants of Emeny's energy rapidly drained away as pain clawed through his face. He felt as if he had been dropped, from a great height into the most diabolical nightmare.

He was taken to the back of Dr Salmon's big house, which was also called

Chateau Renard. The doctor, a leading member of the Maquis, gently bathed his eyes and got one eye open. The doctor could not speak English but his sixteen-year-old daughter, Alliette, spoke it well. She told Emeny they had sent a message to London through the Resistance, for medication. The gunner was cleaned up and given soup. His burned battledress and flying boots were destroyed and he received a fresh set of clothes.

Next day a package was delivered to the house. Containing sulphanilamide, it had been dropped by a Special Duties Flight Lysander, flown by Flight Lieutenant Martin Verity.

Emeny remembers, shuddering, that first treatment:

'Sulphanilamide is effective, but its application is excruciating. I was taken to the surgery at the back and held down on a couch as the doctor dusted sulphanilamide powder all over my face. I have never known such terrible agony. It was as if my face was being torn open. They held my arms behind me so I couldn't touch my face and until my yells subsided after five or ten minutes. Then they gave me a glass of Cognac. That happened once a day for five days.

'My burns ranged from first degree: my nose and right ear, through to third degree: my eyelids and the rest of my face. The burns came down to my right shoulder. The left side of my face was not so bad. I had been saved by the clothes I had been wearing, the mae west and my helmet. Eventually a crust formed over the wounds and the sulphanilamide didn't penetrate.'

To say that Dr Salmon and his family's lives were in perpetual danger from being discovered by the Germans is an extraordinarily frivolous understatement. The right side of their ten-bedroom house had been commandeered by the Germans for their officers' mess. Eight officers shared the house with the Salmons and Emeny, who lived in the east wing.

Emeny says: 'Upstairs my bedroom was next to a bathroom. The bedroom immediately on the other side of the bathroom was the German commandant's. We used the same bathroom, but Alliette told the gunner not to use it between 10pm and 7am. She said: "You must understand you must keep to the times because my father does not want a confrontation in his bathroom".'

Emeny watched the Germans through the venetian blinds in his bedroom.

'The soldiers of occupation were a scruffy lot. They had the arse out of their trousers, patches on their clothes. The commandant, short, tubbyish, was an engineering officer in charge of the local garrison. Every night when the curfew started I heard the German patrol stop outside and the NCO in charge stamped inside for his orders from the commandant. I heard them talking. When I was in the Salmons' living room having a meal, after coming down the back stairs, the commandant was twelve feet away in a room across the passage. If I'd been found the doctor, his wife, Genevieve, and Alliette, would have been executed. The doctor carried on his normal duties, which included going to farms. This was marvellous for the Resistance because he carried messages and information everywhere.

'One day there was a kerfuffle in the street. A local man was shot and left lying there. The doctor brought him into the surgery and did what he could, but the man died.'

After Dr Salmon received a message that the Germans were planning to search the village Emeny was taken on the back of a motorbike to Churilles, where the Maquis were hiding at an abandoned railway station. The gunner was plunged into further drama after the group received a supply drop from a Halifax. Six containers were carried to the church and hidden under flagstones beside ancient coffins.

It was Norbert Carminac's sixteenth birthday, the day his father had said he could join the Maquis. Norbert, brother of Luce, was left alone in the church, proudly entrusted with his first job, sweeping away any evidence of the unusual burial.

The Germans, responding to a tip-off, raided the church and shot Norbert dead. The boy's father, who lived opposite the church, rushed out with a gun and killed a German officer and a sergeant in their car. The rest of the Maquis swooped into the village on bicycles and started a fierce gun fight. Twenty men died, eleven of them Germans.

Emeny was spirited away from Churilles and handed over at Montargis to Etienne, a boy of sixteen, who took him by rail to Paris.

Emeny again: 'Etienne could speak good English. I had no identity cards and was done up in bandages. My story was that I was a Frenchman injured in an RAF raid. I had some pain-killing tablets and sulphanilamide powder.'

At the station Etienne said: 'There is a blonde lady outside. She will have two bicycles. You go to the lady and she will say: "Can you ride a bicycle?" You will say: "Yes." And she will take you.'

Virginia D'Albert-Lake, a pretty Amerian woman in her forties, and Emeny cycled across Paris, round the Arc de Triomphe, to Maison la Fitte. There was little traffic in Paris, apart from the odd German kubelwagon. They were not stopped.

The woman said: 'I have another man hiding in my house from London, you must know him.'

'I probably do,' said Emeny kindly, not adding that there were many thousands of Londoners serving in the British forces.

He says: 'We got to her place and a voice suddenly said: "Hello, Ron." And I replied: "Hello, Len." Len Barnes, a pilot at 630 Squadron, East Kirkby, had lived five doors away from me in Bow, we had been in the same class at school. He said if I'd been there a couple of days earlier I would have met Reg Lewis, a navigator, based with the Special Duties Flight at Tempsford. Reg had also been in our class. He'd gone down the Cometé escape line.'

Given identity documents, travel permits and railway tickets they met Michou, real name Micheline Dumon, the young woman who would help get them out of France.

The Germans had been closing in on Michou and Monique Tommi, another guide from the Cometé, and both women were escaping to England with Emeny and Barnes.

On 2 June Michou led them on to a train heading south. Most seats were occupied by Germans. Emeny and his companions stood in the corridor for the twelve-hour journey. By now they had been joined by three American pilots: Lieutenant-Colonel Eugene 'Speedie' Hubbard, former Eagle Squadron pilot Major Don Willis, and Lieutenant Jack Cornett.

Emeny says: 'We got into a little local train which was going to Cibour, a village at the foot of the Pyrenees mountains. It stopped everywhere. I was in the corridor and two German soldiers came out of a compartment and asked me in bad French for a light for their cigarettes. I said I didn't smoke but they'd had a few drinks and started nudging and pushing me. When the train stopped in a station I thought: "Soddit!" and got off to avoid any trouble. I saw Len inside wondering what the hell I was doing. I could see the Pyrenees in the distance and the railway track ran parallel to the road. I started walking.

'On the outskirts of town an old boy was digging his garden. He looked at me and said: "Monsieur!" I stopped. He said: "Soldat?" I said: "Non." He said: "Aviateur?" I said: "Oui." He said: "I served with the Tommies in the First War. You do not walk like a Frenchman, you march like a soldier. A minute".

'He went into the house and came out with a black beret. He put it on my head, pulled it down, put my hands in my pockets and gave me a packet of Gauloise cigarettes. He said: "Now you look like a Frenchman".

'I carried on walking until two blokes came towards me on bikes. One was also pushing another bike. It was for me. We cycled into Cibour and met the others sitting at a table drinking coffee.

'Next day we cycled over a bridge, guarded by German soldiers, up into the foothills of the Pyrenees, to a little Basque house. I've never seen anything like it. The animals were in the house. There was a byre in the corner with a cow and a donkey, and chickens and ducks pecking at the dirt floor. We slept upstairs in a loft full of straw, picking fleas and bugs off ourselves all night. Next morning they gave us some really rough clothes and Basque spadules, rope-soled sandals, which are made for climbing. Our guide was Florentino Giorchi, a big fellow, a professional smuggler. We walked for two days then Florentino left to get food. He never came back. We decided to carry on.'

On the third night they sheltered in sheep pens from a torrential downpour. Basque shepherds took them into their house and gave the travellers a pint of curdled milk to share. There were two men, two women, three children and little food. One man disappeared, returning later to talk animatedly with the second Basque.

The American major, who spoke Spanish, said: "We've got to get out of here. This fellow has sold us out to the Germans and they're coming to pick us up tomorrow". We left quickly. They tried to stop us and Len had to thump one of the Basques.'

They got lost on the mountain before spotting the town of Pamplona far below. They also saw a man sitting on a rock with a big hand of bananas and a skin of wine, both of which he handed over without speaking. He was Raymond, son of Florentino, who was in hospital after being shot in the leg by the Germans.

The little group were put into a town hotel but soon afterwards the men were wrenched out by a Spanish Army officer and put in prison where they joined another six escapees in a small cell, its floor covered in rancid straw, with a small malodorous corner cleared for a toilet, and bugs on the walls waiting for night when they would drop down to enjoy the taste of human flesh.

Next morning, news of the D-Day landings and the advancing Allies, led to the group being moved back into a hotel by engratiating Spaniards. Driven to Madrid, the Americans went their own way, leaving Emeny and Barnes to meet the British Consul, Sir Samuel Hoare, a former British foreign secretary.

Hoare glowered at the two airmen across his desk and said, darkly: 'I'll be glad when you people stop coming over the French-Spanish border. Every time I go to a social function the German ambassador gets on to me about it.'

Emeny passed on Hoare's good wishes for Britain's war effort when he was interrogated in London by Airey Neave at the Grand Central Hotel, Marylebone.

The gunner learned later that his navigator, Jack Pittwood, and flight engineer, Nick Stockford, escaped to England through Portugal and Spain. Stockford died from pleurisy a week after getting home. Wireless operator Phil King was hidden in France until the liberation. Bomb aimer Laurie Wesley was caught, incarcerated in Buchenwald concentration camp and released at the end of the war.

Emeny's parachute was retrieved from its hiding place by Lucien Tripot, one of the men who helped him on his agonising bicycle ride to Dr Salmon's house. Tripot had the 'chute redesigned as a wedding dress. It was worn, in front of the Germans, by his bride, Paulette, on their wedding day, 29 September 1944. The dress now hangs in a museum at Caen.

Ron Emeny's disfigured ear and nose were rebuilt by the New Zealand pioneering plastic surgeon, Archie McIndoe, at East Grinstead Hospital. Emeny's mind took longer to heal. His dreams often focused on his desperate struggles in the burning Lancaster. After enduring nights of her son thrashing about in bed, tearing sheets, the only way Emeny's mother could get him to settle was by putting a single mattress into the bath, where he slept until returning to his squadron.

CHAPTER FIVE

BOMBS STOP PLAY

Air-raid sirens began howling as John Mathews hurried from the railway station clutching his bag of cricket gear. Without breaking step he glanced irritably at the empty blue sky, avoiding the people who were obediently filing into shelters. Already late for the start of the match he saw no point in wasting any more time. The bloody Germans had no good reason to drop bombs here.

Mathews, nineteen, had been picked for a Sussex side to contest a match at the county ground in Hove. His brother, Tom, a medical student, and their father, Kenneth, a capable all-rounder, were also playing. They had all been looking forward to a good afternoon's cricket.

Mathews heard the menacing rumble of an aircraft as he approached the ground and, while passing quickly through the turnstiles, the ground was shaken by four convulsive thuds. The bomber passed out of sight as Mathews ran anxiously on to the playing area.

Over sixty years later he recalls the scene from that hot summer of 1940:

'There were four great craters in the pitch from bombs which had not exploded. My father had been batting and with the other players had, of course, ignored the sirens and carried on with the match. Dad had strolled over to square leg as the bombs were falling. Tom, who had been waiting to bat, ran to help families whose homes had been bombed nearby. The other players had scattered. No one was hurt and the game was reluctantly abandoned.'

Not everyone agreed the match should be halted. The aristocratic Cecil Somerset, who lived in a castle at Goring, demanded, loudly and huffily, that the ground staff should fill in the craters so they could continue the game that day, defying the bloody Huns. Somerset was gently persuaded that playing cricket over four deeply-embedded unexploded bombs might present both teams with a few difficulties.

Even so, spectators and players alike were appalled to think the hated Germans were so brutal and small-minded they would bomb an English cricket ground on such a fine summer's day. Cricket was a game which did not normally succumb easily to mild inconveniences like war and the wanton damage to the Hove square would long remain in their minds.

John Mathews' Uncle Bunny, a civil engineer, and owner of a company which made precast concrete, wanted all his apprentices, including his nephew, to become sappers on the outbreak of war on 3 September 1939. Charles 'Bunny' Mathews had made his fortune by building scores of pillboxes in France during the First World War. During the second conflict, his firm made precast concrete units which would be floated from the south of England across the Channel, on the day after D-day, to help create the two huge Mulberry Harbours off the Normandy beaches. But John Mathews wanted to join the RAF.

Felsted-educated Mathews, a very fit youngster from Worthing, who played many sports to a high standard, rejected the Army and Royal Navy to join the Brylcreem boys in September 1940 because he wanted to wear a tie. He wanted to be smart.

'It was,' he says, 'part of my upbringing. My mother always made certain that we had washed our hands and we were never allowed to come into a meal without a tie on.'

Rejected as a pilot because he was too heavy-handed, Mathews trained as an observer in Rivers, Manitoba.

Mathews' skipper was Sergeant Vic Saunders, a diminutive but athletic man, whose home, in Shoreham, Sussex, was not far from his observer's. Saunders had joined the RAF straight from Shoreham Grammar School. His parents ran a lorry drivers' cafe in the town.

Flying Vickers Wellington IIIs, they were based with 57 Squadron at Methwold, Norfolk, a satellite of nearby Feltwell.

Saunders' wireless operator, Johnny Hitchen, was later admitted to hospital and replaced by Sergeant 'Parky' Parkinson. Bomb aimer and front gunner, Sergeant Norman Wilding, tall and dark haired, joined his skipper and Mathews when they went to a pub on free evenings. Wilding's wife lived at Tangmere.

The rear gunner was Pilot Officer Punchard, known variously as Dreamy or Punch by his crewmates. Mathews, a sergeant, regarded the gunner's rank with disapproval, for although the observer's public school accent suggested he was a likely candidate to join the privileged young gentlemen in the officers' mess, he was firmly against aircrews being commissioned and said so loudly, often in high places. Mathews regularly played tennis with officers, including the commanding officers of Methwold and Feltwell and they did not escape his occasional outbursts against what he believed to be the unwarranted and foolish elevation of very young men, leap-frogging chaps who had been in the service for years.

Punchard's crewmates seldom saw their rear gunner who preferred the banter of his companions in the mess. They thought Punchard an aloof individual, who had a curious sense of humour which could embarrass them and startle the debriefing officers after they had returned from a sortie.

Mathews says: 'We were annoyed because our stories were true. An awful lot were made up at debriefing. Even our head man, Bomber Harris, said one of the troubles with aircrew was that they had only just left home or school and did not yet know how to live the life and tell the right sort of stories without exaggerating. Punch was unique, but a bit of a joke. He told them we had seen airships and barrage balloons over Germany. Eventually, we and the intelligence officers would enjoy a laugh about that, and I would join in by saying we had seen ten airships that night.'

Crews were fiercely loyal to each other, a laudable trait, but it sometimes invoked the wrath of higher authority. When Vic Saunders was ill, languishing in station sick quarters, his crew, told they had been given another pilot that night, refused to fly with him.

Mathews again: 'Our flight commander, Squadron Leader Laird, a regular and a fearful snob, who I never liked, called me aside, knowing I was probably the ringleader. He said, grimly: "You know this is utter disobedience, Mathews?"

'I said: "Well, you'd better take me out and shoot me."

'After a long wait the squadron commander, Wing Commander Peter-Smith, called me in to his office. He said: "What's all this about? Why aren't you flying with this chap?"

'I said: "I would sooner not tell you, Sir, but I do think you ought to take my word and the rest of the crew's word that we do not want to fly with this pilot."

'I didn't tell the wingco this but the pilot we objected to was a Geordie whose father was a Methodist priest in Newcastle. The pilot, a sergeant, was a man of God and we had heard from people who had flown with him that during the most dangerous parts of the flight, when he should have taken evasive action, he never did. He always told his crew: "God will look after us." Well, nobody was going to believe that. If they were attacked by a fighter he kept going straight and level. He would not corkscrew because God was on their side. I did not fancy flying with a pilot who did not look after his crew.

Perhaps God was on the side of the Germans when they later shot down the God-fearing pilot and his unfortunate crew.'

Peter-Smith told Mathews: 'Very well, if you feel you can't tell me about your objections would you and your crew fly with me?'

'My face must have lit up,' says Mathews, and I told him. "Fly with you, Sir? Marvellous." Not only was Peter-Smith a good commander, and fine pilot, he was a real up-and-attem type of chap who always aimed to inflict the maximum amount of damage on the enemy. He refused to return to the station with any ammunition remaining aboard the aircraft. We bombed Bremen that night with several other crews from 57 Squadron. On the return leg the skipper was looking around to pick a likely target for the gunners and, eventually, we nipped down to ground level and shot up a German railway station. We could see a train waiting there. We didn't have a spare bullet when we landed at Methwold, but our little diversion was not mentioned during debriefing.

'We heard later that Peter-Smith had said of us: "There's nothing wrong with that crew, they're a grand bunch of chaps".

'Sadly, Peter-Smith was shot down and killed in the summer of 1942, flying with another crew. It was a daylight raid in cloud. Our instructions had been that if we came out of cloud we should return home. That's what happened. We came out of cloud, about forty miles from the target. Vic immediately saw three fighters coming straight at us and he did a stall turn to port pretty quickly and dived back into the cloud. We went home, hugging the cloud, carrying our bombs. Nobody knows what happened to Peter-Smith. Knowing him he probably refused to come back early and went down to drop his bombs.'

Mathews retains fragments of powerful and troubling memories which can still make his stomach lurch as his mind drifts back to 1942. Once, when they were returning happily at 8,000ft over the Dutch coast after bombing the Ruhr Valley, a night fighter leaped out of the darkness to spray cannon shells into the Wellington's undefended belly.

'Because we did not know any better we had been flying straight and level. We were hit all over but amazingly none of us were hurt. A few seconds before we were attacked I had walked up to the pilot's position to look out. I was there when I saw the German's tracer passing under us. It's odd how one's life can be saved by nothing more than an idle whim. A shell had torn through my position. If I'd been in my seat I might have been badly injured or killed.

'After we were attacked Vic yelled: "I'm going down!" He put the nose down, hoping to escape the fighter. The engines were at maximum revs and Johnny Hitchen, the wireless operator and I, looked at each other. Thinking we were going to die, wondering how long we'd got, we instinctively reached out to each other and held hands. Just that. A silent goodbye. Religion came in and we sort of thought God would look after us.'

Then as the two Bristol Hercules engines stopped screaming, the pilot said, in a strained breaking voice, which was a curious mixture of elation, surprise and tearfulness: 'I've pulled out, thank God.'

The nose came up a few feet above sea level. They had lost the fighter. Life suddenly seemed wonderful and Hitchen and Mathews sheepishly released each other's perspiring hands and returned thankfully to their tasks.

The controls had not been damaged but the fabric which covered the Wimpy's geodetic skeleton of thin steel was hanging in tatters and had to be replaced and the aircraft was unavailable for flying next day.

After a night of kitty pontoon in the mess they were dragged out of bed at 5am on the morning of 27 August 1942. They trudged from the billet for an early breakfast before picking up F-Freddy for an air test before a daylight raid. The raid was cancelled and they either tried to catch up on their disturbed sleep or went for an early lunch. That afternoon they were briefed to attack Kassel.

Saunders carried a second pilot on this operation. He was probably the most experienced pilot on the squadron, having flown on thirty-seven sorties, two more than Mathews. This would be the end of their tour and it seemed sensible that sprog pilot Pilot Officer D. J. Gill should fly with him for experience.

'I hardly knew him,' says Mathews. 'He was standing most of the time in the astrodome. Vic asked him to be another pair of eyes.

'We were driven to the aircraft in a truck by a WAAF called Ginger. She was our lucky charm. Ginger haired, of course, she was tubby and cuddly, big bosomed and a charming smile. She didn't cuddle me before we took off but I think a lot of chaps would have liked to hug her before climbing into the Wellington. Ginger was beloved by us all. She took us to the flights and to Feltwell where we received our instructions for the day. She drove us back to the squadron where we prepared for the journey, waiting to take us to the mess for our meal. She was always waiting patiently for us deep into the night, if and when we returned. Ginger had a tragic end, killed later in the war when an aircraft went into her truck.'

It was an odd feeling for Saunders and Mathews taking off, knowing this would be their last sortie. Thinking ahead to a second tour was unrealistic, his war was conducted a day at a time, but Mathews swiftly ran through his mind what Vic Saunders had told him of a recent chat with the new squadron commander, Wing Commander E. J. Laine.

Laine had asked: 'What do you want to do? And what plans do your crew have after you all come back off leave?'

Saunders had replied: 'Whatever my crew want to do, I'd like to go with them, Sir.'

The suggested alternatives were the crew splitting up to go instructing, joining the Pathfinders, or Saunders and Mathews going as a team with the Photographic Reconnaissance Unit on Mosquitoes.

Matthew recalls the discussion he had with his pilot:

'I didn't really want to go instructing. Nor was I ready to risk my life again with Pathfinders. I wasn't particularly worried about it but thought I'd done enough for a bit. I liked the idea of PRU. It involved going out the day after a raid, taking photographs and bringing back weather reports. We decided to join the PRU. I was quite looking forward to it.

Freddy was among 306 aircraft grinding through the sky towards Kassel that night when German fighters took a heavy toll. Thirty-one aircraft would be lost, twenty-one Wellingtons, five Stirlings, three Lancasters, one Halifax and a Hampden.

They were flying comfortably at 10,000ft between Münster and Hamm when Freddy was struck by the blue radar-controlled beam of a master searchlight. The brilliant light fastened on to the Wellington and remained, as if it had been screwed on. Other searchlights zipped across the sky to join their master and the bomber was held in their deadly grip. Mathews remembers actually hearing the blue beam attaching itself to them with a violent fizz, 'Swssssssh!', as if they had collided with a powerful electrical current. Night became day when the lights drilled savagely through the fuselage as if they had been tipped with diamond cutters.

The bombs were jettisoned before the Wellington dropped so violently, as Saunders tried to escape, that Mathews briefly blacked out, perhaps cracking his head on the fuselage. Flak was funnelled up to the plunging bomber which was framed perfectly in the lights for the German gunners. Mathews believes Gill was also knocked unconscious or killed for when the observer came to he heard Saunders cry out: 'I've been hit, for Chrissake. I can't use my left leg and can't pull us out. Get up here, Norman.'

The pilot, in agony from the wound caused by a piece of shrapnel which had ripped straight through his leg, grinned bleakly as his bomb aimer moved into the second pilot's seat. Together they struggled to pull Freddy out of the spiralling dive, still trailing searchlights and flak.

The taut cries of frustration crackled from the cockpit over the intercom:

'The fucking thing's not going to make it.' And: 'Brace yourselves, chaps. Brace yourselves.'

Mathews again: 'Once we were coned all hell was put up at us, but with Vic and Norman both at the controls it seemed we might pull out at between 1,000 and 2,000ft and I thought we would be able to gain height and get away. Instead we pancaked into the ground.'

The design of the Wellington, with its in-built strength, meant it could absorb tremendous punishment in the air. But even a Wellington when striking the ground at high speed and at an angle a few degrees away from the vertical, offered little hope to the men inside.

The bomber crashed with a shattering roar into a field and exploded. Fire leaped from the punctured fuel tanks and quickly spread. Incredibly, three men escaped. The three trapped inside had no chance.

For sixty years John Mathews has been haunted by a wavering cry that he believes came from inside the bomber.

'Johnny! Johnny!' The words, first heard when he was lying shocked and stunned near the blazing wreckage of the Wellington, have echoed down the years as again and again he has relived that awful moment.

Mathews again: 'I came to lying on the ground. It was a nightmarish situation. I picked myself up twenty yards from the aircraft which was burning like hell from end to end. I remember thinking: "My God, I hope no one is in there." Then I heard my name called. It happened so quickly. I looked at the aircraft being consumed by fire and knew if anyone was in there I could do nothing to get them out. It was a terrible moment.

'It was a miracle that any of us escaped from that. Punch had somehow got out of his rear turret with a broken leg. Vic was lying nearby. I went to him and he said in a voice full of pain: "Don't touch me Johnny, I think I've broken my leg."'

Both the pilot's legs were broken as were a collar bone and his pelvis. His right knee had also taken a vicious pounding and blood was oozing from the shrapnel wound. Mathews had a remarkable escape, heavily bruised at the base of his spine and burned from the left ear lobe to his eye and down to the middle of the chin, but nothing was broken. His mae west had been torn off with the parachute harness and his flying suit was almost ripped to pieces. His boots had disappeared. But he was alive.

Mathews, on his knees, turned briefly from his skipper to stare in anguish at what was the funeral pyre of his three crewmates, Wilding, Parkinson and Gill, even though he still hoped they would later be found alive nearby. At that moment he heard the sound of a truck drawing up and men shouting in a language he did not understand. Figures in dark uniforms suddenly loomed over him. Drawn by the flames from the burning Wellington which could be seen miles away the Gestapo had wasted no time.

Mathews was pulled up and dragged to an open-top Gestapo truck while others bent over Saunders and Punchard, who were later moved to hospital. Held down by two Germans in the back of the truck Mathews heard the familiar drone of RAF bombers passing overhead.

'It was weird hearing them, miserable too. German guns were firing and I was willing every shell to miss its target. In the hands of the Gestapo I was not optimistic about my future. I had heard about their brutality. The only thing that seemed to be in their favour was that they were human beings, but that did not always count for much in war. I was pleased that they took me to a Luftwaffe station. I was interviewed that night in the sergeants' mess by a chap who somehow knew my name and that I came from Worthing. He spoke English well and asked if I would like a drink. I assumed he was planning to screw information out of me, laughed and said: "You'll get nothing out of me except my name, which you seem to know, my rank and my service number." Which I gave him.

'My interviewer, who I believe was a sergeant, smiled and said: "I'm very interested in you because I was in England for a year and worked at a brewery in Brighton which I believe we have managed to destroy. I loved Brighton".

'I said: "So do I. I hope to go back there one day."

'"Would you like a drink?" he persisted.

'After all that had happened I was very thirsty and, eventually, I said: "If you really insist, one of your lovely lagers. Ice cold".

'He went off, returning with an ice cold lager, the best drink I have ever had in my life.

'He carried on talking and again mentioned the bombing of Brighton. I did not want to tell this very pleasant German sergeant that although the bombs which fell on the Brighton brewery, and cricket ground at Hove, inconvenienced a lot of people, such pointless attacks would hardly lead to them winning the war.'

Mathews might have added that many English people took their cricket and their beer more seriously than their wars. But might this have suggested to Hitler, in possession of such classified information, that he had exposed a flaw in the English character? Or might the Englishman's obsession for cricket suggest that his character was even tougher than the Fuehrer had imagined? Mathews steered the German away from beer and did not mention cricket at all.

On a train to Frankfurt with other prisoners of war a sergeant with dark curly hair started asking questions that aroused Mathews' suspicion.

'The others in our compartment were willingly giving him information as they would to someone they knew from their own squadron. He spoke with an East End Jewish accent, but said he was an Australian flight engineer and told us where he'd been shot down. I didn't believe him, said they shouldn't talk to him because he was a German stooge, and told him to buzz off. He left almost immediately.

'We weren't guarded very carefully in Frankfurt and six of us, all with minor injuries, wandered about for nearly half-an-hour before being taken to Dulag Luft for interrogation. I was put in the cooler but the walls were thin and I could hear the interrogation going on in the next cell. An American Spitfire pilot from Eagle Squadron in Fighter Command who had been shot down was telling this very nice German, who you couldn't have distinguished from an Old Etonian, all about the battle and what he did. I banged furiously on the wall, shouting: "Shut up! Only tell him your name, number and rank." But I was ignored. Then I climbed up to the bars at my cell window and there was this bloody stooge from the railway walking outside with my interpreter. If he was English I hope he was found out and dealt with at the end of the war.'

Mathews spent most of his time as a POW at Stalag VIIIb, Lansdorf, in Silesia, where he found a little civilisation in the middle of so much miserable deprivation. He was the proud owner of a cricket bat and ball provided by the Red Cross and Test Matches were played between England against Australia, New Zealand and South Africa. The Australians won most of their games.

Actor Denholm Elliott, who slept in the bunk beneath Mathews at Stalag VIIIb, formed a little theatre group which was so successful it went on tour to other POW camps with Twelfth Night. Mathews had a small part, but struggled to learn his lines. He recalls playing cricket with other actors on the station platform at Gliwice as trains pulled in carrying dead and wounded soldiers from the Russian front.

In February 1945 Mathews was one of several thousand prisoners on the long march west as guns of the advancing Russians could be heard in the east.

'We had been given one Red Cross parcel each and after a march of some twenty miles we were herded into a farm. It was dark and freezing. At dawn next day we had to defrost our boots and were on our way to the next resting place. This routine went on for some time. In the Dresden area we passed many columns of Bulgarian and Hungarian Jewesses who were being herded towards the slaughterhouses. We managed to speak to some and understood the women knew they were on their way to be killed.

'On the night of 13/14 February 1945 we heard the Allied aircraft passing overhead to bomb Dresden. Thousands of Germans were killed, but I don't think the post-war anti-bombers realise what help it gave to the Allies to bring the terrible war to an end. Many of the Jewish girls managed to escape and eventually got back to their own countries.

'Some chaps on the march suffered badly from dysentery. For some it was their own fault, drinking from a stream where I had seen bits of bodies floating.

'To my knowledge RAF aircrew prisoners on the march were not treated too badly and were never beaten up except when we pinched food. We melted snow to drink, pinched swedes from the fields and turned them into soup.

'Ernie Corley, a rear gunner from 57 Squadron, was my mucker at Lansdorf and we stayed together on the march. He'd been a butcher's assistant. When we stayed overnight on a farm we had our spies out watching for guards and the farmer. I grabbed a chicken, took it to the hay loft where we were bedded down and asked Ernie to kill it, but he had no idea, so I wrung its neck. We plucked and ate it raw. One or two Cypriot Greeks joined us and we agreed the liver and kidneys were quite good.

'I thought I was being clever when I went to get another bird next day. I wrapped it up in straw and put it in my kit bag on top of a heap of corn I'd found. The farmer, a big tall Hun, grabbed me by the neck. He led me into the farmhouse where Krupps guns hung round the walls among the heads of boars and stags. I thought he had plans to put my head with them. Then the lads made such a row in the farm buildings that he went off to shut them up and I escaped.

'Towards the end we were in a camp where Russians were being held. They were treated badly and never received Red Cross parcels. Their dead were put outside the barracks and collected by a cart that was wheeled to a pit where the bodies were dumped. Corpses were held up between two prisoners at roll call and they got rations for an extra man. It is difficult to imagine a more terrible scenario.'

CHAPTER SIX

AIRCREW TWINS

After Joe Spurrs qualified as a pilot in Canada he was posted to a unit which patrolled the coast and bays near where the St Lawrence river spilled into Lake Ontario. Not a very exciting job, but it was a safe, comfortable berth during wartime, without the dreary inconvenience of rationing and the blackout that his family and friends were suffering in Britain. Flying Officer Spurrs was happy there and resented being sent back to the austerity of England to be part of the rather more dangerous environment of Bomber Command.

His flight engineer, Arthur Madelaine, remembers his pilot as mild mannered but slightly aloof, a small man with whom it was difficult to form anything but a competent working relationship.

Madelaine, who was a twenty-one-year-old sergeant when he crewed up with Spurrs at 1656 Heavy Conversion Unit, Lindholme, Yorkshire, said: 'Joe was all right, but he was about thirty, and married. I'd been looking forward to having a skipper who was a lot younger, someone who'd be happy to go out boozing on our nights off. But we only saw him when we were flying or at briefing, he spent most of his spare time in the officers' mess. He didn't share my youthful keenness and seemed a little out of place on a bomber squadron. Joe often said he was here because of a mistake at Records and he should really be in Canada. He didn't like it, but he was stuck with Bomber Command, and us.'

Having been plunged reluctantly into the war Spurrs, who came from near Sunderland, took practical steps to increase the expectation of his survival. While he and his crew were stationed at 1 Group's Lancaster Finishing School at Hemswell, Lincolnshire, the pilot spent time in the information room, poring over statistics detailing the losses of bomber squadrons.

He later told his crew with considerable satisfaction: 'I've applied to join 12 Squadron because it's had the lowest losses in the last month in the whole of Bomber Command.'

And so they were posted about twelve miles to Wickenby, the base of 12 Squadron which, by the end of the war would have suffered the second heaviest percentage losses – 171 aircraft – in Bomber Command, the highest losses in 1 Group.

The pilot's best friend on the squadron was his navigator, Flying Officer Joe Cordner, who had a wife at home in Carlisle. Cordner, a year or two older than Spurrs, was a reticent man of rigid habits, neatly laying out his fruit, vacuum flask, chewing gum and chocolate beside the flight plan and charts on his navigator's table before takeoff.

Flying Officer Peter Richardson, the wireless operator, a likeable loose-limbed six footer from Tasmania, enjoyed drinking with the lads. Originally a ground aero fitter he was, like Madelaine, dead keen to get started on ops.

The bomb aimer, Flying Officer Ken Chambers, an incurable romantic, was in love with a WAAF he had met before moving to Wickenby and, while chatting at dispersal, often returned to the subject of her staggering beauty. He probably never told her about the training corkscrew when he was copiously sick in the aircraft and had to pay the ground crew to clear it up. Chambers had a head of thick black hair and always looked as if he needed a good shave, even immediately after he had had one.

Madelaine came from Oldham. His father, a brass moulder, had died from pneumonia when his twin sons, Arthur and George, were aged five. George joined the RAF before his brother and became a Halifax bomb aimer on 640 Squadron at Leconfield, Yorkshire. Arthur Madelaine, a slim confident young man of twenty-one, known as 'Red' because of his curly auburn hair, was an apprentice toolmaker before volunteering for aircrew.

He says: 'I thought, like most other chaps, I was absolutely fireproof. If anything bad was going to happen it would involve someone else's aircraft. I always thought we'd get back. I was never scared and enjoyed flying. I didn't like fighter cannon shells coming at me, but didn't mind the flak. You went in gradually and it built up. It wasn't like pulling back a curtain and you were in the middle of it.'

Brian Dufty, from a farming family in south Devon, was educated at Kingsbridge grammar school until his parents, George and Dorothy, split up. He went with his mother to live at Blagdon, Somerset, joining the RAF as soon as he could.

Sergeant Dufty, nineteen, an only child, quiet and shy, had not told his crewmates that he was courting seriously when he went home on leave. Nor did they know their mid-upper gunner was married to Joyce Penney on 29 May 1944 at Wrington parish church some weeks before they joined the squadron.

The flight engineer once swapped positions in the Lancaster with rear gunner Sergeant Tom Dick on a training exercise. Madelaine recalls the eerie feeling of complete detachment from the rest of the crew when he sat shivering in the frozen turret, alone but for the four Browning machine guns:

'There were only four bolts holding the turret on. You could see nothing but empty space in front of you. When I turned the turret on beam the slipstream caught the guns and it shook so much I thought it was going to fall off. I didn't go in there again.

'Tom was a happy-go-lucky character from Belfast who'd drink until he could barely stand up. Always on the borrow for boozing money before pay day, I lent him ten shillings (50p) before our last trip, but never got it back. Tom and Pete were good pals, spending their leaves together in London.'

Their first bombing operation was on 12/13 August 1944 when they were part of a force of 144 aircraft bombing a concentration of German troops north of Falaise, France. The attack was a success and no aircraft were lost, but Madelaine was impatient to bomb Germany. His chance came four nights later when they squirmed through heavy flak at 18,000ft to hit Kiel. Five bombers did not make it home.

He says: 'On the way back a twin-engine German plane flew underneath us. It could have been a Messerschmitt 410 fighter, but I let it go without saying anything. When we landed I said to the mid-upper: "You didn't say anything about the plane that shot past underneath."

'"I saw it," Brian said, "but I didn't want to alarm Joe."

'All the crew must have been of the same opinion: none of us wanted to alarm Joe. The skipper had such a soft voice he didn't give the impression that he was a man of iron and, although he wasn't a panicky type, you'd only report to him if it was absolutely necessary.'

Madelaine remembers vividly the searchlights guarding Rüsselsheim when they were among 412 Lancasters attacking the Opel motor factory on 25/26 August. Fifteen aircraft did not return:

'There seemed to be hundreds of searchlights in big boxes. We saw one poor devil struggling in the lights doing everything he could to escape. He got away after going straight down in a screaming dive. The crew of another bomber baled out, their parachutes looking like white blobs.

'Flying over Germany the Main Stream was spread out about five miles wide. We were in the middle of the stream where chaps thought they were protected against night fighters. Mosquitoes were said to be patrolling fifty miles on each side of the stream, but fifty miles was a long way from the action. The dangerous time was when all the bombers needed to squeeze into the narrow gap over the target. I kept an eye out across the starboard wing while the skipper looked to port because you could suddenly be wing tip to wing tip with another bomber and collide. We were always glad when we'd dropped the bombs because you were then free to spread out a bit.

'When we got back we were stacked over the airfield and a Lancaster was circling round every 500ft. We didn't have lights on in case German fighters came in behind us. Our lights were switched on when we came in on the final circuit. That's when the Germans moved in behind you. This was another dodgy period because by the time we came in to land the gunners had their guns dismantled, ready for the ground crew to take away. It saved time doing it in the air, but we would've been helpless if a German had come up on our tail. They shot several bombers down this way after following them back to Lincolnshire.'

It was still daylight when thirteen Lancasters, from 12 Squadron, including PD273 H-How, piloted by Joe Spurrs, began lifting off from Wickenby at 8.42pm on 29 August 1944. They were joined by another eighteen from 626 Squadron, also based at Wickenby. The target was Stettin, a Baltic port, with important shipbuilding yards and engineering works. It stood on the river Oder which was linked with Berlin, eighty-three miles to the south. A total force of 402 Lancasters and one Mosquito were briefed to bomb the town. Twenty-three Lancasters would be lost.

'This was our fourth op,' says Madelaine. 'We had been briefed twice before for a raid on Stettin. The first time it was cancelled shortly before we left the briefing room. Next time it was called off when we were at dispersal. As soon as each plane heard the news everyone shouted: "Hooray!", jumped out and waited for the wagon to take them back. After the third briefing somebody said: "I don't like it. We've been briefed three times for this, the Jerries will know we're coming."'

One 626 Squadron Lancaster did not get off the ground when it swung on takeoff. The rudder pedal slipped and the pilot, Flying Officer G. Lofthouse, was unable to regain control. No one was injured. Another crew, from 12 Squadron, aborted after the wireless operator lost his nerve.

Each Lancaster from Wickenby carried an 8,440lb bomb load, which included a 4,000lb Cookie, 660 4lb incendiaries and sixty 30lb incendiaries. They also held 2,154 gallons of high-octane fuel for the long flight.

Madelaine again: 'The Cookie looked like a big elongated dustbin. Our incendiaries that night were known as a J-type cluster. Each one was like a big blowtorch, throwing out a flame about fifteen feet long and two feet wide. The Germans didn't know how to put them out and we were told if they were played on a brick wall it would get so hot the slightest vibration afterwards would bring it down.

'We were taxiing round in a line of aircraft to take off when there was a bit of a mix up at the top. One plane had not got on to the runway fast enough. The voice of a WAAF in the control tower drew attention to the offending aircraft and exclaimed: "Come on, get your finger out!" No one expected that remark from a girl and everybody had a good laugh, lightening the moment.

'We flew at 3,000ft over the North Sea to avoid enemy radar. Everything was going normally until Tom Dick, the rear gunner said his turret doors had jammed. He couldn't open them to get into the fuselage where his parachute was strapped. It was my job to go back and free them but Pete Richardson, the wireless operator said he would see to it. Pete used his axe to chop open the doors.

'Darkness had fallen when the skipper asked the navigator for our position. Joe Cordner reported the Gee set was u/s, did some quick calculations and said we were fifty miles outside the bomber stream. He gave the skipper a new course and we were back in the stream by the time we were flying over Denmark. By now we'd climbed to 20,000ft.

'Many fighter flames were dropped over the stream at the Kattegat. Three aircraft went down in flames and shortly afterwards we were attacked by a German fighter. I saw cannon shells streaking in from the rear, passing between the starboard inner engine and me, standing beside the pilot. I tapped his shoulder and pointed. "Bloody hell, tracers!" he exclaimed and shouted into the intercom: "Rear gunner, which way corkscrew?"

'The rear gunner, sounding panic-stricken, just cried: "Corkscrew! corkscrew!" I think Tom may have been dozing and was shocked to see the fighter. The pilot made up his own mind quickly and calmly, corkscrewing to port. As he brought up the starboard wing we heard and felt cannon shells smashing into the plane, hitting something solid, which I believed was the main spar.

'We lost the fighter and hastily checked for damage. The engines were behaving normally and I couldn't detect any fuel leaks, but the skipper said the controls had no trim on the starboard elevator and the rear gunner reported large sections of the tail unit shot away.

'It was illegal to cross a neutral country, but we'd been briefed to go over Sweden. We saw the lights of the towns below and their gunners were throwing up flak to 10,000ft. Part of the Main Force was going to Königsberg that night and, with luck, the Germans thought every bomber was heading there. We did a loop over Sweden, went across the Baltic and swept round to come in from the east to Stettin. We couldn't see a thing for cloud, then heard the Master Bomber say: "Basement Twelve." We came down to 12,000ft, just under the cloud.

'We were in the second wave, approaching Stettin, when I looked to port and saw a small orange ball, rapidly expanding. It turned white, lighting up a Lancaster a few hundred yards ahead of us. I saw its wings fall off, and the engines drop away from the wings. It exploded, disintegrated, and the skipper moved to starboard to avoid debris.

'The target was already burning furiously with fires reflected in the water beside the docks, a marvellous sight.'

Flak was heavy, increasing in intensity as they started their bombing run. Some crews reported many bursts were so savage they could have only come from high-calibre naval guns. Long sticks of flares illuminated the target at 7,000ft then the aiming point was marked punctually and accurately by green and red TIs. Bombing was good and the fires were fierce, spreading to surrounding areas, leaping high into the sky.

Brian Dufty, the mid-upper gunner suddenly shouted: "There's a bloody big fire underneath me, Skip." The pilot did not reply so Madelaine yelled into the intercom: "Well, put the bloody thing out."

The aircraft lifted as the bombs were dropped and Madelaine decided he must attempt to extinguish the fire.

'I disconnected my oxygen line and was reaching behind the pilot for a portable oxygen bottle when the navigator pulled open the curtain to his little office and came forward. I thought: "Bloody hell!" because his parachute was clipped on and it seemed he was ready to leave. The skipper hadn't given an order to bale out, but Joe Cordner was seeing the flak for the first time and we were in the middle of it. It unnerved him and he was trembling as he tried to force his way past me. Unknown to me he disconnected me from the intercom as he brought his leg up, so I heard nothing more from the crew. He eventually pushed past and went down into the bomb aimer's compartment.

'I fixed on the oxygen bottle, got a fire extinguisher and turned round to tackle the fire. When we'd got the order: "Basement Twelve", some planes didn't bother coming down. It was in my mind that an incendiary from one had smashed through our fuselage. I only had to pick it up at one end, carry it to the rear door and throw it out.

'All I could see down the aircraft was a whitish glow. The fuselage was filled with a thick white vapour and out of this came the wireless operator. He signalled with his hands for me to go forward to the front escape hatch and I noticed he was wearing his parachute. I could have got aft with the oxygen bottle so I stood on one side, pointing for him to come past, then realised I was off intercom. Pete shook his head and barred my way. It was clear he wouldn't leave until I'd baled out. Pete was a decent bloke and I couldn't jeopardise his life. I looked at the pilot and he motioned me to get out, so I reluctantly put my 'chute on, then realised I was still wearing my helmet. I pulled it off, knelt beside the open escape hatch and as I went out head first, falling on my back, I could see underneath the plane. There were no flames so the fire could only have been inside, and I believe there were toxic fumes which killed both gunners.

'What upset me was that the Lancaster had four good engines, in perfect working order. Even today I think we could have got home if I'd got through to put out the fire. But the biggest drawback was being cut off the intercom, not knowing what was happening and being told things by hand signals right at the end.

'I saw Pete drop out, opening his 'chute immediately. It spilled all along the bottom of the plane and looked as if it would catch on the tail wheel, but he was lucky. Seeing him reminded me to release my own parachute. The intercom wire was caught between me and the 'chute and there was a danger of it catching in the shroud lines, stopping some from opening. We'd been warned not to bale out in this condition, but there was no time to think. I pulled the toggle and looked at it in my hand because it was like daylight with the fires below. I thought the 'chute hadn't worked then there was a jolt and the canopy opened.

'I was falling into the target area with the third wave of bombers yet to come in. I saw a huge column of thick black smoke rising to 10,000ft or more, probably from a burning oil tank. I was concerned that I might drift into the smoke or fall into one of the many fierce fires.

'A canal and a railway line were on the starboard side and to port I saw the river Oder. I thought I had a few hundred feet to fall and was taken by surprise when I suddenly hit the ground. I gathered up the 'chute and dashed into nearby bushes. I later found that I'd landed on what seemed to be a peninsular in Stettin's dock area with the river flowing on one side and a canal on the other.'

Madelaine kept his head pressed against the pulsating ground as bombs exploded around him from the third wave, then listened bleakly to the lightened Lancasters pushing on merrily for England.

A ship of 2,000 tons was sunk that night in the port and seven other ships, totalling 31,000 tons, were damaged. Thirty-two industrial premises and 1,569 houses were destroyed. Over 1,000 people were killed and a similar number injured.

Four Lancasters from Wickenby were hit by flak. One of these and another two were struck by incendiaries from other bombers, adding strength to Madelaine's theory that they had been disabled by one of their own aircraft which had ignored the clear instruction to lose altitude.

As shocked survivors emerged from the Stettin air raid shelters and wandered in a daze through their burning town Madelaine heard the sound of angry voices approaching and pressed himself more deeply into the bushes. Eight youths, armed with pick axe handles, paused within a few feet of his hiding place. They had seen a parachute drifting down, but were not sure where it had landed. Madelaine knew if he was caught they would probably kill him. He kept quiet and they began walking away, but one hung back, peering more intently into the bushes. Then he too wandered off and the airman breathed more easily and took stock of his situation.

Madelaine realised that in the morning light he would be easily spotted lurking in the bushes. He crept out, dodging from bush to bush, crossed a railway line, which led to the docks, slipped through tall dense reeds to the canal and found a more secure place to hide. He settled down on the grass, opened his silk escape maps and was dismayed to find they were useless, covering France and the Low Countries.

By now he was thirsty and would have given almost anything for a cold beer, but had to make do with a scoop of water from the murky river to which he added two purification tablets.

Arthur Madelaine only learned after the war that his brother, George, who was on leave, paid a surprise visit to Wickenby over two hours before he had left to bomb Stettin. George was told his twin had gone to briefing and he must wait to see him after they returned from the raid.

George Madelaine recalls: 'It was a disappointment, but they were very hospitable, fixing me up with a good meal and somewhere to sleep and I chatted to a couple of Arthur's friends over a few beers before turning in. I went for an early breakfast and learned that some aircraft had not returned. My stomach took quite a jolt when told my brother was in one of the missing crews. The station adjutant said I could go through Arthur's personal belongings and take whatever I wished to keep, but it was unsettling going through his things. I selected a few minor articles to take home, including letters my mother and others had sent him. I caught the first available train to Oldham and tried to think how I could break the news to my mother.

'I walked into the house and the family all sat there. My mother was in a bad state, crying along with some of my aunts. She had received the telegram from the Air Ministry which said Arthur was missing. I tried to reassure her that he was most likely safe and a prisoner of war, but she was convinced he'd been killed. Someone suggested making a pot of tea and that seemed to break the tension.

'When I returned to Leconfield at the end of my leave the CO said I need not fly any more as the RAF did not want my mother to risk losing two sons. He told me to think it over and let him know in a few days. It was not an easy decision, but I had come so far and decided to carry on. Looking back I think I was a bit selfish not taking his advice as I knew my mother would have felt more easy. About two months later we learned Arthur was a prisoner of war and I felt much better about continuing to fly.'

Arthur Madelaine was awakened early next morning by an FW-190 circling low over the town. He remained concealed throughout the day, waiting for night when he moved cautiously down the peninsular, passing a hutted camp holding what he thought were foreign workers. He believed he had two alternatives: walking west, with the daunting prospect of hundreds of miles crossing Germany, or heading east a few miles to the Polish border.

After deciding to take his chances in Poland he heard the metallic clink-clink of railway trucks and considered the advantages travelling by train had over walking. He went purposefully towards the railway line until a large ferocious dog hurled itself snapping and snarling at a gate and abandoned the idea, quickly retreating over a main road beside which stood rows of wooden prefabricated houses.

'I walked along the road,' says Madelaine, 'until I heard vehicles approach, then dived into the ditch which ran beside the road. The ditch had the stench of an open sewer and I clung to the bank until it was safe to move. In the countryside outside Stettin I thought I was safe. Instead of sticking to footpaths I walked in the middle of the road and that was my undoing. A light flashed in my eyes and a man loomed up, asking for identification. Taken to a house where a young woman wanted to kill me, I was later marched back into Stettin.

'Crossing a bridge I saw a partially-collapsed building where arc lamps shone on men digging for bodies. One of the German guards with me said: 'Why didn't you bomb the bridge instead of people's homes?'

Forced to strip naked in a police cell as his clothes were searched, Madelaine tried to sleep on the bare floor after stretching out, briefly, on the filthy lice-infected bed.

Conditions were worse at Stalag Luft VII, Bankau, near Kreuzburg, in Silesia, near the Polish border. Without the weekly delivery of Red Cross food men would have struggled to remain alive. As winter gnawed on their emaciated bodies, the men in Madelaine's hut took an enlightened decision. They would make a Christmas pudding.

'We needed something to make it in and I was the only chap with a vest,' says Madelaine. 'I took it off and it was run through the tap. It was clean enough, I suppose. It was going to be boiled, anyway. We stitched up the bottom then cut up prunes from Red Cross parcels. This was mixed up with bread, raisins and currants, tied up like a ball and hung beside a window for several weeks.

'On Christmas Eve Jock Nicholls, a Lancaster navigator from 5 Group, stayed up all night stirring a vat of porridge that we'd saved. We put the pudding to steam in the can that had held our breakfast porridge. We poured thick Klim cream over the pudding which tasted beautiful, but we ate too much and half the chaps were sick. I was later given my vest back, but it was so badly stained I got rid of it.'

Russians pushing hard from the east forced the camp to evacuate in January and start the grim march to Luckenwalde. Here Madelaine palled up with other airmen and after being liberated by Russian soldiers, they became proficient looters of food.

Their route home was an adventure. Given a lift to Magdeburg in a fire engine requisitioned by an American airman, they transferred to a broken-down truck which was towed over 100 miles into southern Germany. Here they stole a car from a crippled German and were fired at by American soldiers on an autobahn. Conned in Frankfurt by a cunning American sergeant who took the car in exchange for a flight back to England, which did not materialise, they reached Blighty on a steamer.

Madelaine's four surviving crewmates got home safely and he was soon reunited with his twin brother, George, who had completed twenty-six operations.

On 8 November 1944, ten weeks after Brian Dufty was killed Joyce, his widow, gave birth to their daughter, Christine.

CHAPTER SEVEN

COMING HOME

Navigator Tom Nelson flew back to England aboard a Lancaster on VE-Day after enduring the dreary inhospitality of Adolf Hitler since September 1943. Despite the brutal scars of bombing, England looked fresh and welcoming to a young man who had been away for months, but there was one snag. He and other repatriated RAF aircrew arrived at London's Victoria Station en route for Yorkshire, where they were to be debriefed. Nelson had not heard from his mother for eight months. Refused permission to catch a bus to her home in Stoke Newington, he was allowed a quick telephone call.

He recalls: 'My mother did not have a telephone, but I had a bright idea. She lived in a flat above a shop on Stoke Newington Road, right opposite the Savoy Cinema. The shop and cinema might have been bombed flat, of course. It was a sobering moment. I looked up the number, inserted twopence, dialled and pressed button A after a young woman answered from the box office.

'I said: "I know this sounds stupid but from where you are sitting can you see the shops across the street?"

'She replied, a little surprised: "Oh yes, I can see them plainly."

'I then briefly told her my story and said I hoped to be home in a week or ten days. Would she please dash across the street to tell my mother that I was on my way north, but would get home as soon as possible? She promised to do that and I went off to Yorkshire with a lighter heart.'

Nelson had left England a sergeant; he was now a flight lieutenant. Promotions of aircrews did not grind to a halt when they were cooped up in German prisoner of war camps. As his steam train snorted northwards the slightly-built Nelson reflected on his remarkable mother and the circuitous route which had led him into the bomber war.

He was just eight in November 1926 when his South African-born father, John, died, leaving his pregnant widow, Mary, with four small sons, soon to be joined by a fifth. They moved from Hackney, London, to the Essex villages of Danbury, then Ingatestone, supported by a small allowance from Mary's wealthy widowed older sister, Dorothy.

Nelson's education was taken care of by his popular and erudite scoutmaster Stanley 'Skip' Potts, a bachelor, who paid for him to attend the small private Gate House School in Ingatestone for four years until he was eighteen. Potts had told Nelson's mother he was one of the brightest boys he had ever met.

It was at the nearby village of Margaretting where Tom Nelson became a King's Scout, proficient in signalling and the Morse code. In 1931 his mother married Fred Rich, a farm worker who had lodged with them to help make ends meet. A year later her sixth son was born. Two of Nelson's brothers survived the war in the Royal Navy. Another served in the Merchant Navy.

Nelson joined the Army in 1939 to become a signaller, but became so irritated with the mind-numbing parades with 99th Field Regiment, Royal Artillery, that he volunteered for aircrew and became navigator for Sergeant Larry Cates on 51 Squadron at Snaith, Yorkshire.

The pilot was tall, lean, blond, and came from Heybridge, a village no more than fifteen miles away from Nelson's home.

Nelson again: 'We knew little about each other's background, but were all bound together by our love of flying. None of us lost the chance of going up for a flight, even on air tests when, sometimes, the gunners were not required to go. We were a relatively quiet crew. We played snooker in the mess, went to the camp cinema and occasionally drifted into the village of Pollington for a couple of pints. At twenty-four I was one or two years older than the others.'

Cecil Manning, who answered to the name of Curly, was wireless operator. From Putney, south London, he was short and handsome, with dark curly hair.

Three of the crew were Lancastrians: six-footer John 'Mitch' Mitchell, from Oldham, who squeezed into the mid-upper turret; bomb aimer Leslie 'Robbie' Robinson, whose home was in Ulverston, and Burnley lad Jack Watson, the flight engineer.

They were all sergeants except Warrant Officer Lloyd 'Junior' Brondgeest, whose tall frame filled the rear turret. His home was in Calgary, which stands in the foothills of the Canadian Rockies. He and Nelson were particular pals, sharing the same quirky humour and philosophy of life.

Snaith had several memorable characters. Nelson recalls Squadron Leader Charlie Porter, who commanded C Flight:

'Charlie was unusual because he was a navigator. Most flight commanders at that time were pilots. A small chunky fellow, from Uttoxeter, no more than 5ft 5in tall, he was always interested in the crews and seemed different to other senior officers. He came round and talked to us. If there were any problems he sorted them out. We had great faith in him.

'Charlie could hold his liquor better than anyone else on the squadron. They had bets in the mess on what time he would go to the toilet. When Charlie heard about this he held on to it, going for a piss at the last possible moment.'

Their first bombing operation was in Halifax II DT729 when they took off at 12.30am on 27 April 1943 to Duisburg. Nelson remembers the night when nothing seemed to go right:

'The winds we had been given were completely wrong. We were told there would be fairly light winds coming from the east. Instead, all the way to Duisburg they were blowing up to 90mph from the west. Everybody arrived too early, but we dropped our bombs, took the photograph and turned for home into this fierce wind.'

'About ten minutes later, Robbie, the bomb aimer, let out a strangled cry: "Christ, they're all hanging up."'

'We hadn't dropped anything. Every single bomb was hanging on the bomb racks. I had serious doubts at that point whether we'd make thirty operations. Robbie struggled with the 1,000lb bomb and eventually got rid of it over the North Sea, but the incendiaries wouldn't budge. We made it safely back to Snaith, but were feeling gloomy.'

Coincidentally, Squadron Leader 'Skip' Seymour, a World War One pilot, who debriefed them that night, was a schoolmaster from Ingatestone, who had examined Nelson for his various King's Scout badges. The navigator was astounded to meet him at Snaith and had not even known he was in the RAF.

Their confidence was restored on the next trip on 28 April when they laid mines in the Frisian Islands and everything went right.

On 28 June 1943, aboard Halifax HR839, heading for Cologne, they ran into the heaviest flak they had experienced.

'It was,' says Nelson, 'like being in the middle of a heavy hail storm. Flak ripped through the curtains in my compartment, and Jack Watson put out a fire in the electric circuits of his engineer's panel. At Snaith, 300 holes were found in the fuselage and wings, but none of us had been touched and the Merlin engines kept going. We were told the aircraft was so badly damaged it would be dismantled for spare parts.'

On 3 July, Brondgeest shot down a Junkers-88 as they approached the Dutch coast on the way home. They began weaving as the fighter attacked then the rear gunner fired a burst into it and, as flames shot out of the fighter and it started going down, he cried: 'I've got the bastard!'

Window was used for the first time on 24 July when 791 aircraft attacked Hamburg. Window was thin strips of aluminium foil stuck to black paper which, when dropped in huge quantities out of the invading aeroplanes, jammed the Germans' defensive radar system.

'At the briefing our intelligence officer told us that Window was absolutely foolproof', says Nelson. 'Window had been ready for over a year but we were afraid to use it in case the Germans retaliated with it over Britain. All the aircrews flying at that time felt a profound sense of relief. At last we had something that would save our necks. This Hamburg op went like clockwork, but a lot of people, including my own crew, were lulled into a certain amount of security by the apparent magic of Window.

Twelve aircraft were lost that night, but by the time the Battle of Hamburg had ended on 2/3 August, it was estimated that Window had saved over 100

Bomber Command aircraft.'

Larry Cates and his crew went on all four raids to Hamburg in which over 42,000 Germans were killed.

In the early hours of 31 August they slumped into bed after returning from Mönchengladbach, their fourth operation in nine days. About midday they were wakened with the dispiriting news that they were on again that night.

'We were shagged out,' says Nelson. 'We couldn't believe it when we knew we were going off again that night. No crews should have been made to go on operations two nights in a row. We needed one good night of sleep in between.

'That afternoon Mitch went sick, which meant we'd have an odd bod mid-upper gunner, never good news. We met Mitch's replacement, Flight Sergeant Ken Murray, a well-built Canadian, at briefing.

'Briefing was done in a rather theatrical manner. As usual, when we arrived at the briefing hut the big map was covered by curtains. A cry of disbelief went up as they were pulled back. The target was Berlin, which was not what anybody who had just come off a six-hour flight wanted to see. Worst of all, the route we were given was out of this world. We were to fly to a point east of Berlin, having passed sixty miles north of the city. Then we had to come back over the German capital to bomb. The idea was to make the night fighters think we were going somewhere else. People like me just wanted to drop the bombs and get home as quickly as possible. The briefing officer said on this operation we would wake up everybody in Germany. I reckoned we'd be flying over enemy territory for nearly five hours.

'We didn't do an air test. There was time for a bit more shuteye, but not enough to make any difference, we were still very much below par. We collected our 'chutes from the parachute section. We were handed them, as usual, by Kathy Cripps, a good-looking WAAF with dark hair, dark eyes and a nice smile. She was the kind of girl you'd sit in the pub with for a pleasant chat. She knew us all by name and always said: "Good luck, boys. I'll see you when you come back."

'We were driven in a truck to the aircraft by Winifred Ryder, a Yorkshire lass. We all called her Freddie. Her eyes always filled with tears as she quickly drove off and everybody pretended not to notice. Bigger than Kathy, Freddie was a buxom blonde. She had waited in her truck for a lot of chaps who had not come back. That night we were flying Halifax HR931 F-Freddie.'

Two aircraft from 51 Squadron were among the forty-seven which did not come back out of a total 622 sent on the Berlin raid.

Nelson was always puzzled by the mysterious disappearance of aeroplanes during a bombing operation:

'We always seemed to be on our own until the rendezvous points, when other aircraft appeared. This was one of the strange things about night operations. Generally speaking, you took off from your station, and there would be rendezvous points, first somewhere on the English coast, secondly on the enemy coast. You took off and flew towards the first point, not seeing any other aircraft. As you got closer to the first rendezvous you suddenly saw them: aeroplanes in front of you, behind you, to the left and the right, all the way around you. Somewhere over the North Sea they'd disappear. At the enemy coast they would all be back. Given the number of aircraft meeting at certain points it was surprising there were not even more collisions and mid-air crashes.

'It was a textbook flight to Berlin, but something was wrong. Normally when you came in over the target there was flak. We were at 18,000ft and could see the flak bursting at least 3,000ft below us. Somehow we were fooled into either thinking that we were doing a good job or Window was confusing the German gunners. In fact we were exhausted and could not think clearly. What we didn't realise was that the flak was being kept deliberately low. The fighters were massed high over Berlin. As our bombers came over the city they were being picked off one at a time. It was the luck of the draw whether you or somebody else was hit.

'The red target indicators dropped by the Pathfinders sparkled below, right on our flight line. Robbie, the bomb aimer, took over the plane, lowered the bomb doors and nudged the aircraft left and right until the TIs were in the cross hairs of his bomb sight and released the bombs.

'I wrote in the navigator's log "Bombs gone, 0002." We breathed a sigh of relief and continued straight and level for sixteen seconds until the photoflash went off. The picture it took was important. It proved that not only were you there but, with some luck, showed exactly where your bombs had fallen. The bomb doors were closed and I gave Larry the course home, heading due south for some distance before turning west. Suddenly, just as we got on to the new route, there was a tremendous "kerumph" which shook the aircraft, and that was it.'

The black curtains beside Nelson were jerked violently aside. Jack Watson stood there, his face contorted with horror, shouting: 'Jump! jump! jump! jump!'

Nelson looked beyond the engineer and saw the entire port wing being consumed by leaping flames. The aircraft was still purring along straight and level as if the burning wing was an optical illusion. There were no instructions from the pilot over the intercom and Nelson was grateful to Watson for giving him vital seconds in which he could escape.

'The escape hatch was right underneath the navigator's seat,' says Nelson. 'I had to clip on my parachute, push up my seat, fold it back, then we both opened the escape hatch. Jack got his feet into the hatch and I was waiting for him to drop out, but at that moment the bomber turned straight on to its nose and began diving.

'Jack fell back into the aircraft and I toppled backwards towards the bomb aimer's position. I saw the escape hatch above me and put my hands up to try and grab hold of it and pull myself out. But the G-force was so great I couldn't get my hands above my head. It was as if an elephant was sitting on me and I was struggling to push it off. I let my hands fall back and knew I was going to be killed. I was absolutely certain of this.

'That was when this strange thing happened. I've talked about this with different fellows who went through the same experience and exactly the same thing happened to them. As soon as I knew I could not save myself I felt an air of absolute calmness. Not only calmness but sheer love. It was as if someone had put their arms around me and said: "Don't worry about it. Everything is going to be fine."

'This had never happened to me before, nor have I experienced it since, but I knew with absolute certainty that when you die you are going to be all right and are going somewhere else.'

As they plunged towards earth and annihilation Nelson's sweet dreams were interrupted with sudden brutal violence as he was grabbed by gargantuan forces and flung out of the aircraft, to tumble helplessly through the air like a wisp of straw. His scattered senses then focused on his parachute pack floating in front of him. He grabbed a strap, hauled the 'chute back to his chest and pulled the D-ring. No more than five seconds passed before he struck the ground and was feeling lucky as the sweet thoughts of death were swiftly consumed by much sweeter thoughts of staying alive.

He says: 'I was a bit dazed when I hit the ground, but apparently unhurt. At first I was completely deaf, I could not hear a thing. I could see Berlin in the distance with flames coming up, painting the sky red. I ran away in the opposite direction.'

He ran into pitch darkness and across fields which with a little imagination might have been fine Yorkshire meadows. He ran for nearly four hours driven not by panic nor fear, but by the knowledge that he must put as many miles as possible between himself and the bombed city. Some aircrews had been beaten to death or strung up from trees by vengeful German civilians. Death no longer seemed the sweet prospect of inevitability. Life gave him something more positive to think about. When rain began tipping down, the navigator's pace slowed dramatically as his flying boots became saturated. He fell into a ditch and was immediately up to his waist in filthy water.

As it began to get light he cut the tops off his soggy boots, turning them into soggy shoes, and removed his stripes and brevet. Nelson recalls his uncomfortable stuttering progress across the German countryside:

'I hadn't realised that when you got water in these things, especially with their fleecy kapok lining, they got very wet. The shoes fell off after every ten steps. It was like trying to run in an old pair of slippers. I was so annoyed with the man who had invented them I was writing a letter in my head to him, explaining that this was a problem which had to be solved. It was then I discovered a cut about three inches long on the right side of my head. It was superficial but the blood had been running into my collar.

'I saw an old mill without any sails and went inside. Nobody seemed to be around. I climbed steps into a loft, sank wearily into some hay and went to sleep. After waking I lay there all day. No one came near. I planned to move that night but when I got up in late afternoon I couldn't walk. I think the straps of the parachute buckle must have hit me in the groin and upset a few muscles. I hadn't felt any pain before. When it got dark I knew I had to go on. I hobbled west throughout the night.

'At dawn I couldn't find shelter but limped into a wood and lay down on some bracken. I was very tired.

'I was wakened abruptly by a sharp prodding in my back. Two unfriendly German farm labourers, armed with forks, forced me to march to a village about a mile away. They knocked on a farmhouse door which was opened by a middle-aged woman in a night-dress. I was led into the kitchen. Her husband and their daughter, of about eighteen, were there. They were both dressed. They didn't speak a word of English, nor did I know any German. We communicated by signs. I must have looked a mess because they brought a big tub into the farmyard and filled it with warm water. I took my shirt off, had a pretty good wash and felt a lot better. Then they gave me a magnificent breakfast. The coffee was awful, but the bacon and eggs were absolutely gorgeous.

'They were very kind, friendly and smiling. My only objection was that the men with the forks stayed in the background. One had been to a police station to telephone for the Luftwaffe and eventually a young pilot, who spoke good English, arrived to take me to Spandau prison in Berlin, where there were another dozen RAF fellows.

'Next morning we were taken one at a time into a little room on the first floor where a kind-looking man in his sixties, wearing civilian clothes, sat at a desk. He said he was from the Red Cross and needed to take details to make sure everybody in England knew I was alive. I gave him my name, rank and number, and my mother's address in Stoke Newington. I clammed up when he started saying it was impossible for the RAF to continue to take such heavy losses among bomber aircrews.

'In the next room a German said, in English: "How do you like broadcasting home?" He took me to a window and I was horrified to see cables running down into a recording van. Everything I said had been recorded. That same night Lord Haw-Haw gave my mother's name and address on the German radio and said I was a prisoner of war.

'Next morning a lorry shrieked to a halt outside my mother's flat and a man jumped out. He told my mother that his son was a POW and he listened to Haw-Haw's broadcasts from Germany every night. He had heard my name and her address. And so my mother knew I was a POW three days after I was shot down on my twenty-fifth operation.'

Tom Nelson eventually joined the inmates of Stalag IVb at Muhlberg and, to his delight, was reunited with Curly Manning and Robbie Robinson. They believed the whole nose of the aircraft had blown off, hurling the three survivors into the night. The other two had been picked up almost immediately after they had landed, near Nelson, in a German Army training area near Döberitz, a town about sixteen miles west of the centre of Berlin.

Their German captors had taken Manning and Robinson next morning to their wrecked bomber and forced them to go inside and remove their crewmates' bodies. It was a distressing task. Their skipper, Larry Cates, still in his pilot's seat, was burned all down his left side. They also brought out both gunners, Ken Murray and Junior Brondgeest, and Jack Watson, the flight engineer, who had been within seconds of baling out before he was flung back into the aircraft and trapped.

John Mitchell, the gunner languishing in sick quarters, recovered, was given a new crew, finished his first tour, and was decorated with a DFM. His luck did not hold. On 30 July 1944, flying with 97 Pathfinders Squadron, his aircraft was shot down over France. There were no survivors.

Shortly after arriving at Stalag IVb, Nelson and another 200 new arrivals, were deloused and had their hair cut short by a machine which appeared to have been used for sheep shearing.

'We felt absolutely low,' says Nelson. 'More planes were being shot down at this time than any other. There were so many prisoners they could not all be accommodated at any of the normal aircrew camps which were run by the Luftwaffe. The German Army was in charge of this one which was like a concentration camp in almost every detail except there were no gas chambers. About 20,000 men were crammed into big accommodation huts.'

He heard many staggering stories of survival including that of a man who landed across a telephone wire which caught under his chin, slicing him from ear to ear. When angry German civilians picked him up they found a man with his tongue hanging out underneath his chin. He was stitched up before being sent to Stalag IVb.

In late 1944 Nelson learned that he and Larry Cates had both been commissioned a month before the crash, but the papers had not come through. At the end of the following February Nelson was moved to an officer's camp, Oflag VIIb, at Eichstätt, near Nuremburg, where conditions were markedly better and he shared a room with three other men. He had mixed feelings about this because among wild rumours circulating at Stalag IVb had been one that claimed Hitler was going to gather British officers around him as hostages for his last beastly stand in Berlin.

It did not happen and on 8 May, VE-Day, Nelson boarded a Lancaster at Reims bound for Manston, Kent. The flight almost ended in disaster.

Nelson recalls: 'One of the soldiers going home, who had been a prisoner for five years, went to the Elsen toilet and did his business. He saw a handle nearby, pulled it, a ten-foot raft flew out of the wing and banged against the aircraft's tail. The pilot, wondering what had happened, dived towards the Channel. The raft broke loose and disappeared and the Lancaster levelled out at 100ft above the water. I thought we were going straight in and was beginning to think that maybe flying was a dangerous business.

'Shortly after arriving back in London I discovered something that had not occurred to me before. All over the country people were still clinging to the hope that their loved ones might still be alive. And why not? There had been a lot of evaders. Some were still with the French or Belgian resistance. Many more had been passed along the lines to a neutral country or simply captured and not notified to the Red Cross.

'My two dead gunners were both Canadians. Jack Watson came from Lancashire, but Larry lived no more than fifty miles away in an area I knew well as a boy. Like so many people those days his parents were not on the telephone so I decided to visit and tell them I knew for certain Larry would not be returning.

'I made the journey by train and bus and arrived at his modest home just before lunch. His mother was there. She was a tiny woman which surprised me because Larry stood over six feet. Without going into any details I said that if she had any lingering doubts it was my unpleasant duty to dispel them.

'She looked at me very calmly and said: "It was so kind of you to come, but it really wasn't necessary. I have known since the night you were shot down that Larry was dead. I woke up suddenly in bed that night. The luminous hands of my alarm clock pointed to ten past midnight. Larry was standing in the bedroom looking down at me. Dressed in his flying suit he was burned all down his left side.

'"I woke up my husband and told him what I had seen. We sat up most of the night and the next morning, just holding hands, waiting for the dreaded telegram which we knew would come. It arrived shortly after lunch."'

It is around 650 miles in a straight line from Berlin to Heybridge, Essex. It had taken about five minutes for Larry to come home.

CHAPTER EIGHT

THE DEATH CAMP

Douglas Jordin was hiding quietly in the field's long grass when he saw the head pop up. Swallowing his excitement, he slowly raised his rifle, took aim and squeezed the trigger. The rabbit fell dead. At the age of six Jordin had made his first kill, using a .177in air rifle. Thirteen years later he was in charge of four .303in Browning machine guns in the rear cockpit of a Lancaster bomber.

He says: 'I was the ideal person to be a rear gunner because I enjoyed being alone and my main hobby and purpose in life was to shoot. After that first rabbit came pigeons, waterfowl, pheasants, partridges, hares, crows and starlings. A lot of these I killed on the twelve-acre smallholding I had when I was seventeen, at Culcheth, between Warrington and Leigh, Lancashire. I became quite a good shot.

'I tried to join the Home Guard but they said I was too young at fifteen, so I got prepared in case the Germans invaded. I had a device for creating balls of lead and modified my .410 shotgun ammunition. I emptied the shot out of several cartridges and put two lead balls into each one. They could rip through a two-inch plank. Whenever we had a raid I went into the middle of a field, laid on my back and waited for Germans to come down on parachutes. I never saw any, but if they'd appeared I'd have rattled their ribs at thirty yards.

'Initially, I wasn't going to join up because I thought it would be better to stay at home and make a bob or two. But one night, in 1942, Jerry bombers missed the munitions factory at Risley, two miles away, and dropped a lot of incendiaries on my smallholding. It was irritating having to put out so many fires and I thought it would be appropriate to throw a few in the other direction.'

Aged nineteen, Jordin was a stockily-built sergeant stationed with 12 Squadron at Wickenby. Rabbits he potted on the airfield with his .22 rifle were skinned expertly by wireless operator Sergeant Bob Yates and deep fried on the billet's black stove, with lard and potatoes scrounged from girls who worked at the sergeants' mess.

Yates, from Melbourne, Australia, two years older than Jordin, was slim with reddish curly hair and prominent teeth. He did not seem to have a great deal of fun in him, but he could skin a rabbit while Jordin was thinking about it.

Their skipper, Pilot Officer Mike Guilfoyle, thin faced, lanky, from Kingston, Jamaica, was always complaining of the cold. A good pilot, he reacted instantly to abrupt demands to corkscrew from Jordin when their Lancaster was pursued by a German fighter.

Sergeant Joe 'Sunshine' Sonshine, the navigator, from Toronto, Canada, had his jaw wired up after breaking it during a game of American football. A Jew, he was a powerfully-built man of sixteen stones, who always flew in his blue and gold football jersey.

Flight Sergeant Steve Stephens had a wife and child at home in Aberdeen, but still enjoyed the company of pretty girls in Lincolnshire. Wiry and short tempered, the bomb aimer went to sea on a trawler as a youth. Always ready to pick a fight he was once dumped fully clothed by Jordin in a bath to cool off.

The flight engineer, a sergeant, was known simply as Taffy. With his dark curly hair and pretty girlish features the Welshman bragged excessively about his conquests of women, but these romantic assignations ended abruptly when he was killed before the end of the war.

Sergeant Les Faircloth, a Londoner, was the mid-upper gunner.

Many aircrews' early experiences helped shape their characters, giving them confidence and spirit to deal with difficult situations later on. Doug Jordin, not easily ruffled, did not turn a hair when he was ordered into the pilot's seat, while trundling across the Scottish countryside aboard a twin-engine Anson. The training pilot cried: 'Come out of that bloody turret. I'm sick of flying this thing. I want to get in there and have a few shots. You come and fly it for a bit.'

Jordin did as he was told, vacating the mid-upper turret to take up the unfamiliar position at the skipper's controls.

'Just keep it straight and level,' said the officer, happily, before disappearing rapidly into the gun turret and running his hands gleefully over the two Brownings.

Jordin says: 'I heard him firing off, shooting seagulls or whatever he could find over the sea. I flew back to base, the gunnery school at Dalcross, near Inverness, and he came back into the cockpit to land it. It was quite a jolly experience and I think the pilot felt better for letting off steam.'

Their first training trip from Wickenby was in O-Orange, a brand-new Lancaster which had been delivered to the squadron that day. Jordin recalls the flight:

'Joe, our navigator, was not very good with H2S so we did a tour round the north of Scotland that night using it while the rest of the squadron went somewhere else. We flew into a thunderstorm at around 15,000ft, the Lancaster put its nose down and took us into a hellish dive over the Hebrides. We were told to stand by to bale out as we hung on, but fortunately the pilot and flight engineer pulled us out of it at 3,000ft.

'We arrived back at Wickenby shortly after the rest of the lads had landed. As we approached the flare path I noticed an awful lot of sparks behind and thought we must have hit some cables. Then I realised it was tracer.

'By this time we were on the flare path. I couldn't see terribly well but fired straight back up the tracers and must have got close to the intruding German fighter because he broke off his attack during which I felt a blow under my left foot. I thought it was a shell and told Mike to watch out for a possibly damaged tail wheel, but we got down safely.

'A shell had badly gouged the turret inches from my foot, without exploding, but ricocheted off to destroy the starboard outer engine which, luckily, had not caught fire.

'I was having my supper in the sergeants' mess later that night when Mike was sent by the group captain to collect his rear gunner because he wanted to congratulate me personally for saving his aircraft. This rather irritated me because he wasn't interested in the poor sods whose lives had been spared. I said: "Tell the old bugger I'm eating my supper." The next time I saw Groupie he snarled: "Get your hair cut, Sergeant"!'

The best gunners were those with sharp eyesight, able to quickly spot an attacking German fighter, which might be almost indistinguishable from a swirl of cloud.

Jordin again: 'I can only remember one lad having a better night vision score than me on the training course at Bridlington. The secret was to try not to look directly at the object speeding towards you. At night you can see better if you look beside the thing rather than straight at it. Then you must estimate the range and correlate the sight, all in a split second.'

On their first sortie, attacking a military base in the Normandy area, Jordin saw several bombers falling in flames, then glimpsed one of the fighters responsible for the mayhem. It streaked in from port, intending to rake their belly with shell fire. Jordin fired his Brownings and saw bits of metal fly off the Messerschmitt which veered off and disappeared, without using its guns.

Never satisfied with the amount of ammunition he was allowed in the rear turret' Jordin begged and scrounged from the armourers to make sure he had twice the normal supply for every op.

Mike Guilfoyle and his crew returned refreshed to Wickenby on 27 June 1944 after several days' welcome leave, but they were propelled quickly back into the arduous routine of war. They were on ops that night and their aircraft, G-George, which had been given a major overhaul during their absence, was already bombed up. Guilfoyle was dismayed when the ground crew told him George had not been on a flight test since the overhaul. He was denied permission to have the bombs taken off so they could take it up and his vehement protests fell on deaf ears. The Lancaster was in perfect order, it would fly sweetly to France, and the armourers were too bloody busy to sod about for fussy pilots.

One of the ground staff, a Welshman, had wanted to sneak aboard Guilfoyle's Lancaster that night to experience a bombing raid. Notoriety gained from a bombing trip would ensure him free beers in the Valleys for years. Such a dodgy venture was totally illegal and the pilot would have been jumped on from a great height by anyone of superior rank if the stowaway had been discovered. The pilot was not afraid of upsetting brasshats, but he cancelled the Welshman's flight after an intelligence officer said German fighters were expected to be busy in the target area. A dead fitter, without dog tags, found by Germans on French soil would take some explaining to his grieving family.

The target was railway yards at Vitry, east of Paris. The squadron had been told the importance of bombing accurately, making a mess of the railway while avoiding casualties among French civilians.

They had not got far when an engine began overheating, a problem which would have been picked up during a simple air test. Guilfoyle ground his teeth and thought of a few sharp comments to make when they were back at Wickenby. He consulted the crew and they decided, as the target was only in France, they could manage on three engines. When, after thirty minutes, another engine overheated and that too had to be feathered, the situation became more serious.

They struggled on to Vitry, switching the two sick engines back on as they headed into the target to give them stability for the bombing run. The bombs were released and the pilot hauled the reluctant George round until they were heading west on two engines. The limping Lancaster would be easy prey to any predatory fighter.

What really niggled the worried crew was that their predicament was solely the result of an ignorant prat at Wickenby being too preoccupied with his lofty rank and smug self-importance to consider the bomber's air worthiness a top priority.

Jordin recalls the tension which enveloped the aircraft as they switched off the two faulty engines:

'The route home took us over the fighting which followed the D-Day landings. We could not maintain height and would soon be in danger from the Germans and our own soldiers. The pilot, navigator and flight engineer talked briskly about our options because Mike had trouble keeping George stable. We were all brought into the discussion and agreed if we went on it wouldn't be much fun ditching in the Channel. The aircraft was an old one and had been reassembled once or twice before we got it. We believed it would go straight down as soon as it hit the water. The immediate worry was whether we would get over the fighting zone intact. We decided it might be better to bale out while we had solid ground beneath us.

'With the benefit of hindsight we might have got farther, baling out behind the Allied lines. An engineer who worked on Merlins and understood bearings told me the engines would stand more heat than regulations allowed before they disintegrated. With that in mind we might have flown across the fighting area at a reasonable height, avoiding the unpleasantness that followed.'

'We dropped out one by one from 10,000ft as Mike stayed at the controls.

The plane was still flying, it seemed a shame to leave it. I sat in the rear doorway and my feet were immediately whipped by the slipstream and clamped to the side of the fuselage. I glanced at the tailplane which seemed near and brutal and thought I'd give it a bit of time before I pulled the ripcord.

'The floating down sensation was pleasant and relaxing until I thought of the possibility of rifle fire waiting for me below. I saw our Lancaster burning on the ground, avoided a spiky fence and landed on a hard cobbled surface. Dogs began barking. I pushed the 'chute under a bush, climbed the fence into a field and walked quickly away.'

While other escaping aircrew might have quailed at a field of dairy cows Jordin's eyes lit up. He walked up to one, talking gently, nustled its head, knelt down, took hold of a teat and squirted the warm milk into his mouth. He put some half-grown sugar beet into his pockets and carried on across country. Behind, the sound of exploding ammunition in the blazing bomber rumbled through a nearby cowering French village.

Jordin again: 'After walking an hour or two the sky was lightening and I thought it would be sensible to find somewhere to go to ground. Seeing a light in a cottage I knocked on the door and there was a scuffling behind it. An old woman opened it, saw my uniform, whipped me inside, talked to someone behind another door, then Mike walked in. He was last out at the front of the Lancaster and I was first out at the back which makes it an incredible coincidence that we should end up at the same place.

'We were escorted from the cottage by a young lad, Jean Bousquet, who took us into a wood where there was something I can only describe as an empty poultry arch, less than four feet high. We were locked in there with a bottle of water. That night Jean returned with food and next morning he took us to his home where we met neighbours who could be trusted. We spent the night here and the following day enjoyed a picnic in a field with Jean and his family. You could hardly believe we were in occupied France.'

All the crew had baled out safely, although wireless operator Bob Yates was knocked out landing in a tree and hung there helplessly for several hours. Five successfully evaded the Germans. Jordin and Guilfoyle were given clothing by villagers and Bousquet's mother bought two rail tickets to Paris.

They travelled alone, waiting outside the station in the French capital for the man who was supposed to contact them. A man in his fifties turned up, smartly dressed, and said to Jordin: 'Say something in English.'

The gunner replied: 'What the bloody hell would you like me to say?'

The man grinned. 'That'll do.'

The following days were spent in a dizzy whirl. They went to a party of high-ranking guards officers, and were billeted in a luxury apartment off the Champs Elysée, where they met two other airmen, an American gunner, A. J. Paletier and an Australian navigator. All four eagerly anticipated the nightly entertainment by a shapely girl in a bedroom across the road who slowly stripped down to her brassiere and knickers every night. Sadly, she always unsportingly closed the blinds before the pulsating climax.

When Jordin and Paletier were moved to Rose Vivier's café at Levallois Perret, they were introduced to caviar which she had hidden from her German customers. Noisy German troops were billeted on the floor above, and in the cellar Madame Vivier kept a smelly billy goat. They went to another party given by the middle-aged editor of a sporting paper, whose beautiful young wife had an awesome cleavage and wept miserably when they left at midnight, legs buckling from a surfeit of Cognac, narrowly avoiding a squad of German troops.

Jordin, Guilfoyle, Paletier and three others were brought to a hotel room and told they would be picked up by a German Army wagon and driven south as a working party to get to the Spanish border. Twenty-eight airmen piled on to the wagon. It was only when they were delivered to the Gestapo headquarters in Paris they realised they had been betrayed.

After a month in Fresnes prison they were taken to a railway station. Jordin will never forget the misery of that journey.

'The whole prison population, including ordinary criminals, was stuffed into cattle trucks. Our truck was crammed with sixty men, we could only sit down in shifts. It was the middle of August, very hot, with little to drink. At one stop, when we were allowed out to crap and piss, I drank rusty water from the long trough in the middle of the lines which was scooped up at speed by locomotives. I came second in a competition for the longest chest hair, one of the few lighter moments.

'The trucks had narrow ventilation holes, covered by barbed wire. We were stationary in the countryside, still locked inside when an American in our truck was idly messing with the wire. He was spotted by a guard outside who shot him in the hand. The door opened and a German called out for the injured man to get medical treatment. The American went outside and was immediately shot three times. They dug a shallow grave at the side of the track and his body was rolled into it.

'Before he was killed we'd loosened two floorboards with the only tools we had, a few spoons. We'd planned to drop through the floor and escape. But the Germans promised to fling a hand grenade into the truck if anyone tried to get away. Some were prepared to draw lots to see who would escape, the others were not, so the idea was abandoned.

'Further on the line had been bombed and a tunnel blocked so we walked, covered by machine guns, carrying the loot the Germans had accumulated. I had a heavy crate on my shoulder.'

During that walk Jordin enjoyed one sweet moment of sanity among the deluge of madness. In Alsace, two Alsatian dogs trotted past the prisoners shepherding a flock of sheep. Unaccompanied, they took the sheep out of sight.

Herded aboard a train on the other side of the damaged track they shuffled through the summer heat across Germany to their destination, a station near Weimar. The men got out, gaunt, hungry, blinking nervously in the sun, faced by the grim stone faces of men in SS uniform and whiplash roars of:

'Schnell! schnell!' They were prodded, kicked and beaten by rifle butts into a shambling run towards a huge camp several hundred yards away where drooping hordes of shabby lethargic men watched the newcomers through large sad eyes which had witnessed many undefined horrors.

Jordin had heard stories about prisoner-of-war camps which were run in a civilised fashion according to the Geneva Convention, but in the middle of a boiling hot day, this camp lacked warmth and humanity.

'Where is this?' someone asked, cautiously. 'Buchenwald,' came the reply. 'One of Hitler's holiday camps.'

Jordin again: 'I think the Germans wanted us airmen out of the way. It was simpler than dealing with us in the usual manner and we'd been picked up in civvies and had caused them a bit of trouble. We were stripped, shorn all over, then doused in sheep dip to smarten us up.

'There was not much food. We had one-seventh of a loaf of bread each day and a bowl of soup. Sometimes we had ersatz coffee which some chaps said was made out of grass. The soup came in containers of about thirty gallons. The Frenchmen in our eating area fought over small bits which could be scraped out with their hands after we'd been fed. It took three months before one or two of our blokes had joined the scavengers. I would have died before giving the bloody Jerries the satisfaction of seeing me reduced to that level.

'We turned down jobs at a nearby factory, where we would get better food. It was making parts for the V1 and V2 missiles. The Yanks bombed the factory, unfortunately setting fire to our food store and cutting off our water supply. We helped put the fire out and extracted a lot of food.

'That summer we slept outside on the ground with a threadbare blanket between five. Buchenwald stood on high ground and got pretty chilly towards morning. During a spectacular thunderstorm we took off all our clothes, rolled them in a ball and crouched naked. It was nice to have something dry to put on afterwards. We were moved into billets for the winter.

'A kapo, a rough lanky individual, spotted an airman who had bad dysentery and was late getting out of the bog for appell. Holding a length of wood, he approached our lad to biff him with it. Our group, about sixty of us, suddenly moved quietly to protect him. The kapo stopped and backed off; it was quite impressive.

'The ovens were constantly running. We had a good idea of what was going on. Thirty British agents were there at one time. One day they were missing and we learned they'd been hanged the night before. They were probably put through the ovens. Fifty prisoners died every day from various diseases, including typhus. I saw their piled-up naked bodies waiting for the ovens. We lost two men: one Brit and a Yank.

'When we arrived I saw what I thought were monkeys running round in our compound, but they were gipsy kids. Filthy and naked, they had all been neutered.

'One of the little buggers pinched my breakfast one night. I had a slice of bread wrapped in a bit of rag I used to dry myself after washing. I also wore wooden clogs. This kid, of about twelve, took my clogs and bread while I was asleep. I saw him wearing the clogs later and grabbed him to get them back. A pack of sixty of his mates fell on me and would probably have done me in if some pals hadn't rescued me.

'A man ran past me one day with an eye torn out of its socket hanging down on his cheek. He was pursued by a mob of 100 or so, who he'd annoyed in some way. They were frenzied in their attacks on him and eventually tore him to pieces.

'A little Estonian lad of about eighteen, who spoke good English, said his parents and sister had been murdered by the Germans and he'd not been working hard enough so his hand had been rammed into a machine. He'd lost three fingers. I did my best to convince him that we'd win the war and he would get out. To my great satisfaction, after the war I saw a news sheet with a photograph and interview of his release from Buchenwald. I can see his face now.

'There were an untold number of Jewish musicians in Buchenwald, kept alive to entertain the Germans. There was a brass band which led a working party out of the camp before dawn. The Jerries provided all the instruments.

'We were given a couple of tickets to a concert, which demonstrates what a weird place it was. We drew lots for the tickets and I won one. I saw some of the best musicians in Europe playing on a platform in this building. A pianist played *Run Rabbit Run* for our benefit. He kept sticking in little bars of other music, like *We're Going To Hang Out Our Washing On The Siegfried Line*. The Germans applauded with the rest of us. As we enjoyed the music the smoke continued to pour out of the oven chimneys.'

They were in Buchenwald nearly four months. An agent who went out on a working party got a message to the Red Cross which informed the Luftwaffe. The airmen were moved in October to Sagan, Stalag Luft III, an officers' prison where Jordin and Guilfoyle were separated. NCOs from Buchenwald were allowed to stay as batmen. Jordin had a cushy number sweeping out the padre's bunk once a week.

The card which Jordin sent to his family on 25 October was the first news they had received to say he was alive.

That winter they flooded part of the parade ground with water from the ablutions, turning it into a skating rink with snow banked up around it. One man, who found a record of *The Skater's Waltz*, played it on a gramophone to the surreal scene of skating prisoners watched by their German captors.

They left on the winter march west on an icy day in January during a blizzard. They walked 16km, spending the first night in a church. Jordin and his companions had each been given two Red Cross parcels and a blanket before leaving Sagan. He wore a helmet made from a pair of underpants tied under his chin, and an Army greatcoat. They made sledges at Hobau to carry their things but had to abandon them three days later during a thaw.

Several guards got frostbite and Willie, a Canadian, carried the rifle for one German whose feet were suffering. A German woman left her house with a bucket of water but the guards sent her away, weeping, because her son, a POW in England was being more kindly treated.

Jordin saw fawns skipping across a glade caught by a weak sun while collecting fuel for a fire and remembered the nightingale he heard at Wickenby when, unable to sleep after a raid, he had slipped quietly into a wood.

Their hut guard at Sagan, a German they called Pop, aged about fifty, always turned and winked at them after giving the Nazi salute at appell. Jordin believes they were his only friends. The German had lost two sons in the war and did not know what had happened to his wife and farm. Told he was to be posted with others who had been given the impossible task of halting the advancing tide of Russians, Pop shook hands with his fifty charges, weeping bitterly.

Spring daffodils saw the march continue. Jordin had made a haversack using the top an old pair of Army trousers, tying up the legs, but they needed transport for their accumulated equipment.

Jordin says: 'We rested in a village near a blacksmith's shop. Outside stood a four-wheel pony cart, absolutely ideal. Nine of us tried to buy it, using cigarettes and D-bars – American blocks of good chocolate. The blacksmith's wife said he was out and she couldn't sell it. When she wasn't looking we took it. It was a grand light-weight cart, easy running, with all our clobber in it. After 5km we were resting again when she appeared on her bike, panting. We quickly emptied the cart and left it, leaving her very upset because she didn't know how the hell she would get it home.

'We stole a sack of barley which made excellent soup or porridge. The column was shot up and bombed at night by a Mosquito which killed a load of Germans in their wagons, and some Fleet Air Arm chaps died when we were strafed by a Typhoon during the day.

'Before being officially released we had collected around 300 Germans who had given themselves up. We got into a Dakota at an airfield near the Danish border and flew home. It seemed totally unreal after what we had been through.'

CHAPTER NINE

EVASION

Neville Donmall's childhood ended abruptly when he was thirteen. After his accountant father, George, died the boy became the man of the house in Surbiton, Surrey. Money was short and after his mother, Daisy, eventually found secretarial work in the town, the boy hurried home from school every afternoon to cook dinner, helped by his nine-year-old sister, Norah. When Mrs Donmall was in bed, suffering from a debilitating bronchial illness, she became hysterical from the increasing worry of their worsening plight. The boy calmed down his mother and promised they would pull through.

With new responsibilities young Donmall grew up quickly, learning the merits of doing a job well without flapping, while building up his self-confidence and determination, all good grounding for anyone destined to fly in Bomber Command.

Donmall was known as Titch at the Hawker aircraft factory in Kingston Upon Thames where, as a diminutive sixteen-year-old, he was an apprentice draughtsman. Three years later, a navigator flying with 578 Squadron at Burn, near Selby, Titch topped six feet, weighed over fourteen stone, and was extremely fit, a powerful swimmer, shining at rugby and athletics.

Conscientious, but impatient, he was always prepared to short circuit King's Regulations if he thought of better ways to get things done, while biting his tongue in the company of dim or less resolute senior officers.

Pilot Officer Donmall was pleased to be teamed up in north Yorkshire with pilot Flying Officer Chuck Watson, of Whitley Bay, Northumberland.

Like any young aircrew who was planning to be alive and healthy at the end of the war Donmall needed luck which, though essential, was not usually enough to give a fellow an edge over his mates in the precarious steeplechase towards survival. Luck was a major factor but it often needed to be linked to an acute sharpness of mind and the ability to act swiftly, decisively and coolly.

Luck was on board one night when they were heading for the Ruhr with a Lancaster at the same height, 400 yards ahead. The bomber suddenly disappeared in an enormous explosion, except its inflated yellow dinghy which rushed past on the starboard side of Watson's Halifax. Someone muttered an incredulous: 'Bloody hell!' over the r/t as they realised, yet again, that death could strike without warning. Seven men and their aircraft, which had probably been hit by a shell in the bomb bay, had been reduced to fragments whirling about the sky.

Luck needed a competent assistant another time when Donmall had a compelling itch to climb into the cockpit to see what was happening. He recalls the horrifying moment:

'As I came up the stairs I saw a Lanc on the starboard side at the same level, no more than fifty yards away, coming closer. There was no time to shout at the pilot because if Chuck had dived the tail would have come up and the other Lancaster would have hit it, curtains for everyone. I knocked back the throttles for all four engines and we immediately sank straight down.

'The skipper yelled: "What the fucking hell do you think you're doing?" Then the dark shadow of the Lancaster went across the top of us and Chuck was speechless. He later said: "I thought you'd gone bloody mad doing that, but thank God you saw it".'

Once, a 1,000lb bomb fell between their wing and tail plane, only feet from disaster. And during one rough ride through a storm of flak a piece of hot shrapnel burst through the perspex nose, missing the bomb aimer by inches, and another embedded itself wickedly into Donmall's seat.

On 22 December 1944 Watson and his crew were among ninety Halifaxes from 4 Group briefed to attack the marshalling yards at Bingen, on the Rhine, some thirty miles south-west of Frankfurt. They would be joined that night by fourteen Lancasters and two Mosquitoes of 8 Group. Two Halifaxes and one Lancaster would not return.

The crew had bought and delivered most of their Christmas presents on the last leave a month ago. They were among crews on duty over Christmas, with no chance of getting home, but there were the parties at Burn to look forward to. The parties would be clamorous and boozy, with riotous games, a lively combination to help forget the bloody war.

A smoothly confident intelligence officer had told them they would encounter little flak on the way to the target and they left briefing convinced Bingen would be a decent in-and-out target, wrapped up in Christmas paper.

The day was bitterly cold with a miserable drizzle of rain and sleet which clung sickeningly to their clothes, inspiring no one to work up a modicum of festive feeling. Burn was a wartime camp, inhospitably mucky in winter. They kept warm by pinching extra coke from the storage compound for the hungry stoves in their charmless Nissen hut billets.

That night the cold had, as usual, penetrated the Halifaxes and they shivered an hour or so before the 4.11pm takeoff while clambering through the echoing fuselage which could be equated to a seventy-one-foot-long refrigerator. The Halifax had an eight-man crew. A third gunner was in the mid-under position, operating a flexible .5 Browning machine gun.

Donmall recalls: 'Fifty miles from Bingen the clouds started to disperse and we did a beautiful run in. There was enough moon for us to make out the marshalling yards and the Rhine, the TIs went down on time and we bombed from 18,000ft. We continued until we were clear of the target area, turned south and after ten miles pointed west to clear the stream still coming in.

'We thought ourselves lucky, it was an easy one. We were buoyant, we'd bombed smack on the aiming point. Near Bad Kreuznach, the rear gunner reported a Ju-88 on our tail, coming in to attack. Our gunners opened up and thought they'd hit it. We sustained minor damage in the tail unit and rear of the fuselage. But another Ju-88 plunged in, machine guns and cannons blazing, and a starboard fuel tank caught fire. We returned fire, and the mid-upper reported long flames streaking from the fighter which sheered off, but our starboard wing was ablaze. Our position was hopeless and Chuck ordered the crew to bale out. Everybody acknowledged that call.

'I had been at my desk using the H2S, but turned into a whirlwind. I had my 'chute on in microseconds, making sure the D-ring was on the left-hand side. I knew of a chap who put his 'chute on the wrong way round, and was found on the ground dead with claw marks on his parachute made as he tried desperately to find the D-ring. Now my aircraft was on fire and I was determined not to be inside when it blew as I knew it would.

'There was someone right behind me ready to go as I flipped up the seat, released the twist mechanism of the escape hatch at my feet and sat down. Facing aft, I pushed myself out and ducked, to avoid hitting anything. I counted to three, pulled the D-ring and knew nothing more until I came to feeling as sick as a dog, my chin hurting like hell, very dazed. I'd been walloped under the chin by the parachute pack as it deployed and had a graze right up the side of my face. I looked round for the ground, but couldn't see anything and believed I was in cloud or fog. I hit the deck with a terrible whack and my knee clouted me under the chin. Luckily, I'd landed in a foot of snow, which absorbed the impact. I knew I had to clear the area so, gathering up my 'chute, I started running. I discovered I'd landed in some hills, near Trier, and kept moving until I came to the shelter of a wood, and stopped for a rest.

'I didn't see the wreck of our aircraft, but found out later that all three gunners were killed. As Chuck got out the aircraft blew up, breaking his leg. He wrapped himself up in his 'chute until the Germans found him. The others also became POWs.'

The raid on Bingen successfully stopped all movement of supplies by rail through the town to the Ardennes battlefront. No civilians were killed.

The night was bitterly cold and Donmall was only wearing his battledress and a roll-neck sweater.

'I cut panels from the parachute with a sheath knife which I kept strapped to my leg inside a boot. I wrapped them round my body and quickly got away from the area, getting a westerly heading from my large luminous compass. I decided to get into the Ardennes where the battle was on, but I knew they were on a pronged attack which left gaps that I might be able to slip through. I set off at a run.

'After climbing higher into the hills I found a small road with a thicket of bushes and slit trenches to one side. Gathering branches, I laid them across the trench at one end, spread 'chute panels from my body over them and added a layer of snow. I built up a wall of snow to keep out the wind. Using a branch to sweep away my footprints I settled down to sleep, but awoke after an hour or so. It was dawn and there had been a fresh fall of snow.'

Two people with a horse and cart passed on the road before Donmall checked his escape kit. It included Horlicks tablets, glucose sweets, water bag, tablets for purifying water, soap, razor, needle, cotton, waterproof matches and benzedrine tablets, together with German, Dutch and French currency.

He pulled his pullover sleeves over his hands and sewed between the fingers, making himself a pair of mittens. He put snow in the water bag which he shoved inside his battledress to melt for drinking. Remaining in the trench all day he slept fitfully, disturbed by passing farm vehicles and pedestrians.

He set out at dark, skirting a village, through a wood and, after several hours, into a valley where he rested, leaning against a tree, sucking Horlicks tablets, and refilling his water bag with snow. Hearing what he thought was snow falling from trees he noticed he was surrounded by a ring of baleful yellow eyes. Waving a heavy branch he charged a snarling pack of starving stray dogs. They scattered and the navigator found sparse shelter in some bushes. As darkness closed in he set off again, heading west.

'About two hours before dawn I heard the crackling noise of a pulse jet roaring behind me. From a small wood a V1 was taking off, flying directly towards me. I threw myself down and watched it climbing above my head. I left the area in a hurry, knowing German troops must be close by.'

Early on the morning of Christmas Day Donmall stared down into Trier where fires still burned after the attack on 23 December against the town's railway yards by 3 Group Lancasters. He watched German soldiers and two young women collecting Window, the metallic strips dropped by Allied aircraft to jam enemy radar. The Window, hanging thickly from trees, was being harvested for festive decorations.

Donmall again: 'I had little sleep that day, it was far too cold. I thought about the Christmas dinner the squadron were having in the mess as I drank water and sucked Horlicks tablets and a glucose sweet for mine.

'I had ascertained there was only one bridge over the river Moselle and at dusk saw there was a guard on either side. I made a note of the markings of two tanks that went by among a number of military vehicles and approached the guard who'd been watching me. I asked him the way in a garbled version of the Spanish I'd learned at school and was amazed when he gave up trying to understand and waved me across. The guard on the other side ignored me.

'I passed a German officer when we were both going round a large bomb crater. I pointed and shrugged, as if to say: "Those bloody RAF bombers." He just nodded.

'After about eight hours I stumbled across a large area of barbed wire and trench defences. I cleared these and was faced by a daunting anti-tank trench, about twelve feet deep and fifteen feet across that stretched in both directions as far as I could see. I jumped down but had to dig out hand and footholds with my knife the other side.'

Donmall negotiated barbed wire and more anti-tank obstructions, called dragons' teeth, then pillboxes and realised he had stumbled on Germany's heavily fortified Siegfried Line which ran along its western frontier from Holland to Switzerland.

He spent the day in a small farm hut, sleeping under sacks, and watching the movement of German troops who disappeared into pillboxes as the light faded. The navigator slipped like a ghost between the pillboxes and at the bottom of a valley stopped short at a series of notices between a road and the river: 'Minen – Verboten!'

Avoiding the mined area he crept through a trench into a village, found two large gaps in the barbed-wire and decided to cross the river. He searched several empty houses looking for anything that would float. He found five hefty planks of wood in a back yard, a ball of string, a straw-filled sack, and half a pot of plum jam, which he ate heartily.

It was almost dark as he carried his booty to the water's edge, whispering a prayer that he would not set off a hidden mine. He could see the mines, almost hidden under mounds of snow. Ice had formed at the edge of the swiftly-flowing river, where Donmall began assembling his raft.

'I tied the planks together with the string, launching them as quietly as possible. I took off my flying boots, removed clothing below the waist and put them in the sack of straw, which I tied round my neck before boarding the raft. Sitting astride it I started paddling across the river with great difficulty. Since the planks were almost submerged the raft started breaking up half-way across. I was thrown into the icy water and forced to swim the rest of the way, the sack trailing behind me. I sighed with relief as I reached the opposite bank.

'Shivering and gasping in my wet shirt and battledress top I emptied the sack, pulling on my trousers and socks which, luckily, weren't too wet. My flying boots were full of water so I walked in my socks and by the time I had reached a village, 200 yards away, my battledress was starting to freeze. It was imperative that I took my wet clothes off before succumbing to the intense cold, so I went into an empty house and, incredibly, found a duvet quilt. I stripped off, wrapped myself in it and ran round a room to get my circulation going. My fingers and toes were numb and my manhood had temporarily disappeared, but I felt better after an hour and sank down, exhausted, on the floor inside the duvet.

'I must have slept for eight hours when I was wakened at dawn by machine gun fire. I looked through a window and thought the guns were being tested from the pillboxes, firing at targets on my side of the valley.

'Upstairs I found a pair of old boots that fitted, some matches, but no food. I broke up furniture which I fed into the kitchen wood-burning stove and lit a fire, hoping it would not make too much smoke. I put my wet clothes on top of the stove, heated some water and had a shave with the razor from my escape pack. After a good wash and a drink of hot water I was ready to go. The day before I noticed the troops vanished around lunchtime. That was when I made my move.'

He climbed a road leading from the valley and a bend took him out of sight of the pillboxes. Mines lurked in the frozen ground and thin wires were stretched over the road. He stepped over the wires, which he would have blundered into at night, and walked between the mines. In mid-afternoon he left the road in sunshine and saw a long convoy of German soldiers and vehicles moving along a road a few hundred yards away. Aircraft flew overhead and with the sound of bombs whistling down upon the convoy, he dropped flat on his face. One stick under shot and fell close, sending bomb fragments screaming over his head.

Later, hearing the sound of machine gun and cannon fire, he saw a blazing American P-38 Lightning being pursued by a German FW190 fighter and again dropped down as shells and bullets shrieked overhead. Donmall watched helplessly as the P-38 fighter-bomber crashed in a wood and exploded. He moved away quickly before the area was swarming with Germans. He hid that night out of the wind in a hollow surrounded by bushes, disturbed by a battle raging between heavy guns on either side of him, some shells dropping near his hideout, shaking the ground on which he laid.

He spent next morning dodging German troops and after mid-day spotted more soldiers in thick bushes. He tried to get round them, but a shot was fired over his head. Donmall's long solitary ordeal was over. It was not until he got closer that he realised they were Americans.

'Safe behind the American lines I was told they'd been watching me through binoculars for some time and couldn't make out my uniform. Still suspicious they kept a gun trained on me until an officer interrogated me thoroughly about London and shows that were on there. I gave him details about German gun positions and markings on tanks. He took me to lunch where I met General George Patton, a big bluff bloke, who insisted I sat next to him. After I'd told my story he turned to his officers and said: "Here's a limey who's got some guts. But if he got through the Germans can get through. See we close that gap".'

Put on an Anson in Paris for Northolt wearing an American officer's uniform, just before New Year's Eve, Donmall went home for a fortnight's leave. The door was opened by his mother who immediately fainted. The telegram he had sent from Paris had not arrived. She had thought he was dead.

He joined his second crew, which was skippered by the popular Pilot Officer Douglas Wood, on 158 Squadron at Lissett, Yorkshire, where he was precipitated into more drama.

On the night of 7 March 1945 they were among 256 Halifax and twenty-five Lancaster crews briefed to attack the Deutsche Erdoel refinery at Hemmingstedt near Heide, about fifty miles south of the Danish border.

Donmall recalls: 'We had to fly at 1,000ft right across the North Sea to avoid the German radar, before climbing to around 15,000ft to bomb. When we took off it was murky, drizzling and miserable. We ran into a thunderstorm with heavy rain and passing the end of Flamborough Head were struck by lightning. We lost our radio, the H2S, Gee and the giro compass. We had a little discussion and decided to carry on using DR.

'We climbed when we got to what we thought was the Danish coast, but there were no TIs going down on time. You can always see them, but there was nothing there and Woody said: "Where the hell are we?" I left my desk, looked to the south, saw coloured TIs falling, and thought we'd been blown north by strong winds. So we turned and went south. We saw the target burning but the Main Stream had gone. We were the only aircraft there and all the flak was coming our way. It was ferocious stuff, bursting all round us. Woody cried: "Let's get on and drop our bombs and get the hell out of here."

'Our run in was perfect although we were hit by small stuff. We dropped the bombs using the aiming point where all the fires were. Then we got coned. The radar-controlled master searchlight clamped on to us, the other searchlights followed and Woody lost his night vision. He put the Halifax into a dive to escape the blinding blast of light and I remember someone yelling: "Corkscrew port, go! Fighter on the tail!"

'We were in a steep dive as Woody kicked the rudder, the aircraft twisted to port and we went on to our backs. Now we were in an inverted dive and not looking good. I found myself spreadeagled with the bomb aimer, Russell 'Rusty' Hudson, on the roof of the nose. I dragged myself along the ribs of the Halifax until I got to the stairwell leading to the cockpit. I could see Woody with his feet against the instrument panel desperately trying to regain control, but nothing was happening except we were going down at high speed.

'I pulled myself into the cockpit, got the second pilot's seat down and strapped myself in. I put my feet on the rudder bar, my hands on the control column and started pulling back. The pilot looked over, gave me the thumbs up and started winding the trimming tabs to pull the aircraft through. He continued to wind until the aircraft pulled through, shuddering and shaking like mad. Woody told me later he'd been praying because he knew he couldn't pull it out himself and thought we would go straight in.'

They had pulled out at less than 1,000ft, still over Germany on a curious crabbing course which took them breathlessly over Bremen and Wilhemshaven, where they were welcomed with intense flak and escaped, still believing they had bombed Hemmingstedt. When a bright fighter parachute flare lit up and drifted down they gazed at it in dismay for the Halifax was as vulnerable as a wounded buffalo might be to a tribe of starving Red Indians. Seconds added up to one minute, then two, and no fighter appeared. Then the pilot turned to Donmall and said, anxiously: 'I've no artificial horizon, no turn and bank and no air speed indicator. How the hell can we hold the aircraft straight and level?'

Donmall again: 'I said: "I can tell you." I could see by the light flak that was coming up whether the wing tips had dropped or were going up against it. I said: "Pick up your starboard wing. Bring up the port. Your nose has dropped; pick up your nose." I had turned into his artificial horizon and turn and bank. Eventually we came out over the sea. Luckily the North Sea was rough and, standing beside the pilot, I could use the white horses to bring the wings and nose up. We were at no more than 1,000ft. An engine cut and we tried to climb, but the aircraft shook and shuddered. Woody was flying on rpm which was working on all three engines, so he knew our approximate speed.

'We didn't recognise the land when we saw it, then realised we were on the north side of The Wash. We changed course, turned in and found they had no lights on at the airfield. They had written us off, we were forty-five minutes behind the others. We had no r/t so we fired off a red and the airfield lights came on. We got down all right and were glad to get back in one piece.

'In the debriefing room an intelligence officer said: "You don't need to talk to us, you missed the target, it was a dummy." We told him we hadn't and when we began arguing he snapped: "I don't want to hear any more, forget it." So we went to bed.

'We looked at the aircraft later that morning and found the ailerons and elevators were twisted, there were ripples on the wings, which had also become twisted, hundreds of rivets were sheered and the tail was slightly out of alignment. In the ops room we saw the squadron photographs of the bombed target. One picture was pinned up to one side. It was ours and looked different. We were told it had been sent to group headquarters.'

Wood and his crew later learned that the rest of the squadron had indeed bombed a dummy oil refinery. They alone had attacked Harburg to the south, near Hamburg, which had been pounded by a force from 5 Group before the lone Halifax had arrived.

A threat to court-martial Wood for not turning back after his instruments and radio had failed, putting his crew in jeopardy, was lifted when the top brass at group realised his aircraft had done more damage that night than the rest of the squadron. Wood was later awarded a DFC.

The European war had less than a month to run on 11 April 1945 when bombers from 158 Squadron were sent on a daylight raid against Nuremburg. They were among 129 Halifaxes and fourteen Pathfinder Lancasters which, without loss, accurately attacked the city's railway yards. It was the day Donmall left his parachute on the hard standing at dispersal.

'I didn't think any more about it after arranging to clip myself to someone else's parachute if we had to bale out.

'On the run in to the target I stuck my head out as usual and saw one of our squadron receive a direct hit. I saw it tumble, go into a slight spin, and drop around 5,000ft. Their New Zealand warrant officer pilot regained control, went on to attack the target and I told Woody about it when we'd bombed and turned back. I suggested we went down to escort him back, which we did. It had a great hole towards the outer edge of the port wing. The average dining room table could easily have passed through the hole which had damaged an aileron. Three American Thunderbolt fighters came down to have a look at us and stayed for a short while before climbing away.

'We didn't shake hands with the other crew after we got back. We parked in different parts of the airfield at Lisset. It was just something that happened.'

Seven days later a 1,000lb bomb was hung up after they had attacked Heligoland with nearly 1,000 other bombers.

Donmall says: 'As we were leaving the target we saw three E-boats in line astern, leaving the harbour. We did a run over them, released the bomb and after the explosion only two boats could be seen. That was very satisfying.'

CHAPTER TEN

FOGBOUND

In the winter of 1942 when snow swept belligerently across shivering Leicestershire, groups of young aircrews, whooping with excitement, raced on to the airfield at Wymeswold. All Australians, they had not seen this strange white stuff before and wanted to make the most of it before a thaw set in.

They rolled and slid in it, pelted each other with snowballs and made stolid grinning and grimacing snowmen, some of which, with a few telltale additions, bore a passing resemblance to the station commander of 28 OTU, and one or two of their instructors.

Sergeant Frank Smith was among those yelling and capering airmen. The pilot, in his late twenties, was a long way from his home in Newcastle, a town in New South Wales, which stood at the mouth of the Hunter river, on a great coalfield. Thickset, normally a sober and serious sort of chap, with a reputation for thoroughness, he was known to blow a little wild occasionally with his Australian pals. Married before the war he nevertheless enjoyed the companionship of pretty WAAFs at different airfields.

Smith's crew were all sergeants at Wymeswold. Many were later commissioned and went on to second tours.

Don Hanslow, from Yardley, Birmingham, first saw service with the Army and was among the thousands of soldiers who escaped across the Channel from Dunkirk. Back in England, bored and thirsting for more excitement, he was right to think he would find action in the RAF. He later became Smith's navigator. Before each operation Hanslow allowed himself plenty of time to fastidiously plan a course which avoided all known trouble spots.

Jack Dix, the hale and hearty wireless operator, came from Consett, County Durham. Pipe-smoking John Studd worked as a clerk with Ipswich Corporation Electric Supply and Transport Department before training as a bomb aimer. After the war he became brother-in-law to the rear gunner, Harry Quick, who married his sister, Jean, a midwife.

Quick, brought up in the north Devon village of Atherington, had done various odd jobs, including cleaning out hens at a poultry farm, after leaving school at fourteen. One of five children, he was only eighteen months old when his father, Charles, a postman, died of exposure on a wintry Devon road after an accident. Quick's great-great grandmother, Annie, was sister to Richard Doddridge Blackmore, whose best-selling romance, *Lorna Doone*, was set on nearby Exmoor.

Everyone in bombers had nicknames and Quick might have expected to be called Swifty or Flash. Instead, his skipper said at OTU: 'You'll have to be re-christened. We've got to change your name to Harry because it's easier on the intercom than Harold.'

Quick had never been called Harry before, but the name stuck, except among his relations in the West Country.

After joining up in 1941, Quick found it was not easy to get at the throats of the Germans when he was posted to Ford, near Littlehampton. He kicked his heels here for six months on guard duty, and as an orderly room runner, until a place was found for him on a gunnery course.

For luck, Quick had pinned an ivory elephant the size of his thumbnail, to the inside of a battledress pocket. The charm, given him by a girlfriend, came in useful at Ford, where he was given his first taste of flying. Although the hair-raising experience might easily have propelled him afterwards towards station headquarters with an urgent request to remuster to a ground job.

He was standing idly chatting with a group of other bored gunners-in-waiting, complaining bitterly about how the bloody war would be over before they got their fingers on the trigger of a Browning machine gun, when a Polish fighter pilot appeared with a cheerful grin and an irresistible invitation.

He said, in crushed English: 'I'm just going up. Anyone like to come?'

Quick hastily stepped forward, failing to notice that the men who had been waiting patiently at Ford longest, displayed a curious reluctance to grab the chance of a gash flight, while wearing unfathomable smiles.

The Pole briskly led Quick to a twin-seater Boulton Paul Defiant. They got in, taxied down the runway, took off and Quick's heart swelled with excitement and pride as the fighter skittered pleasantly a few hundred feet above Hampshire. Then they turned upside-down and the pilot's toothy grin widened as a long wavering howl from his terrified passenger burst down the intercom.

The Defiant did a slow roll back to normal and the pilot told Quick, quite reasonably: 'Don't worry, I was just tipping the leaves out of the cockpit.'

It was too late for the white-faced Quick to be advised by his chuckling companions on the ground that while Polish pilots' courage was unsurpassed, they possessed the most wicked sense of humour among flying men, and a wild recklessness that bordered on insanity.

By 28 November 1942, Smith and his crew had yet to see a German aircraft. Their heads had been filled with awesome facts and figures, plus considerable bumph, which one day might be useful. They had flown in some very creaky Wellingtons on circuits and bumps and cross-country exercises since arriving at Wymeswold earlier that month. They looked forward to the day when they were sent to an operational squadron, but today they anticipated more grinding circuits and bumps when they climbed into another tottering Wellington IC, T2896.

John Studd had been excused this flight and lay slumped happily on his bed in the crews' Nissen accommodation hut, reading a book when Smith turned the old Wimpy on to the runway and waited, building up the revs.

Quick recalls the terror of a routine trip which did not go according to plan:

'We used to go off individually at Wymeswold. I think it might have been a bit dangerous to have two training crews above the airfield at the same time. I remember rolling down the runway and looking out of my turret. Everything was normal and I made a gentle turn of the turret for a look round. We lifted off and had got very little height when there was a hell of a rattle and thump, followed by an almighty bump. It happened without warning. I was sitting there a bit dazed, wondering what had happened, realised we'd crashed, and knew it was time to get out a bit smartish.'

Studd looked up sharply at the kerumphing sound of the crash, said to himself: 'I bet that's Frank Smith,' swiftly calculated the distance to the far side of the airfield, then returned to his book. The excitement would all be over by the time he got there.

The Wellington had struggled to no more than 200ft when the starboard engine caught fire. The bomber immediately turned its nose down and went straight in just off the end of the runway, inside the perimeter track. Amazingly, no one was hurt but the four men all had a tremble in their legs as they scrambled to get out of the crumpled wreck. Quick, cocooned in the tail, found the rotating mechanism had failed and his turret would not move.

'It must have been buckled when we hit the ground. I don't recall being scared as I dragged desperately at the doors into the fuselage until they opened wide enough for me to squeeze through. I didn't see the others. They probably left through the escape hatch in the top of the cockpit and I was a minute or two behind them. By now the Wimpy was burning quite merrily and there were one or two items of ammunition going off as well which was rather frightening. The fire was spreading rapidly as I got out, not even bruised. We were all very lucky, especially those in the front. The aircraft was a total write-off.'

Later, at 1656 HCU, Lindholme, they were joined by a mid-upper gunner, Ron McCord, a lanky forthright Australian, who came from the small town of Gympie, north of Brisbane, Queensland, and the bluff genial flight engineer, Jack Ingram, the only member of the crew with a moustache. They were a relaxed crew, happy in each other's company. Harry Quick cannot remember a bad or awkward moment which was generated by any quirk of character.

On 12 April 1943 they were posted to 101 Squadron, which was based with Lancasters at Holme-on-Spalding Moor, in Yorkshire's East Riding. Their initial enthusiasm was a little deflated when told they were replacing a dead crew. Their predecessors had returned from ops a few nights previously, crash landed on the airfield and died horribly, consumed by flames.

On 20 April they took off on their first bombing trip, to Stettin, but this was aborted halfway across the North Sea in pitch darkness at 1,000ft on the way to a turning point over the Danish coast when the starboard outer engine caught fire and resisted all attempts to put it out. They climbed slowly to a height at which they could safely jettison the bombs and headed for base, praying that they would not suffer the same fate as the crew they replaced.

Their first completed sortie was to Duisburg on 26 April. Quick again:

'We were frightened the whole of the time on that raid. I don't believe anyone who says they were not frightened on ops. The first operation was something very spectacular for most people, it certainly was for us. We were always warned not to look down at the target, partly because you were being distracted from what you were supposed to be doing and partly because it could ruin your night vision. Sometimes you were drawn to it, you just had to look. It was horrific what was happening down there. There were explosions, huge fires: a monstrous bubbling stew of reds, oranges and blues, and searchlights. I did not feel in any way for the people who were being bombed, nor did I hate them. I had no hate in my heart, but I disliked the Germans for what they were doing to other people after they had invaded Poland and the Low Countries.

'We saw a Wellington blow up and could see a large number of our aircraft flying over the target. We didn't notice any Jerry fighters, which was a bit of good luck on such a clear night. We collected one little hole from flak in the starboard fin.'

There were no safe places in a bomber which was being attacked by a German fighter, or pummelled by ack-ack, and the rear gunner was more vulnerable than his companions.

Quick recalls: 'There was a theory that the night fighters always tried to knock off the tail gunner but to me, that was a fallacy. The Germans shot at the aircraft, not an individual, although the rear gunner was usually first in the line of fire. More than anything I was frightened of being in thunder clouds or in a thunderstorm when you had static electricity playing around the aircraft. When it struck my four Browning machine guns it streaked to the end of the flash eliminators and surged off like flames from a gas jet. I tried in vain to crawl down out of the way when St Elmo's Fire was leaping about on the rivets inside my turret, while outside our trailing aerial appeared to be an inch wide, wrapped in flames.'

The Duisburg trip took 5hr 50min. They bombed, returned safely to base and went to debriefing with the sound of the mighty Merlin engines still hammering in their ears.

Apart from the occasional outburst of exuberance from their pilot this was a quiet and thoughtful crew. Unlike so many men in Bomber Command who believed death and serious injury only happened to the other fellows, they understood that death might strike on operations at any time without warning. This did not make flying to attack enemy targets any easier, but they could see no reason kidding themselves that they were immortal. They did not dwell on the fact that the odds were stacked heavily against them living until the end of the war. It was an unpleasant thought which lurked sinisterly at the back of their minds, but they bombed, relaxed with a few beers, then went off to bomb again. It was their job.

Their next trip, on 30 April, to Essen, was uneventful, apart from the novelty of bombing through ten/tenths cloud. On 4 May they went to Dortmund in their new Lancaster III, ED830 X-X-Ray, joining another 595 aircraft in the first major attack on the Prussian town, the largest on the Ruhr coalfield. Thirty-one aircraft were lost, including six Lancasters from 101 Squadron. Another seven crashed at airfields in the grip of bad weather.

At least 693 people were killed in the raid, including 200 prisoners of war, and 1,075 injured. Among 1,218 buildings destroyed and 2,141 seriously damaged, were factories important to the German war effort.

Smith's Lancaster bombed from 20,000ft, but as they pulled away from the target area they were suddenly coned. The fierce glare from several searchlights struck with shattering force and the pilot snapped to the engineer: 'Jack, through the gate!' Ingram pushed all four throttles forward to get the emergency boost and the Lancaster began its desperate tumbling corkscrew to escape.

Quick, huddled petrified in the rear turret, saying his prayers, was told later by the engineer that they had touched almost 400mph before pulling out at 4,000ft, comfortably cloaked by the dark, but with ack-ack damage to the ailerons. They crossed Germany, hearts thumping, pointing towards England, reflecting on the split second it takes to be transported from a comfort zone into a situation that might end in disaster.

Former navigator Don Hanslow takes up the story as they approached the English coast:

'Control advised that our base was fogbound and we would be required to do a beam approach landing. We had every confidence in the skipper's ability to put us down safely on the runway, so we picked up the beam and proceeded to approach the airfield listening for the blips of the outer marker beacon.

'The beacon came up as expected and we continued a perfectly-controlled descent into the dense fog with eyes glued to the altimeter as we listened intently for the very welcome sound of the inner marker beacon.

'At an indicated height of 300ft there was an ear-splitting crash, a great rush of wind and the interior of the aircraft appeared to be full of broken perspex, the branches of a tree, twigs and leaves.

'Throttles were rammed forward for full power and we remained airborne, but had no idea of how much longer we could carry on. The air speed indicator and altimeter needles dropped to zero, presumably due to the pitot head being ripped off, and the starboard engines were overheating at such an alarming rate that they had to be switched off and feathered.

'We were now right up the creek and the skipper asked if we thought we should bale out. At this point a rather apologetic voice was heard asking if it would be all right for him to leave the rear turret. In the excitement up front we had completely forgotten poor old Harry sitting back there in complete isolation and without any clear idea of what was going on.

'The prospect of baling out at an unknown height and which for all we knew might only be a few feet above ground level held no appeal at all and we decided to stay put and take our chances.'

John Studd says the crew were later firmly convinced that after calling base to check ground pressure they were given a wrong reading. When the Lancaster charged blindly through the upper branches of a tree a height of 300ft was showing optimistically on the altimeter.

Quick tottered bleakly towards the cockpit and was stunned when he saw the devastation to the front of the aircraft. The nose was caved in and Frank Smith was sitting in the open air, with Jack Ingram, the engineer, standing beside him, and a fierce gale blowing through the aircraft. The chances of making a safe landing in fog in this condition seemed remote.

The bomber appeared to be slowly gaining height but with two dead starboard engines it took the combined strength of the pilot and engineer on the control column to keep the aircraft on a reasonably straight course. But where were they?

As they climbed clear of the fog a searchlight, which they believed might be standing on an airfield, was spotted to port. They turned and radioed for permission to land but got no reply and realised that the trailing wireless aerial had also been torn away when they ripped through the tree. As they drew near, with what seemed to be a reasonable chance of making it, the searchlight was switched off and they were lost again.

Hanslow again: 'With the constant roar of cold air blasting endlessly through the aircraft the situation now seemed hopeless. The pilot and engineer remained up front to wrestle with the controls while the rest of us took up crash positions and braced ourselves in the darkness behind the main spar.

'After what seemed to be an eternity we heard a yell from the skipper as a huge black mass of hillside suddenly loomed dead ahead. "This is it! We're going in! Hang on!".

'The throttles were closed and the nose of the plane was pulled sharply upwards as we struck the ground and buffeted our way up the hillside in a screeching sparking mass of metal and equipment.

'Faint daylight appeared as the rear section of the fuselage was torn away from the main section and it trundled along noisily behind us, held for a short time by the control cables. The screeching stopped as the aircraft came to an abrupt halt. The stillness was intense as we stayed in position for a few seconds listening to the creaking of the fuselage while it settled into the ground. We were stirred into movement by the crackling of a fire which had started in the region of the starboard engines.'

The Lancaster had crashed a few miles from Linton-on-Ouse, narrowly missing the village of Little Ouseburn. They had been airborne for 6hr 30min. Another two 101 Squadron bombers also crashed that night in the Yorkshire fog.

They remembered that earlier, John Studd, the bomb aimer, had reported a number of incendiaries remaining hung up after leaving Dortmund. They were still in the crumpled bomb bay and would create an even more explosive situation when the flames reached them.

For those huddled behind the main spar the amputated tail section had provided a speedy and unobstructed exit. They raced away from the wreckage, glancing back to see the pilot and engineer bursting out through their escape hatch in the roof. A quick head count revealed one man was missing: the rear gunner.

They returned at a gallop to the burning Lancaster and, fearing an explosion at any moment, groped around inside for a body. They found the unconscious prostrate figure of Harry Quick lying with his head against the main spar. It seemed clear that his skull had smashed into the spar at the moment of impact. They grabbed his arms and legs and rushed with the gunner to the opening.

The men stopped abruptly when their patient released a sudden sickening howl and they realised they had overlooked the vertical steel pole which stands halfway along the fuselage. Quick's legs were on either side of this pole and a crushing blow had been delivered to his private parts. Quick was still unconscious, but the placid expression on his face had changed to that of a man suffering awful pain and a barely-suppressed fear of the consequences of the ultimate violation.

They carried him a sensible distance away from the burning Lancaster, laid him gently on the grass, decided that his brutalised wedding tackle would best be examined by someone with medical qualifications and wrapped him with all the warm clothing they could muster.

'We then attempted to take stock of our situation,' says Hanslow. 'We seemed to be on a hillside surrounded by fog miles from anywhere with thousands of pounds worth of wrecked and burning aircraft nearby and one member of the crew who looked frighteningly lifeless. For reasons totally incomprehensible to the rest of us the pilot suddenly insisted that he must return to the cockpit and satisfy himself that all the switches had been turned off. As far as we were concerned the plane was a wreck from which we were all only too glad to be clear and nothing on earth would induce us to return to the potentially explosive hulk.'

They blew blasts on their whistles and yelled: 'Hello! hello! hello!' to attract attention and shortly afterwards became aware of a khaki-clad figure, armed with a rifle, emerging cautiously from the fog.

'It is difficult to say whose relief was greatest: his at finding us not to be Germans, or ours at being found at all,' says Hanslow. 'He said he had been on night picket duty at an ack-ack battery guard post when he was startled by the roar of an aeroplane passing low overhead followed by complete darkness as the lights in his hut went out. He hurried outside and found that the electric cable between his and another hut had been severed by the bomber. Hearing the crash he set out with the rest of his section to search the hillside.

'We were quickly surrounded by a team of Army helpers who, having surveyed the wrecked plane from a safe distance, set about organising an ambulance to take Harry to York Military hospital.

'We had been extremely fortunate. The only other crew injuries except, of course, to our nerves and personal pride, were the engineer's bruised forehead which bore evidence of being thrown with considerable force against his instrument panel, and the finger nail which Jack Dix, the wireless operator broke in the scramble from the wreckage. We might easily all have been killed.

'Our immediate problems were now virtually over. A telephone call from the Army camp to our squadron headquarters speedily brought a lorry to transport us back to base. At debriefing we were delighted to find that we were not being held to blame for the crash and that everybody's main concern was for our safety. Unknown to us a number of other aircraft from the group had also crashed that night, most of them with tragic results.'

After a few days Frank Smith was in the cockpit of another new X-X-Ray with a spare bod in the rear turret.

Harry Quick, who spent several weeks at a spinal unit in Sheffield, says:

'I remember little of the minutes leading up to the crash and nothing of events that happened after we hit the deck. I gather the aircraft was scattered over a couple of fields and my turret had been torn off. It's amazing we all got out alive.'

The squadron was posted to Ludford Magna, Lincolnshire, in June 1943, when Quick was still nursing his spinal injuries although happily, after a temporary problem urinating, his genitalia were now in full working order. Fully recovered, he rejoined his crewmates for his fourth trip – their thirteenth – on 12 July, when again they had to deal with an engine on fire. The flight to attack Turin dragged itself out to ten-and-a-half hours and nerves became taut when Quick's rear turret became unserviceable.

They remained together until the happy day when the last entry in six of their logbooks, signed by the squadron commander, read: 'First operational tour completed.'

For Quick it was far from the end and he flew as an odd bod rear gunner with several different crews before finishing his tour.

Three of the original crew were decorated: the pilot, Frank Smith, received a DFC. A DFC also went to Harry Quick, while navigator Don Hanslow picked up a DFM.

After a period instructing they started their second tours. By now Quick had been commissioned and was a flying officer when he joined another pilot, Squadron Leader Roland 'Roly' Newitt, DFC and Bar, from Vancouver, Canada. They had met at 1662 HCU, Blyton, where they had been instructing. Newitt became C Flight commander with 550 Squadron at North Killingholme, Lincolnshire in November 1944.

The pilot was a quiet man whose favourite occupation after harassing Germans was taking his crew for a drink, providing they went to Scunthorpe where he had a crush on one of the landlord's pretty daughters at The Oswald pub.

Quick would complete fifty bombing operations, twenty with Newitt, and finished as a flight lieutenant. He has never regretted that his second tour was less hairy than the first, and the moment that sticks in his mind is not drawn from a ghastly night battling through terrifying flak over the Ruhr, nor desperately corkscrewing to escape enemy fighters or manic searchlights. It is of a moment when Frank Smith suddenly sprouted horns when thundering in their Lancaster over the countryside no higher than 100ft. He spotted a double-decker bus, filled with drowsing passengers, ambling innocently along a twisting road, and roared over it with a demonic gleam in his eye.

With the satisfying vision of a squeaking and squawking tumble of startled passengers, the bus driver screeching to an undignified halt and the conductor shaking his fist at an empty sky, Smith, smiling contentedly, looked forward, more than usual, to an agreeable dinner in the mess that night. He might even stand a round of drinks for the boys. There was definitely something to be said for a chap occasionally letting his hair down.

In September 1995, the day before 101 Squadron's annual reunion, Harry Quick and John Studd, his brother-in-law, both in their seventies, drove to north Yorkshire, searching the first time for the spot where they had crashed fifty-two years before.

Quick says: 'We had never been able to find any official documentation about what happened to X-X-Ray that night. It was as if the aircraft had just disappeared. On the squadron's battle orders only the two other Lancasters that came down that night were shown as "crashed". "York Military" had been written against my name, but there was no other information about our predicament.

'We talked to a few villagers then went down a lane and found the crash site. The bomber had gone through two hedges bordering the driveway up to a big farmhouse before plunging across two fields. The gaps in the hedges were still there, which seemed strange. It was as if no one in all those years had wanted to put in a new hedge or, if they did, nothing wanted to grow there.'

CHAPTER ELEVEN

SPLASH DOWN

They were posted to North Africa just before Christmas, 1942. They might have been sent to the moon. No one on 150 Squadron would have chosen such a time to leave England; Christmas has a special significance for men fighting a war. Given a spot of festive leave it is a brief and welcome haven with families, girlfriends and wives, away from the madness of killing and being killed. And yet the posting, so far from home, saved lives.

Navigator John Morton had flown Wellington IIIs from Snaith, south Yorkshire, on raids to Reims, Duisburg and Berlin. He says:

'The raids were getting progressively more difficult and many crews were lost. It was certainly less horrendous over targets we attacked from North Africa than flying over Germany. We did not face the withering ack-ack fire and rarely saw fighters when we were night bombing. The enemy fighters only appeared to operate in daylight. In October 1941 I had been at 10 ITW, Scarborough. In 4 Flight of 4 Squadron there were fifty-eight of us. It is possible that I was the only survivor, saved by my posting.'

Morton and his crew were new boys on the squadron without a regular aircraft, remaining in England when the others took off en route for the staged flight to Blida, Algeria.

They picked up a brand new Wellington X, with two 1,675hp Bristol Hercules engines, at Moreton-in-Marsh, Gloucestershire, and after landing at Blida were much envied by the more experienced aircrews who were still flying the old less-powerful Wellington IIIs.

Their skipper was Sergeant Jack Alazrachi, a British Jew who had lived most of his life in North Africa and Paris. Young women responded warmly to his dark good looks and the merry twinkle in his eye. He had a brother, Joe, also a pilot and, unusually, on the same squadron. It was a tense and difficult time for the Alazrachis who could expect to be roughly handled if they were picked up after being shot down over Germany. Their sister, Christina, had already been snatched from her home in Paris by the Germans and put into a concentration camp. Blida was not a soft touch, but the brothers felt less vulnerable when flying from here.

Born in the Old Swan district of Liverpool, Morton was a skinny

FIELDS OF CONVENIENCE

Above: Spitalgate, 1940: the war beckons. Four proud young pilots display their new wings. From left: Sgts Fulton, Hedley Hazelden, Foster and Hipperson. *(Hazelden)*

ESCAPE OVER BERLIN

Above: Unavoidably detained at Stalag Luft III, Sagan. Underwood is tenth from left on the back row. *(Underwood)*

Top: A wedding, delayed by months in a POW camp. From left: Reg Wilson, Joyce Ellis, George Griffiths, Laurie and Beryl Underwood, Sylvia Pope, Johnny Bushell, Laurel Pooley, Norman Pooley.

(Underwood)

Right: A premonition warned Laurie Underwood that he would not be back for a long time. *(Underwood)*

Opposite page: 2 May 1945: Gosh, we are coming home. Underwood's letter to his fiancée, Beryl Pooley, on the day he became a free man.

(Underwood)

My own darling Beryl, I was ~~relieved~~ liberated to-day at one o'clock by the British. Gosh darling I feel as light as air. I do not know how, when or where I shall be coming home but quite possibly I shall be home this month. Gosh darling I have not heard from you since October and there are thousands of questions rushing through my brain first my darling I must let you know that I am fit, well and happy. I have lots of food in fact I shall have to give some of it away. Gosh Beryl, the air around this place is electric I can hardly think, and may possibly be home in a few days. If you are still at Salmons darling, tell "Timmy" you will shortly be taking a long holiday. We have a lot of lost ground to cover darling. For the last 3 weeks I have been walking through Germany just ahead of the Allies. Finally we were billeted here in a barn about a week ago and have been waiting with baited breath for this big moment. We have been hearing gunfire and seeing our planes flying around for several weeks when to-day at one o'clock two army boys came rolling into camp in a wireless car. Our guards immediately became our prisoners. A Spitfire pilot flew low over the camp, rolled and waggled his wings in salute. Last night we heard Hitler was dead. Gosh darling give my love to the folks at home I can't write any more, oh yes it is dad's birthday to-day please wish him many happy returns from me. Beryl darling I still love you with all my heart and I can hardly wait these last few days. Bye for now my own 'Dearly Beloved' your ever loving and devoted sweetheart,

Laurie XXXXXX

Stan Hauxwell: the shuddering bang came before they turned on the bombing run.

(Hauxwell)

Top left: Mid-upper gunner Ron Emeny plunged into a mass of flames. *(Emeny)*

Top right: Happier days. Back, from left: Ron Emeny, Laurie Wesley, Jack Pittwood, Nick Stockford. Front: Ron Ellis, Les Lissette, holding the crew mascot, which hung in the cockpit, Phil King. *(Emeny)*

Bottom left: Lucien Tripot, of the Maquis, who helped Emeny escape on a bicycle.
(Emeny)

Bottom right: Ron Emeny returns to the family vault where he sheltered after baling out. *(Emeny)*

Emeny's parachute was turned into a wedding gown for Lucien Tripot's bride, Paulette.

(Emeny)

Top: Luce Carminac (left) showed Ron Emeny (centre) his 'grave', and Lucien Tripot. *(Emeny)*

Bottom: 'Michou', of the Cometé Line, and Ron Emeny, in the 1980s. *(Emeny)*

Above: A tearful reunion. From left: Len Barnes, Florentino Giorchi, Ron Emeny, former Cometé Line despatcher Catilina Agourre.

(Emeny)

BOMBS STOP PLAY

Two Worthing R.A.F. Sergeants Missing

Eldest son of Mr J. K. Mathews, prominent Worthing sporting figure, and of Mrs Mathews, Sgt.-Observer J. B. F. Mathews, R.A.F.V.R., has been reported missing on active service.

Mr Mathews, who lives at Cam-owen, Parkfield-road, Worthing, has for many years been captain of Worthing Cricket Club, and is one of the best known members of Worthing Golf Club.

Also missing is 20-years-old Sgt. Tony Cursett-Sutherland. He is the son of Mrs J. N. Howard, of Belmont, Littlehampton - road, Worthing, and has taken part in many raids over enemy territory. Educated at West Buckland School, Barnstaple, he came to Worthing three years ago.

New Army Chaplain

After completing two years' work as curate of St Mary's Church, Broadwater, the Rev. Robert William Alfred Coleman will, on October 1, take up duties as an Army chaplain.

He will be succeeded by the Rev. Arthur Hurd, who is at present at Clifton Theological college.

Above left: Bridge Farm, Downham Market, was a meeting place for off-duty airmen. Back, from left: 'Dreamy' Newell, Ray Stoodley, farmers Mr and Mrs Bennett, Derek Inman, John Mathews.

Front: Bill, 'Tiny' Rettle, Vic Saunders.

(Mathews)

Above right: A cutting from the *Worthing Herald*.

ohn Mathews: early days.

(Mathews)

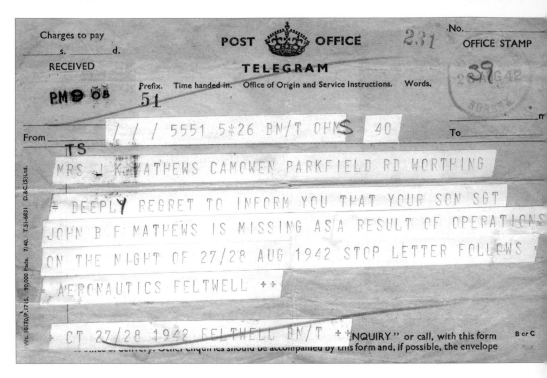

Above: This telegram devastated the Mathews family.　　　　*(Mathews)*

AIRCREW TWINS

Above left: Arthur Madelaine regretted abandoning his Lancaster.　*(Madelaine)*

Above right: Brian and Joyce Dufty after their wedding.　*(Bill Dufty)*

Dulag-Luft. Kriegsgefangenenkartei.

	Gefangenen-Erkennungsmarke	Dulag-Luft Eingeliefert
	Nr. 790	am: 13.9.44 L.

NAME: M A D E L A I N E

		Vorname des Vaters:
Vornamen:	Arthur	Familienname der Mutter:
Dienstgrad:	Sgt. Funktion: Ing.	Verheiratet mit:
Matrikel-No.:	1 892 568	Anzahl der Kinder:
Geburtstag:	1.5.23	
Geburtsort:	Oldham	
Religion:	C of E.	**Heimatanschrift:**
Zivilberuf:	Werkzeugmacher	Mrs.E.Madelaine
		254 Leestr.
Staatsangehörigkeit:	britisch	OldHam Lancaster

Abschuß am: 31.8.44 bei: Stettin   Flugzeugtyp: Lanc.

Gefangennahme am: w.o. bei: w.o.

Nähere Personalbeschreibung

Figur:	mittel	Augen:	grau
Größe:	174 cm	Nase:	gerade
Schädelform:	oval	Bart:	
Haare:	rotblond	Gebiß:	3 Zähne fehlen
Gewicht:	72 kg		
Gesichtsform:	oval		
Gesichtsfarbe:	rötlich	Besondere Kennzeichen:	

Rechter Zeigefinger

Front   Profil   Fingerabdruck

K/0257

The POW record of Arthur Madelaine.   (Madelaine)

Top: Bound together by their love of flying. From left: 'Junior' Brondgeest, 'Curly' Manning, Tom Nelson, John Mitchell, Larry Cates, Jack Watson, 'Robbie' Robinson.

(Nelson)

Bottom left: Navigator Tom Nelson: 'I knew I was going to die.'

(Nelson

Bottom right: The eyes of truck driver 'Freddie' Ryder always filled with tears.

(Nelson

Above: Starving Russian POWs, bereft of hope.

(Nelson)

THE DEATH CAMP

Above: Their Lancaster was refused an air est. Back, from left: Steve Stephens, Bob Yates, Taffy, Les Faircloth. Front: Joe

Sonshine, Mike Guilfoyle, Doug Jordin.

(Jordin)

Doug Jordin was kicked and beaten by the SS. *(Jordin*

Top left: Doug Jordin found the rear turret less draughty on the ground.

(Jordin)

Top right: Inside his turret Doug Jordin entertains some ground crew.

(Jordin)

Left: This letter was received by Doug Jordin's father.

(Jordin)

Ref :
12S/5/2/185/Air.

No. 12 Squadron,
Royal Air Force,
Wickenby, Lincoln.

28th. June, 1944.

Dear Mr. Jordin,

It was with the deepest regret that I had to inform you by telegram this morning that your son, Sergeant Douglas Foster Jordin, has been reported missing from last night's operations, and I am writing to offer you my most sincere sympathy in your anxiety.

He was the Rear Gunner of a Lancaster bomber which took off last night on a mission against the enemy an we have had no news of this aircraft or of its crew since they left Base. We are all hoping that the crew may have escaped with their lives and been taken prisoners of war or are even endeavouring to return to this country, but in saying this I do not wish to raise hopes which may later prove to be groundless. Should any news be forthcoming you will be notified immediately.

Your son's personal effects will be forwarded to the R.A.F. Cenrtal Depository at Colnbrook, Slough, Bucks., from which department you will be hearing shortly. It is regretted that for security reasons I am not now allowed to disclose the names and addresses of the next of kin of the other members of the crew.

I had every confidence in Sergeant Jordin's ability as a Gunner and his courage and devotion to duty. The loss of such men as he will be greatly felt by the Squadron, especially at such a time as this. All Officers and Men join with me in tendering our most profound sympathies.

Yours sincerely,

J.C.B. Brown,
Squadron Leader,
Commanding,
No. 12 SQUADRON.

Mr. F.H. Jordin,
Twiss Green Farm,
Culcheth,
Near Warrington.

Navigator Neville Donmall negotiated
minefields and a freezing river while
evading the Germans.

(Donmall

Above: Donmall's second crew. Back, from left: Bob Saiger, Russell Hudson, Douglas Wood, a Canadian rear gunner, known as 'Pop', Harold Wiltshire, George Cannon. Front: Neville Donmall. *(Donmall)*

FOGBOUND

Above left: Rear gunner Harry Quick's first flying experience was horrifying. *(Quick)*

Above right: They ripped through a fog-shrouded tree. Back, from left: Jack Dix, Jack Hill, John Studd, Harry Quick. Front: Ron McCord, Don Hanslow, Frank Smith. *(Quick)*

Above left: Pilot Frank Smith enjoyed the company of young women. *(Quick)*

Above right: The second tour. Back, from left: Roly Newitt; mid-upper gunner; Levin, Bill Hill, Glyn Williams. Front: Johnny Wright, Harry Quick. *(Quick)*

SPLASHDOWN

Above: While instructing between tours John Morton (front, second from left), was sent on a course at Hereford. *(Morton)*

Navigator John Morton did not need his flying kit in North Africa. *(Morton)*

A GUINEA PIG

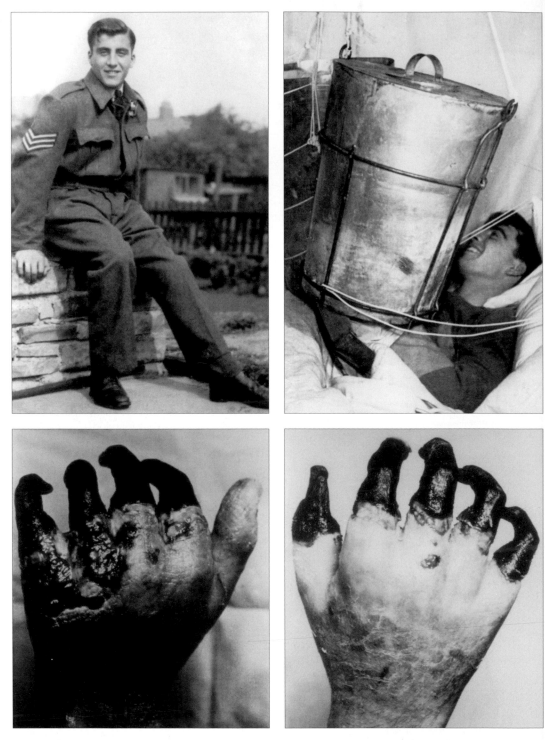

Top left: Alan Morgan enjoys a break from the war at home in Audenshaw. *(Morgan)*

Top right: Alan Morgan's frostbitten hands were kept in buckets of ice. *(Morgan)*

Bottom left and right: Alan Morgan's hands were blackened claws before all his fingers and the right thumb were amputated.

(Morgan)

All smiles for the wedding of Alan Morgan and Ella Broadbent.   *(Morgan)*

LUCKY THIRTEEN

Above: It was tricky coming in to land with only two engines and the controls up the creek. Back, from left: Jim Wright, Larry Guthrie, Dave Stoddard, Bob Purvis; a spare bod engineer for the injured Sam Leary; Vernon Scoble, Ken Scholefield. Front: ground crew. *(Purvis)*

APPOINTMENT WITH DEATH

Above: These wireless operators/air gunners were on a course at Cottesmore. Bob Dack (back, second from right), lived within a bike ride of the airfield. *(Dack)*

Above left: Bob Dack would soon become a wireless operator. *(Dack)*

Above right: Home on the farm in 1943, Bob Dack and his daughter, Sheelagh, feed kale to a calf. *(Dack)*

THE GOERING FACTOR

Above left: Jack Forrest landed in a marsh up to his neck in water. *(Forrest)*

Above right: Pilot Kim Roberts took immediate evasive action. *(Forrest)*

Top: Collecting rations at Stalag IIIA, Luckenwalde. Jack Forrest and Reg De Viell had marched here from Bankau. *(Forrest)*

Bottom: Liberated by the Americans at Stalag IIIA. *(Forrest)*

Top: Charlie Kaye (front row, second from right) has his first taste of the RAF at 1 Aircrew Reception Centre at Lord's cricket ground, on 25 September 1941. *(Kaye)*

Above: Waiting for the crew bus to take them to dispersal are: Don Ince (third from left), right next to Norman Marsh and Bill De Brock. *(Kaye)*

Left: Australian pilot Norman Marsh, an extraordinarily charismatic young man, whose boisterousness often overshadowed a gentle and thoughtful nature.

(Fred Marsh)

Above: They received an unfriendly welcome over Berlin on January 29, 1944. The ground crew cling to Lancaster V-Vic above while below, left to right, are: 'Glen' Glendinning, Don Ince, Charlie Kaye, Norman Marsh, Middleton, Bill De Brock, Geoff Watson. *(Kaye)*

TAFFY'S WAR

Above left: Bill Thomas discovered he had a natural talent for learning Morse. *(Thomas)*

Above right: Few air gunners were as old as Tommy Allen. *(Thomas)*

Above: They shared several hairy adventures on 25 (SAAF) Squadron. Back, from left: Tommy Allen, 'Jock' Rudd, Bill Thomas. Front: Pete Askew, Dick Richards, Mac MacIntosh. *(Thomas)*

BOMBING HITLER

Above left: An early start for pilot Wilf De Marco. *(Cole)*

Above right: Checking on Lancaster D-Dog.

From left: Freddy Cole, Ted Norman, Arthur Sharman. *(Stephanie Roll)*

Above: Their last raid was against Berchtesgaden. From left: Norman Johnston, Freddy Cole, Gordon Walker, Wilf De Marco, Arthur Sharman, Jack Speers, Ted Norman. *(Speers)*

DUTCH COURAGE

Above: Bob Haye, aged nineteen, at home in London, with his mother, Johanna Stein, and stepsister, Clarissa Stein. *(Haye)*

Top left: Sentenced to death: Elly De Jong.
(Haye)

Top right: Bob Haye (fourth from right), with most of those who escaped across the North Sea. Alfred Hagan is second from right. Tonny Schrader is also pictured. The fighter pilot son of Mrs Burgwall (front) had previously escaped, but was later shot down and killed.
(Haye)

Bottom: Bob Haye joined 83 (Pathfinders) Squadron at Coningsby for his second tour. Back, from left: Lewis, Jemmett, Richardson, Bob Haye, Ted Stringer, Anderson, Smith. Front: the ground crew.
(Haye)

Together at last. Bob and Elly Haye on their wedding day. *(Haye*

Top left: Norman Clausen was blown out of his aircraft. *(Clausen)*

Top right: Stopover at Blida. Norman Clausen (left) and Duncan Moodie. *(Clausen)*

Bottom: The crew with Lancaster W4268 Q-Queenie. From left: Les Melbourne, Norman Clausen, Arthur Hughes, Jimmy Bundle, Len Drummond, Tom Stamp, who was cut in half by photographer Duncan Moodie. *(Clausen)*

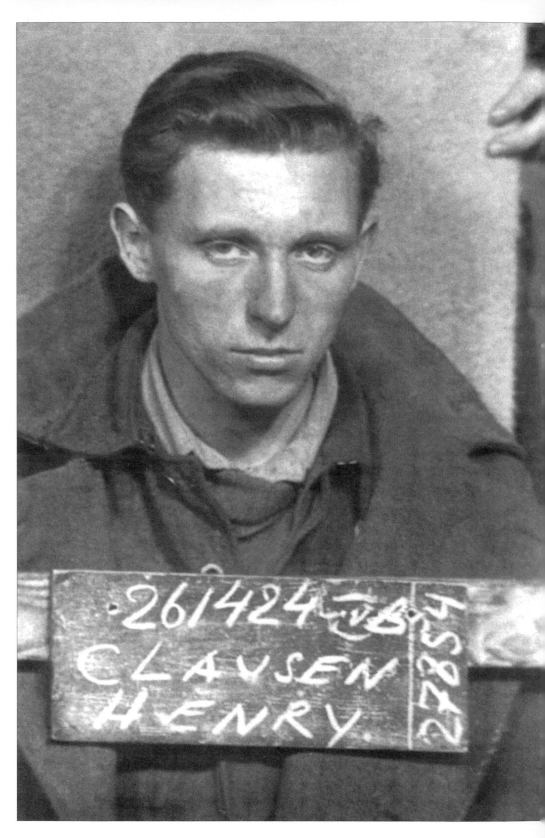

Norman Clausen at Stalag IVB, December 1943.

individual of eight stone who, straining every sinew, just topped 5ft 8in. At twenty-two he was the same age and height as the pilot, but Alazrachi was more broadly built. Grammar-school-educated, meticulous and good at figures, Morton had initially been classified as an observer. He also released the bombs and, as if he had nothing else to do, manned the front gun turret in an emergency.

He says: 'I never really liked that. I was a navigator who always liked to have a course ready for the pilot. I couldn't do that behind a gun in the front turret. Fortunately, we were joined later in Blida by bomb aimer Pilot Officer Ron Payne, a Londoner, who had been in banking before the war. He always wanted to do well and made sure he got right on the target no matter how difficult or dangerous it was. The skipper often cursed Ron, asking him to get on with it, but he'd say he couldn't see the target and we'd have to go round again, sometimes three or four times. That would have been very dodgy over Germany.'

Sergeant 'Ossie' Osborne, a tall twenty-year-old West Countryman, the wireless operator, was often irritated by the unreliability of his equipment which prevented him from doing his job.

'I'll fix the bloody thing,' he always snarled, to whoever was listening when his radio was playing up, and gave it a crunching kick. This was standard procedure for a wireless operator plagued by duff equipment. It often worked, too.

Sergeant 'Andy' Andreas, an RAF regular, had remustered from a ground job to become an air gunner. Quiet, intelligent and an efficient rear gunner, he spent most of his spare time reading. Morton was best man at his wedding in 1942.

Blida, south-west of Algiers, was not an attractive posting for anyone seeking night life or excitement, but Alazrachi and his crewmates merely shrugged at the sand, the heat and the flies and got on doing the job for which they had been trained.

Not all the Algerians were friendly. Morton says: 'We slept in chalets and kept what money we had in our bush shirts folded under our pillows. One night we were asleep and an Arab crept in on his bare feet, lifted Jack's head off his pillow, drew out the shirt and took his wallet. By now we were all awake and Jack gave chase, but the Arab ran off like a hare and got away with his money.

'Our sister squadron at Blida was 142 which went out with us on raids. There was also a Free French squadron which we always felt was a waste of time because they didn't do anything. Not only did they do nothing but when we were taking off with a full bomb load they were always lined up beside the runway grinning and waving.

'Jack Alazrachi, who had lived with the French in Casablanca, used to say: "Look at the rotten buggers, wishing us all the best and make sure we do the job for them".'

On 14 May 1943 they took off from Blida at 7pm to attack oil installations at Palermo, the capital and seaport of Sicily. This was the thirteenth operation for Morton, who recalls the sortie that went horribly wrong:

'We took off in daylight and got out over the Mediterranean in the dark. We didn't fly as a squadron or in a stream. We always went as individual aircraft. It was every man for himself. So much was different here than in England. The weather was different too. It was bloody hot in North Africa and I wore shorts in the air most of the time with a battledress top over a singlet.

'It was hot that day when we were over the Mediterranean three-quarters of the way to the target and the starboard engine began giving trouble. We carried on but the pilot was not happy and, of course, we didn't have an engineer. The engine was spluttering and hiccuping. The skipper tried to clear it and cool it down. He dropped the revs, then gave it a boost, but the problem remained.

'We reached the target and bombed at 11,000ft. There was a lot of ack-ack fire that night and it is possible our wonky engine was further damaged by shrapnel. Certainly an hour or so after heading for Blida the engine was in worse shape and the pilot told us to throw out anything that might help us maintain height. All the guns went, the bed, the Elsen toilet, even the astrodome was dropped into the sea. None of it helped, but it had given us something to do to take our minds off what might happen later. The Wellington continued to lose altitude and when we were halfway back to base the starboard engine stopped. Jack tried to start it again, but it was hopeless. He told me when he had feathered the engine and I made a note in my log.

'We were at about 8,000ft. The pilot said if we couldn't make it to Blida we might get far enough to make an emergency landing at Bône which was near the Tunisian border. I just prayed for the best and hoped we could keep going. The wireless operator had been in contact with Blida for a QDM, which was a course to steer with zero wind to reach base, but it was impossible on one engine, really. Taking off from Blida you always had to turn to port to get over the sea. One Canadian crew turned to starboard and flew straight into the Atlas Mountains and that was the end of them.'

Jack Alazrachi told them: 'We'll see if we can maintain height on one engine. If we can't, be prepared to do anything quickly.'

The Wellington droned on, steadily losing altitude. The wireless operator did not send an SOS to Blida because the dinghy carried a radio and they agreed it was sensible to give their rescuers an exact position when they were sitting in it waiting to be rescued.

The aircraft was down to 1,000ft with the port engine blaring when the pilot confirmed that they would not make it to land. Each turn of the labouring propellor brought them nearer to Algeria and closer to the dark waters of the Mediterranean.

Every sortie from Blida took them over the sea and occasionally, in the mess, someone raised the question of ditching. Some old sweats had said cheerfully that landing in the sea was like hitting concrete and if you did not touch down at the right angle an aircraft could break its back.

There was a lot of sea down there and each man had his own bleak thoughts about what it would be like to ditch and feel the water closing over them, never to see the sky again. As the Wellington sank even lower the sea seemed to be reaching up for them and it was at this point Alazrachi told his crew to take up crash positions, facing aft with their backs braced against the main spar. Morton's offer to stay in the cockpit to help the pilot was abruptly turned down and he joined the others, realising that while Alazrachi was strapped in he would be thrown about when they struck with a very good chance of being killed. No more than 100ft above the sea they were still on intercom when the skipper said, tensely, he would shout just before they went in.

Pressed against the metal spar the bellow of the single engine drilled relentlessly into their thoughts which were all focused on staying alive, except when they became entangled with the real possibility that they only had minutes to live. If the Wimpy struck nose first there was a good chance they would continue down to the sea bed. No one would ever know what had happened and their loved ones would forever cling to the hope that one day they would walk, grinning, through their front doors.

When the bomber was a few feet above the water Alazrachi, ever so gently, brought up the nose and yelled to his crew: 'We're touching down!' It was 12.55am when the rear wheel dipped into the water, a moment remembered clearly by John Morton:

'It was the best landing Jack had ever made. He put the tail down first and the rest followed until we seemed to skim over the surface of the sea for a while like a huge flat pebble. If he had gone in hard the aircraft might have broken up.'

The five men, feeling lucky, hauled themselves through the gaping hole where the astrodome had been. The round yellow dinghy had already been ejected from its stowage in the starboard wing and was bobbing invitingly on a calm sea, attached by a rope to the aircraft. The rear gunner was first to clamber along the wing of the Wellington which was rapidly sinking. Andreas pulled on the rope, slipped into the dinghy and was quickly followed by the wireless operator and navigator. The pilot was saturated when he joined the others and rounded angrily on John Morton:

'You didn't tell me the bloody wing was under water.'

Ossie Osborne cut the rope and they floated away from the Wellington which they watched sink out of sight barely five minutes after ditching. It was a moment of extreme loneliness. Morton reckoned they were about fifteen miles north of Algiers and the men screwed up their eyes to stare into the blackness when someone said he could see the city lights. Their concentration was shattered by a roar of disbelief and outrage from the wireless operator who had been searching through the storage compartments in the dinghy.

'There's no fucking radio!'

'What?' The pilot whirled round.

'We haven't got a radio. I can't contact base. Now we're really in the shit.' Osborne ferreted through the compartments again as if the radio might be hiding from him, before sinking on to his haunches. 'Nothing.'

Alazrachi stared at him. 'Then we'll just have to bloody well wait until we're picked up. They knew our course at Blida; when it gets light they'll send chaps out to look for us.'

'The radio had probably been pinched,' says Morton. 'I'm sure it hadn't been done on the squadron. Someone very likely nicked it at Moreton-in-Marsh before we had picked up the aircraft. It should have been signed for by the skipper, but he had other things to think about. There was no point in dwelling on that. We were alone in a dinghy on the Mediterranean, which was a dangerous place to be in those days.

'When it got light we saw quite a bit of shipping, but they never stopped. We had Very cartridges and a pistol for firing them. That was Ossie's job, but we had no joy at all. They went off but no one took any notice. We saw one or two aircraft in the distance, but didn't know what they were and although we waved like mad it was a futile gesture. We were just a tiny dot in a big mass of water.

'We had four paddles and when we thought we were going in the right direction we used them, but with a round dinghy it was difficult to make progress and we were wasting energy. Our last fix put our position fifteen miles north of Algiers, but it was a hell of a long way to paddle. The dinghy did have some emergency food, but we didn't use any of it. There wasn't much and we thought we'd save it in case we were adrift for some time. We talked a lot and wondered what had been the problem with the starboard engine, but time seems to crawl when you are waiting for something important to happen.'

They spent the cringing heat of the day, and that night waiting, exhaustion gnawing into their bones. The talking trailed off as night fell, the air cooled and they slipped into elaborate thoughts which centred on being plucked from the sea and deposited on dry land with a glass of cold beer in both hands. No one slept and next morning, feeling isolated and abandoned, they talked about getting their heads down in shifts that night.

As so often is the case after a series of disappointments their rescue was unexpected. They saw several ships and aircraft going about their business to the exclusion of five men in a dinghy. That afternoon they idly watched a dot on the horizon become larger until it turned into the huge bulk of a destroyer bearing down on them and they were yelling excitedly and waving shirts and trousers which had been tied to paddles. The big ship actually bumped against the dinghy and, for a moment, the airmen were afraid of being capsized. Then seamen high above were bawling unintelligible instructions down at them in a foreign language, and they were shouting back in English with Alazrachi contributing his tuppence-worth in French.

The ship was Polish and the exhausted airmen were hauled aboard. It was about 4pm. The airmen were questioned closely and later learned from an officer on the destroyer, that if they had been Germans they would immediately have been put back into the dinghy, and sunk.

Morton says: 'When, at last, the Poles accepted that we had ditched one silly bugger, still suspicious, wanted us to show them our aircraft. We told him where he could find it if he had the time and equipment. Although we hadn't eaten for some time we were not hungry, but absolutely knackered and only wanted to sleep, but they plied us with food and drink.'

They were landed at Gibraltar and Squadron Leader Holmes, their squadron's B Flight commander picked them up and flew them back to Blida where the sand and flies had never looked more appealing.

They had little time to recount their exploits in the mess. The next night they were sent nickeling – dropping propaganda leaflets – over Rome, but returned to base with engine trouble. They were not taking any more chances.

Their last sortie from North Africa was on 6 June when they bombed Naples. It was John Morton's thirty-eighth operation.

After a spell of welcome leave Morton spent a few months instructing until it was time to start a second tour. Now a flying officer, he was posted to 214 Squadron at Oulton, Norfolk, with a new skipper, Flying Officer Peter 'Andy' Anderson DFM, who was married with one child. The radio counter measures (RCM) squadron, equipped with Boeing Flying Fortresses, had the job of jamming enemy radar and night fighter communications, hopefully creating confusion among the German controllers, while giving RAF bombers a better chance of arriving safely at their targets.

The B-17G Fortress IIIs were used rather than Lancasters because it was the only aircraft available which had room to hold the three tons of special equipment. The Fortresses were powered by four supercharged Wright Cyclone GR-1820-97 nine-cylinder air-cooled radial engines, with a service ceiling of 35,000ft. They each had a ten-man crew which included four gunners, and two specialists who operated the jamming equipment.

They were Flying Officer 'Bernie' Burnett DFM, who had been trained as a bomb aimer, and Flight Lieutenant Ted Cryer DFC, a wireless operator, who spoke German. Cryer's wife was expecting their first child.

John Morton was not a fan of the Fortress, but he does concede that it was the only aircraft which could do the job.

He says: 'We didn't carry a bomb load, we jammed the fighter belts for the Main Force. We dropped Window occasionally and jammed the searchlights and the ack-ack. The gear we were carrying was so secret I learned more about it years after the war ended than I knew at the time.

'Because we were the slowest aircraft we left earlier than the Main Force, earlier even than the Pathfinders, although the PFF boys usually overtook us on the way. Our altitude depended on the height from which the Main Force was bombing. We were always above them, up to 5,000ft higher, in a jamming position before they got into the target. We could go well above the height of the Lancs. We might be patrolling in an area where the fighter belts were, or where they were likely to be coming from, or circling to one side of the target. Circling was not too bad because it was difficult for anyone to get a bead on us. Jamming the fighter belts which might be well away from the target was our worst job.

'Our jamming was very effective. Ted usually started his jamming by yelling "Balls!" or "Bollocks" over the radio, which the German fighter controller would hear.

'What I most disliked about the Fortress was when the blokes in the Lancs or Hallies were leaving the target they came out at high speed, much lighter without their bombs. We still had our heavy equipment aboard and were soon left behind.'

By the middle of March 1945 they had become an efficient jamming machine and Morton had completed his fiftieth operation. The war appeared to be grinding towards a satisfactory conclusion, but men were still being killed on the ground and in the air, and 214 Squadron continued to do its dangerous job.

Morton was not a superstitious man but a girlfriend, Winnie Dunne, had given him a St Christopher to wear every time he flew and, almost without realising it, he joined the ranks of airmen who carried lucky charms into battle. He had it on when they took off from Oulton at 5.15pm on 15 March to protect bombers in the Misburg area.

'When we finished our jamming the Main Force had left and we flew after them. We were the last aircraft out and this may have been our downfall. We were losing height from about 23,000ft to gain speed when our ordinary wireless operator, Warrant Officer Bob White, saw a blip on his screen and said: "Hostile aircraft at 1,000 yards." No one else saw it charging in from the rear, not even when Bob reported it at 800 yards. The next thing I knew in my blacked-out little office was "br-rer-rer-rer-rah!" as shells and bullets from a German fighter ripped into the floor of our fuselage. One shell smashed into Bob's compartment, and the intercom was cut off.

'The top gunner, Flying Officer Len Moran, was supposed to come and tell me to get out if the aircraft was in the shit, but he'd already pissed off out of it. Bernie Burnett was sharing my office with his jamming equipment and we were not aware of the damage to the aircraft until Jackie Hunter, the flight engineer, dragged our curtain back and yelled: "For fuck's sake Johnnie, get out. We're on fire from arsehole to breakfast time." Without his warning we could have been left sitting there. We dropped everything and took his advice.

'Ted Cryer, the special wireless operator, was going a little bit berserk, running up and down the fuselage. I understood his behaviour later when I learned that his parachute had been burned or shot full of holes. One of our two waist gunners, Warrant Officer Ginger Wheeler DFM, had been quite seriously injured. He had been hit by several bits of shrapnel, but offered to take Ted out on his parachute.

'We'd been hit right in the middle of the fuselage, through Bob White's position. The others had seen the fire and scarpered. Bernie followed me out as I dived headfirst through the escape hatch which had been opened by the top gunner. I saw an aircraft going down in flames and presumed it was ours. It looked like a burning cross. Tracer was coming up at it, gunners wasting their ammunition.

'I came down about 20km west of Koblenz, landing awkwardly, straining my right ankle. I couldn't see a ruddy thing, but there was a bloody dog barking and I thought I would have no chance here. At the time I thought I was in Germany and knew if I was caught by civilians they might literally tear me apart.

'A crew from our squadron which had gone down in Germany the same night were all murdered except the pilot, Flight Lieutenant Wynn. After getting home he reported how a police sergeant had handed his crew over to the SS or Gestapo who shot them. The Germans responsible were caught and dealt with at the Nuremburg Trials.

'I found a farmhouse early that morning and they took me in. They were French, so I was pleased not to be in Germany. They swapped a workman's jacket for my battledress top, but after three hours I was told to leave because the area was being searched. I nicked a push bike down the road and got up a bit of speed, but it was difficult to ride. When I stopped pedalling the brakes were activated. I dropped the bike and resumed walking. I was hungry and took parsnips and sugar beet from fields, anything I could find that was edible, I even tried eating grass, which didn't stir my taste buds.

'I slept at night in hedges, walking during the day. When anyone saw me I was ignored and I didn't try talking to people. I heard guns firing on the front line and thought I must be getting nearer to the Allied positions. I came to a path where there were red and white tapes. They didn't mean anything to me so I kept going. I was told later that I had walked through a minefield and across No Man's Land.

'I had discarded the old jacket I'd been given. While I was walking I always had my trousers over the top of my flying boots. When I got to the American lines after fourteen days on the run I tucked my trousers into my boots thinking that I'd be recognised as a British airman. I went over to a sentry and told him I was an RAF flier. He just left with his gun and returned with a sergeant, chewing gum, who exclaimed: "Waal George, before you shoot the bastard I'll have his boots".

'For one terrible moment I thought I was about to be shot as a spy. It appeared that Germans dressed in American uniforms, speaking English, had recently infiltrated Allied positions and these fellows were naturally a bit cautious.

'Bernie Burnett, the bomb aimer turned up here at about the same time and we were asked to help identify bodies that had been found. We were taken by Jeep to a field where a lot of Negroes were piling bodies into holes. Ted Cryer's body was lying there. He was black although we recognised him straightaway. They had also found some bones in our crashed aircraft. We were shown Bob White's shin bone and a ham bone. Everyone else had got out of the Fortress before it hit the deck and burned out. The pilot had broken a leg and was picked up by the Germans. He was in dock for six weeks, but by then the Allied armies had gone through.

'Bob White was probably wounded or killed when we were raked by the German fighter. Ted Cryer and Ginger Wheeler went out together. Ted was clinging to Ginger's back and came off on the way down. He was probably thrown off by the jerk from the canopy opening. Ginger was alright after the shrapnel was dug out of his body.

'Bernie and I were flown back to England and I was told I had flown my last op. Although I had not been in the hands of the Resistance there was a theory that if you had the Germans would get you to talk and drop the French in the shit. I was sent on extended leave for six months before being pushed off to do admin work in India. I was demobbed in June 1946. It had been a long war.'

CHAPTER TWELVE

A GUINEA PIG

On 20 February 1944 a couple in Audenshaw, Manchester, were getting ready for the happy homecoming of their son, Alan Morgan, on his twenty-first birthday. Morgan, a flight engineer, and his Lancaster crew, were due to start their leave that morning. Bill Morgan, a printer at the *Manchester Evening News*, had laid on some drink, and his wife, Dorothy, had done her best with the meagre fare which could be screwed from their ration books to provide a good spread. Morning drifted slowly into afternoon and soon, without a word from their son, they were forced, sadly, to draw the blackout curtains on the cold darkening street. They waited up late, imagining his cheerful voice at the door, but he did not arrive. They could not know that the next time they saw him he would be in hospital, struggling for his life.

In the middle of 1942 Alan Morgan and his pal, Gerry Dineen, had volunteered to join the Royal Navy. They were rejected because they were in a reserved occupation.

The friends were apprentice toolmakers, making jigs which would be used by another factory for manufacturing Lancaster bomb doors. It was precision work which needed steady hands and sharp eyes. They enjoyed their jobs which brought them close to the war, but not close enough. They were young and craved adventure.

Morgan says: 'Three months later we were told we could join the Royal Navy or RAF aircrew. It was a time when the Navy was losing a lot of ships to German U-boats, while casualties mounted in Bomber Command. Gerry and I decided to go into the RAF.'

Dineen was killed on his first bombing raid. Morgan survived the war, but he would be scarred for life.

He was soon swept up in the excitement of Bomber Command: training, crewing up and being posted on 6 December 1943 to Fiskerton, joining 49 Squadron, the only unit on the airfield at that time.

RAF Fiskerton had been completed in November 1942. Standing five miles east of Lincoln, between the villages of Fiskerton and Reepham, it was one of the first two Lincolnshire airfields to have FIDO (Fog Investigation Dispersal Operation). Petrol, pumped into pipes which ran the length of the runway, was ignited and the intense heat dispersed the fog above, enabling aircraft to land.

Alan Morgan's skipper was Pilot Officer Jack Lett, who would be decorated with the DFC at the end of his tour. From Romford, Essex, he was tall, slim and assertive. In February 1944, he was twenty-one. Commissioned at Fiskerton, he was like a brother to all his crew, endeavouring, not without difficulties, to keep them out of trouble. Before the war he was in the tea business, a salesman for Brooke Bond.

The navigator, Sergeant Andy Andrews, from Bath, a pre-war council surveyor, was a pleasant round-faced lad, who faced every crisis with unruffled calm. His only mistake had been directing them into the depths of France when they should have been going to England, in the opposite direction. As his pilot went berserk over the intercom, Andrews coolly gave him the new course. The navigator had a problem with his ears and did not fly on every sortie.

Sergeant Frank Campbell, at thirty-one, was inevitably known as Grandad. From Manchester, the wireless operator was married and, in addition to the skipper, was a steadying influence on his crewmates.

The mid-upper gunner, Sergeant Tommy Woods, about twenty-five, was married, but that did not prevent him driving his Morris 8 sports car into Lincoln looking for girls.

Rear gunner Sergeant Andrew 'Jock' Irving, nineteen, from Annan, Dumfriesshire, was typical of thousands of bomber crews.

Morgan again: 'Jock was my best pal, but he would have given his life for any of us. We were all closer than brothers and would do anything for each other. When somebody needed help you would give it without question.'

Compared with many impoverished aircrews at Fiskerton they were well off. Woods ran his small car while Morgan had a 350cc Sunbeam motorbike which his father had bought brand new in 1936. Petrol rationing was strict and rather than lay it up until the war ended Bill Morgan gave the machine to his delighted son in exchange for a few tools.

Flight Sergeant Gerald 'Mack' Mackew, the bomb aimer, also had a motorbike, a 250cc Triumph which he had bought for £12. Totally inexperienced, he asked Morgan to accompany him on the pillion for his first ride and promptly hurtled into a dense hawthorn hedge on the Lincoln to Newark road. They emerged shocked and bleeding and were patched up in sick quarters, but the accident did not prevent them going on the next training flight.

Mackew, of Finchley, London, had failed his pilot's course in Canada before switching to bomb aiming. His father sent him £100 for his twenty-first birthday, a small fortune in wartime.

Morgan, known by his crewmates as Darky, because of his jet-black hair, recalls: 'Mack started spending money at a terrific rate, buying drinks all round in the mess, getting everyone drunk, as if he thought something was going to happen to him. Jack took him to one side and told him not to be such a damned fool.'

Petrol rationing hardly effected Morgan and his pals who scrounged fuel from American negroes who were digging trenches in which the FIDO pipes were laid at Fiskerton. They were happy to fill five-gallon cans from a huge storage tank for the young men, demanding nothing in return. The free petrol was not sufficient for Woods to drive to his home in Liverpool and back. He solved this problem by selling underwear and blankets that he had acquired from friendly storemen at Fiskerton.

The despairing pilot told Woods: 'You'll end up in prison if you keep pinching RAF stuff to sell for your damned petrol.' The gunner grinned and replied: 'It doesn't hurt anyone, Skipper.'

Their first sortie was not a soft touch. They were sent to Berlin on 16 December 1943 and, for a time, as they crawled agonisingly slowly over the German capital it seemed every anti-aircraft gun within 100 miles was firing at them.

Morgan, who had not been scared about flying into the hell of Berlin, says:

'The German searchlights were busy, so were their ack-ack guns, but we were sailing along at 22,000ft with most shells exploding below. The only time we needed to take evasive action was when the searchlights caught us. Two Bf-109s and a Ju-88 trailed us for ten minutes, but Jock gave them a blast from the rear turret and scared them off. When we spotted enemy fighters, we watched them and sometimes Jock or Tommy fired a burst to get rid of them.'

Lett and his crew became familiar with Berlin over the next few weeks. Their second trip was to Frankfurt, but the following five were to Berlin. They returned unscathed each time and began to feel lucky.

Morgan says: 'We were more excited than scared. We were doing a good job and I enjoyed every minute of it. We had been down for ops eleven times in December and when some were scrubbed because of bad weather we were all disappointed.'

On 19 February 1944 they were sent to Leipzig. They were in good spirits as Lancaster JB421 took off a minute before midnight to join the second wave of bombers. Signed passes for their first leave from the airfield were waiting in the orderly room and Morgan had a birthday party to look forward to. His girlfriend, Ella Broadbent, would be at his parents' house and he anticipated having a fine time. Some presents, including a fountain pen, had already been sent to Fiskerton, and he was wearing the gold signet ring Ella gave him three weeks before.

Morgan recalls the Leipzig raid which involved 823 aircraft.

'It was a terrible night with seventy-eight aircraft lost, two from our squadron. I can remember seeing many go down. We saw several big explosions in which two bombers had collided. Tracer fire came up like sheets of water. We weren't scared because we were above it all. We always flew as high as we could and were comfortable at around 23,000ft. Some chaps got even higher. We saw plenty of German fighters and flew through lines of flares dropped by them, but they didn't attack us. Leipzig was lit up by fires and every now and then there was a big red flash where a Cookie had fallen. It took us half-an-hour to get over the target once we started seeing some action, and another twenty minutes getting out of it.

'With so many aircraft on the raid other bombers passed above and Jock screamed from the rear turret: "Jack! There's one above us. Its bomb doors are open."

'Jack said calmly, over the intercom: "We can see them, they can see us. They'll not drop."

'The bomber was no more than twenty feet away, it seemed I could reach out and touch it. Jack was right. We had been seen. The other bomber moved slowly away and released its bombs safely. There was 10/10ths cloud, but good visibility above it and we bombed on Wanganui flares, which had cascaded down.

'This was Mack's moment, the reason for him being there. And he made the most of it, having the skipper fly this way and that: "Steady, steady, left, left, steady, steady, right, right." And Tommy Woods always used to bellow: "Get the bloody bombs down and away!" But Mack kept Jack at it until he was absolutely certain and ready before pressing the bomb tit.

'Then we turned, dived as fast as we could to around 18,000ft to get the speed and were off. We got home safely, although we had to join a queue circling above Fiskerton waiting for the signal to land.'

They touched down at 7.05am and went to debriefing where the intelligence officers did not believe they had seen so many bombers going down. They said the Germans had probably been dropping 'scarecrows' to frighten the crews. Intelligence sources claimed the Germans occasionally used shells which went off like exploding bombers. After the war this theory was discredited. The explosions were, indeed, bombers blown to pieces, although many former aircrews still believe the scarecrows did exist. The myth was a comfort to them.

Dog tired, Jack Lett and his crew went to bed, but in three or four hours they were wakened and told they would be on again later that day. Their precious leave slipped quietly into limbo. They were shocked by the news, but there was no question of anyone protesting to the squadron commander. They were needed to attack Stuttgart that night. It was their job and they must go. England expects, and all that.

Morgan was a little worried that he had been unable to contact his parents or girlfriend to explain that his ten-days leave had been delayed by twenty-four hours, as neither his parents nor Ella was on the telephone. In any case the station was closed down in the hours before takeoff and access to public telephones would not be allowed again until the squadron was well on its way. Morgan had heard of some crews being briefed to attack enemy targets for three nights on the trot and hoped they would not draw any unwelcome short straws next day.

Everyone needed adequate sleep after a draining seven-hour trip in which they had been exposed to many anxieties, but they soon got back into the routine, checking the aircraft, going up for an air test, briefing, dinner, and a few precious minutes trying to relax, writing letters, reading a newspaper or book, or chatting aimlessly in the mess to soak up the dwindling time before leaving.

They clung to the cosy vision of getting back and going straight on leave as they bumped uncomfortably across the airfield in the cold truck and clambered through the echoing interior of Lancaster JB421 K-King, which had already brought them safely back from Berlin and Leipzig.

Fifteen bomber crews from 49 Squadron were briefed to attack Stuttgart that night. Only eleven got airborne. Lett lifted off safely at five minutes to midnight, but as they climbed over Fiskerton, the undercarriage of Lancaster ND498 R-Roger collapsed and caught fire, dragging itself clamorously along the runway. Its skipper, Pilot Officer Frank Clarke, and his crew escaped before their Cookie exploded at the end of the runway. The three waiting Lancasters aborted.

A wide column of 598 aircraft headed towards Stuttgart. They included 460 Lancasters, 126 Halifaxes and twelve Mosquitoes. Cloud hung over the German city but bomb damage was considerable and included the Bosch factory which manufactured dynamos, magnetos and injection pumps. Seven Lancasters and two Halifaxes were lost and another five bombers crashed in England.

Mackew announced the release of their bombs and, turning for home, they were rocked by a blast of heavy flak over the target.

The intercom crackled as the rear gunner, Jock Irving, snapped: 'Skipper, the bloody rear door's been blown open.'

Already icy cold, the temperature inside the Lancaster plummeted. Irving could not be spared from his job of quartering the sky looking for enemy bandits. Wireless operator Frank Campbell, who had least to do at that time, was sent back through the dark fuselage to close the door. Stumbling through the interior of a Lancaster bomber at 22,000ft to shut a heavy metal door was rather different to moving from one's snug fireside to shut the back door on a sudden draught. Yet few airmen would spare the time to clip on a parachute before tackling such a task, which should not be difficult, provided they did not fall out. Campbell was not wearing a parachute, but was experienced enough to be sensible. He undid his mask, shoved an oxygen bottle into his Irvine jacket and disappeared. Ten minutes passed. The aircraft became even colder and Campbell had not returned.

The pilot became anxious. 'Alan, you'd better see what's happened to Frank.'

Morgan collected an oxygen bottle and switched on his torch.

He says: 'I always carried a torch in the Lanc, it was useful for working at my instruments and dials. I found Frank lying unconscious near the open rear door. His oxygen bottle had run out. If this had happened when he was trying to shut the door he might easily have fallen to his death. It looked as if he had staggered a step into the fuselage before passing out. I took off my leather gloves to see to Frank and fix him up with some oxygen from my bottle. I dragged him to his feet, waited for a moment until he grinned, then put an arm round his shoulders. I helped drag him over the high main spar and we slowly got back to his position where I plugged him into his own oxygen supply.

'I returned to the rear door with the same bottle. I should have changed it for a new one, but thought I was okay. The wind was screaming through the door, but I managed to shut it. I was looking for my warm gloves when I passed out.'

Soon after his lungs sucked the last cubic millimetre of oxygen from the bottle he found himself crumpling to the floor, unable to help himself. He fell forward on his chest, hands outstretched, touching the freezing air frame. The last things his mind focused on as he lay helplessly immobile were the roar of the four engines surging through the metal floor of the fuselage and the icy cold seeping into his hands. The temperature outside was minus forty degrees Fahrenheit. It was not much warmer inside.

He lay there unconscious for at least five minutes before the rear gunner turned his turret, saw Morgan lying there and called up the pilot who immediately put the Lancaster into a steep dive. He levelled out at just below 10,000ft, a height at which oxygen was unnecessary, and sent Mackew to the aid of his engineer. Mackew helped Morgan to the rest bed then took over his job, checking fuel and instruments.

Morgan recalls his ordeal:

'Mack sat with me for a while. I could talk, but I wasn't with it, and kept blacking out. I was glad to have a rest and happy for Mack to do my job. He kept an eye on me. My hands were very cold, but I didn't think there would be any problem, perhaps a little frostbite. There was a numbness about them, the sort of feeling I'd got when playing snowballs as a kid. It took about ten minutes to get the feeling back, but in the four hours it took to fly from Stuttgart to England they blistered up.'

Mackew told Jack Lett about the state of the engineer's hands and the pilot contacted Fiskerton which already had a problem with the large hole adorning the end of its main runway. It had started diverting the returning bombers to other Lincolnshire airfields. Because of the anxiety about Morgan's hands it was decided a doctor needed to look at them as soon as possible. They got permission to make an emergency landing at RAF Ford, a fighter airfield near the south coast in Sussex.

Morgan was taken to the nearest big hospital, Chichester, an hour's drive away. After his crewmates had made their farewells they were given a meal and the bomber was refuelled. Despite the four-hour delay at Ford, their Lancaster was first back at Fiskerton after the Stuttgart raid. Relieved to find they were not wanted a third night running, the six men picked up their passes and were gone.

Mackew, the bomb aimer, was killed on 23 April during a sortie against Brunswick when he was hit by a .303 bullet fired from another Lancaster.

Tommy Woods refused to fly after the injury to Morgan and the death of Mackew.

Morgan again: 'He could have been in serious trouble, being branded

LMF, but Jack softened the blow by telling the wing commander that Tommy said his eyesight was failing. Tommy was lucky, he went instructing, still flying, but no more bombing.'

Jack Lett had promised to get a message passed to Morgan's parents and girlfriend, but the engineer's spirits were low as he was driven by ambulance through unfamiliar countryside, regretting that he was not with his pals.

He says: 'I thought my hands were getting better, I wasn't in pain. At Chichester, my signet ring was cut off and, because they were blistering, both hands were put into big warm saline gloves. They thought they were doing the right thing but, as it happened, they were not. Jack and Jock visited me and the skipper had my ring repaired in London.'

Morgan spent ten days at Chichester and his hands looked grim when he was seen by pioneering plastic surgeon Professor Archie McIndoe who was doing so much good work at East Grinstead hospital about forty miles away. He rebuilt bodies which had been brutally violated and burned by war, turning ragged lumps of raw meat back into faces, giving dignity to men who might otherwise have remained no more than a shudder in society. They did not expect miracles. Having looked in mirrors and seen the devastation of their faces all they looked for was a decent rebuilding job, good enough not to be avoided by family and friends. These men were later known as The Guinea Pig Club and members still meet every year.

Morgan's hands were straightaway plunged into two big buckets of ice. It was the treatment he should have been given soon after landing at Ford. His fingers were in a terrible state but meeting McIndoe's other patients he realised he had little to complain about.

He says: 'There were men whose hands and faces were just a mass of completely burned flesh. They were covered in bandages which were changed every day. They were taken out of bed and put into saline baths. Nurses waited until their dressings were wet and floating off. Then they plucked them off with tweezers before putting on new bandages. It was absolute agony for them. Bill Foxley became one of my good pals at East Grinstead. He was a lump of burned flesh. He escaped almost unhurt from a Wellington which had crashed in Leicestershire in March 1944. He went back into the burning aircraft to save a friend and became the worst-burned pilot in the war. He still suffers pain and continues to have operations.

'Visitors were warned not to stare at the patients, but to treat them as normal people. The nurses were wonderful. It was well known that McIndoe had picked the best-looking and most skilful nurses he could find for Wards 3 and 4, where the Guinea Pigs were. Their beauty helped our morale. The nurses were wonderful, the things they had to do. They washed and fed me, wiped my bottom, grabbed my willy to put it into a bottle. I couldn't do anything. I had my hands up in the air inside ice buckets for three weeks. The nurses teased us, of course, they were bloody rascals. The sister, Margaret Mealia, a lovely Irish girl, used to tickle my palms.

'It was very different to normal hospitals in wartime. The doctors, surgeons and nurses were all very open, talking to you about your problems and they laughed and joked with us. We had a piano and a big barrel of beer in Ward 3. You could help yourself and those who couldn't were given beer by those who could. As people came in after an operation other patients gathered round with kind words. It was so friendly. We never had to wear hospital blue, McIndoe didn't believe in it. He encouraged us to go drinking at The Whitehall pub in East Grinstead.

'I learned that Frank and I had passed out in the aircraft because of a problem with the oxygen bottles. I talked about it with Archie McIndoe and he checked with Air Ministry who found out it was normal on the squadrons to check emergency bottles by turning them on. If the needle went to full they turned them off. They lost oxygen every time the bottle was turned on and no one made a note of how many times they were checked, it could have been twenty or thirty times. The bottles used by Frank and myself had only lasted six minutes instead of twelve. That's why we collapsed. After my accident a memo was sent round every station in the country, telling them to find a new method of checking the bottles.

'I remember McIndoe telling me that I was due for the chop. The tips of my fingers had gone black with gangrene and he said I had to lose them.'

Not long afterwards the hospital contacted Morgan's parents to say he was very poorly with pneumonia. The Morgans and Ella hastily packed bags, caught a midnight train from Manchester Piccadilly, and arrived at East Grinstead hospital where they were shocked to be told he was unconscious with only a fifty-fifty chance of survival. They kept a vigil throughout the night at his bedside. After he came out of the coma and appeared to be making progress his father went back to work, but Dorothy Morgan and Ella stayed until he was completely out of danger.

When McIndoe operated he removed all Morgan's fingers and one thumb, but the engineer soon joined the other Guinea Pigs having fun.

Morgan says: 'Within a month I was back on my feet, going to a London theatre at least once a week with tickets we had been given by top stars, including Tommy Trinder, Arthur Askey, Ann Sheridan and Vera Lynn who also entertained us at the hospital. I went with Bill Foxley, and Les Wilkins, who was severely burned after his Lancaster crashed. The plane was in flames with Les trapped in the rear turret until he was dragged out.

'In London, people were a bit shocked when they saw us, but queuing outside the Palladium a fellow came up to me and stuck a pound note into my jacket pocket when he saw my hands were in bandages. I kept the note which has a lot of signatures on it, including Tommy Trinder's.'

Three months after he had been at East Grinstead, on 10 June 1944, Alan Morgan and Ella were married. Guests included two nurses from the hospital. After their honeymoon he returned to the hospital for further operations to tidy up his hands.

Time passed and Morgan told McIndoe that he wanted to get back to flying. After being admitted to hospital the RAF had grounded him and placed him in the category of general duties, effectively stopping his flying pay. Annoyed by this insensitive bureaucracy McIndoe made a telephone call to Air Ministry and roared: 'I'll tell you when my lads are not fit for flying duties.'

The surgeon arranged for Morgan to attend a special medical board in London.

Morgan recalls the day:

'I went before the board of high-ranking officers feeling as fit as a fiddle after over ten months at East Grinstead. One said: "Well, Sergeant, after your terrible injuries, why do you want to go back to flying?"

'I said: "I want another crack at the enemy."'

They were satisfied. I was posted to the Empire Air Navigation School at Shawbury, Shropshire, and started flying Mk III Halifaxes as a flight engineer. I got my back pay and was promoted to flight sergeant. It felt good and in the mess the WAAFs put my dinner on the table for me while the other fellows were queuing. I had suddenly become special.

'I learned fast. I could soon handle a knife and fork and managed to dress myself, including putting on a tie. I was the first to have zips at East Grinstead where the nurses sewed them into the flies in my uniform. I was going to be posted from Shawbury to a heavy conversion unit as an instructor, but the war ended and I was demobbed – not invalided out – later that year.'

Morgan's biggest test was yet to come. When he returned to Cooke and Ferguson, his pre-war employers in Audenshaw, his mutilated hands were regarded with horror. Some probably thought the young man was incapable of holding down any job. Alan Morgan, resourceful and determined, imbued with the unquenchable spirit of The Guinea Pig Club, picked up some tools and demonstrated how nothing had really changed. Soon afterwards he took up his old job as a precision jig borer.

CHAPTER THIRTEEN

LUCKY THIRTEEN

However skilful Bob Purvis was as a pilot he knew there was no guarantee that one night he might not avoid being shot out of the sky by a determined German fighter. But he could cut down the odds against being killed by the RAF.

This was a lesson he learned one grim moonlit night early in his career with 550 Squadron on the bombing run over a German target. He recalls the moment every Bomber Command aircrew dreaded:

'We saw one Lancaster above another, both with their bomb doors open. The top one dropped its bombs, slicing the wing clean off the bomber below. The wing just fluttered down like an ash seed and the aircraft went into a spin. We didn't see any parachutes. Seven men just wiped out.

'After that our motto became: "Don't let anyone get above us". Our normal bombing height was 20,000ft. We always had a good aircraft, well maintained, and we got as high as possible over the target. Obviously all our bombers were heading for the same spot on the map. You might have four or five minutes to bomb in our wave, but it's difficult because they are all converging. There was always a danger of collision or catching the bombs from an aircraft at a higher altitude.

'Approaching the target I always had the navigator stand behind me looking out the port side, with the engineer covering starboard. The wireless operator was in the astrodome peering above. Both gunners were also vigilant. We did all we could to avoid tragic accidents.

'We were first to arrive back on the squadron after most raids. You were supposed to hold your altitude until leaving enemy territory then start descending. I used to keep the throttle settings the same but tilted the nose down very slightly, which increased the air speed while losing height gradually.'

They were based at North Killingholme, a wartime station, north-west of Grimsby, where building work had not been completed when, on a dreary day in January 1944, the squadron flew in from nearby Waltham, where it had been formed in November. Home only to 550 Squadron, in 1 Group, the North Killingholme airfield was so close to the Humber estuary some runway approach lights stood in the water. At least one Lancaster landed in the Humber. This was one murky night when an Australian pilot was deceived by lights shown by creeping barges. After the Lancaster's wheels splashed into the water the bomber heaved itself to the edge of the estuary, where it flopped into the mud, lucky not to tip over. The crew were filthy, but alive and their pilot became known as 'Downstream' Hopkins.

Purvis was five when his father took him for an exciting five-minute trip in a biplane. Sir Alan Cobham had brought his famous flying circus to a field outside Warkworth, near the boy's home at Amble, Northumberland. It was a flight which stuck in the boy's memory and fourteen years later, aged nineteen, he was in Terrell, Texas, learning to fly in PT-18 Stearman biplanes and AT-6A Harvard monoplanes. Here he was intrigued to learn that each town had its name painted on a water tower, which meant navigation was a piece of cake until young trainees ventured to a point which extended beyond the map they were carrying.

Some youngsters did not survive their training. Purvis again:

'One day two of us were in a Harvard on a low-level cross-country training flight. We were both trainee pilots but I was flying that day, Terry Murch was navigating. We had to go through a valley as thick cloud started coming down. We debated whether to turn back, but would that go against us getting our wings? At the last minute we got a recall. Back at the airfield we heard that two of our aircraft had crashed, killing four people.'

In Amble, Purvis's father, Robert, ran a store which combined newsagent, drug store, off-licence, book seller and a library, that lent out books for twopence a week. He died in February 1944 and his widow, Margaret, continued running the business until her son, Bob, took over after his demob in July 1946.

Purvis, tall, thin, fair haired and blue eyed, joined the RAF, full of enthusiasm after wasting much of the Christmas 1939 term digging slit trenches under the trees at Alnwick Duke's Grammar School.

He was encouraged, almost immediately, to smoke because the medics said cigarettes were good for the nerves and aircrews received regular free supplies.

German bombing of Britain was at its most ferocious, amidst growing fears that Hitler was poised for an invasion when Purvis, waiting to join a course, was sent for a week to Brighton. Billeted on the seafront with a bunch of other lads they were given wooden batons with which they were expected to defend Sussex when the German hordes began pouring on to the beaches.

Aged twenty when posted to 550 Squadron on 17 May 1944, he and his new crew were all sergeants. They included navigator Dave Stoddard, from Kirkaldy, Fifeshire, who had been a clerk with an aluminium company.

Purvis says: 'Dave was an excellent navigator, a stickler for doing things by the book. Above the Lanc's navigator's table there was an air speed indicator which Dave watched very closely. If I was one mile an hour out in speed he would come over the intercom and complain: "How do you expect me to plot a course if you can't keep at the right bloody speed?"'

Larry Guthrie, from Hackney, east London, who wore his dark hair slicked back was the wireless operator.

Purvis remembers his bomb aimer, Ken Scholefield, from Oxford, as the man who held the unofficial title as the wrecker of more bicycles than anyone else on the squadron.

'He was,' says Purvis, 'always tight and could never keep the wheels on the narrow path that led to the billets. He fell off regularly, usually giggling, but the bikes suffered.'

The flight engineer, Sam Leary, from Chesterfield, was known for his dry sense of humour, and rear gunner Jim Wright, from near Wrexham, could see something funny in the blackest situation. Purvis recalls a hairy trip across the Ruhr, being blinded by searchlights, swept by a hail storm of flak and being glad to get out of the target. As they turned, Wright, who had so far seen little of the German activity from his turret suddenly squealed excitedly: 'Weeeeeh!'

'What's up, you daft bugger?' exclaimed the pilot.

The gunner burbled: 'There's a smashing fireworks display.'

Vernon Scoble, also married, had worked in the housing department of his local council in north London before throwing in his lot with the RAF. Now a mid-upper gunner he was a balding ancient of thirty-nine, over six feet tall, but making sure he kept up with the youngsters, especially with his intake of booze.

'At the start of one trip,' says Purvis, 'Vernon was drenched in hydraulic oil when a pipe burst in his turret. He couldn't use his heated suit in case of fire and at 20,000ft he would have frozen to death. We had to turn back. The aircraft was supposed to be checked, then it happened a second time when we had the extra booster on climbing. The pressure just built up and the pipe burst at the weakest point. The outraged gunner exclaimed: "Gor blimey Bob, I'm soaked to the fucking skin in bloody oil again." That was another aborted op. The trouble was caused by somebody putting the washer in the wrong way round in the release valve, a simple little thing like that.'

Purvis was the proud owner of a Triumph Gloria car which his father had bought in 1934. He helped keep it going in the days of strict petrol rationing by mixing pool petrol with high-octane fuel from Lancasters. Chaps at North Killinghome had been known to surreptitiously drain a tank in a Lancaster to keep their cars going for such vital missions as visits to special watering holes and trips home at the weekend.

The four-seater Gloria had a wooden frame and aluminium body and sagged a little disconsolately when he and his six flying companions crammed into it for a day of prolonged boozing, often in Grimsby.

'We went to a poky little pub, a bit of a dive, near the harbour that we wouldn't normally have visited. But we had been told that if we wanted to know the target for the next op we would find out here. As soon as we walked into that pub, even in the morning, they would tell us where the target for our squadron was for that night and how many aircraft were going.

It was secret information and annoyed us intensely because whoever was leaking that information was putting the operation and the aircrews in peril. We did a bit of ferreting around and next time went at opening time. A leading aircraftman came in sounding off about that night's op. He was a radio operator at Group headquarters in Bawtry. He was getting the gen about the raids and blabbed it to anyone who was prepared to listen.

'We came back early and I went to see the Wingco to tell him about it and the next thing we knew the pub regulars were not getting any secret information. And the LAC was no longer to be seen. He was a fool, thought he was big and important, but how many times over the country was the same thing happening and how many men had lost their lives because of it?'

Being so close to the Humber meant the airfield was often wrapped in a miserable early morning fog, forcing aircraft to be diverted. On such a morning Bob Purvis, returning from a raid, groped his way cautiously over the estuary, searching for the runway, and was startled by an unsettling 'did-er-did-er-did-er' as the wheels ran across an unexpected surface. He opened up, gained height, landed safely and learned next morning that his Lancaster had galloped over the roof of a Nissen hut occupied by a bunch of terrified WAAFs, who believed the airfield was being bombed. Nothing was said officially but a WAAF on duty in the control tower passed the name of the pilot to the angry residents of the billet with the dented roof who took some time to forgive Purvis for disturbing their sleep so tumultuously.

Aircrews at North Killingholme always knew ops were on when their squadron commander, Wing Commander 'Dinger' Bell, left his office window open. It was open on the morning of 12 August 1944 and later they were briefed to attack oil storage tanks behind submarine pens at Bordeaux. It was a daylight raid and they would be bombing at a much lower altitude than normal.

Among established rituals for crews going on ops was picking up the first aid and escape kits.

Purvis recalls: 'When one of us first went to collect these kits we were a new crew and had to take what was left. The kits were all numbered and ours was No 13. We had a good op that first time, to Calais, and afterwards we always looked for No 13. Normally it was the skipper's job, but I was busy doing something and Ken Scholefield went to pick them up.'

They took off in Lancaster I LL800 A-Able at 11.23am for their twenty-third sortie. With another five aircraft from 550 Squadron they joined a small force of sixty-eight Lancasters from 1 Group and two Mosquitoes of 5 Group to attack submarine pens at Brest, La Pallice and Bordeaux. No aircraft would be lost.

By now Purvis had been commissioned and was a flying officer, but he had not changed his routine from when he was a humble sergeant.

'When we took off with a full load of armour-piercing bombs we got up to height and I switched on George, the automatic pilot, which had not yet been perfected and was not totally reliable. One of the crew used to stand in for me and I went to the Elsen at the rear of the fuselage. There was no second pilot unless you trained them yourself. I usually left the bomb aimer or the engineer in charge. They could both take over in an emergency. Whether they could land or not is another matter. I chatted to the crew on the way to the toilet and came back to my seat where I had ten minutes' sleep. I relaxed completely until we got to the other side of the North Sea. Then George was turned off and my hands were on the controls for the rest of the op.

'We were supposed to be escorted that day by Spitfires, but I didn't see any. We were on a route which we'd not taken before. It went over Oxford, crossed the coast east of Exeter and carried on west of the Channel Islands. We kept over the sea as long as we could, to give the impression we were heading further south, before cutting in towards Bordeaux, avoiding a flak ship at the entrance to the harbour. It was perfect weather, a lovely summer's day. I was flying in shirt sleeves. I had just opened the bomb doors and we were on the final bombing run at 10,000ft when we were lifted spectacularly by the force of an anti-aircraft shell exploding underneath us.

'I saw the air speed indicator gradually dropping off the scale and asked the navigator: "What's your air speed indicator doing, Dave?"

'He said: "It's just going down."

'I replied, rather casually: "Oh, that's all right, so's mine." But the aircraft was still flying, it was just the instrument that had been damaged and was u/s.'

They were droning on towards the target when bomb aimer Ken Scholefield reported: 'The electrics have gone, I can't release the bombs.'

The bomber jumped disconcertingly again after being hit by another burst of flak and the engineer, Sam Leary, cried out and collapsed beside the pilot who called up Stoddard and Guthrie to get him back to the rest bed, where the navigator dressed the wounds in Leary's right thigh and arm. Flames began curling wickedly from the starboard inner engine.

Purvis says: 'The procedure was then: petrol off, let the engine run until it had used up the petrol in the pipe, switch off, feather, then press the fire extinguisher. The fire went out. It was so automatic, the training we'd had. I had to go through the sequence again in my mind to make sure that I'd done everything.

'Next thing Jim Wright, the rear gunner, said oil was coming out of the port outer engine. I watched the oil pressure gauge and once that started dropping I feathered that one as well. Then I told the crew: "Hold tight, they're getting too near for comfort, we're getting out of this." I peeled off, turning to port, and cleared out, nose down, over the top of Bordeaux itself, still carrying the bomb load. I don't know if the Germans thought we'd been hit and were about to crash or not, but there were no more shells sent our way and we saw no fighters.'

'I levelled out at 1,500ft and asked Scholefield if he could get rid of the bombs. He appeared holding a fire axe with blood streaming down his face. The perspex had been shattered in the nose by the flak when Ken had been lying on his stomach with his thumb on the bomb tit. Jim brought another

axe from the back and between them they released each bomb manually, one
by one. The hydraulics had gone so the bomb doors remained open, adding
to the drag. The landing gear was also out of action. We thought there would
be just enough oil to pump it down by hand, but we couldn't use the flaps.
The draught from the hole in the nose made life a little more uncomfortable.

'We later realised that the Lancaster would have been in much worse
condition had Ken been able to release our bombs over Bordeaux. The
armour-piercing bombs acted as armour plating when the shattering blasts
of flak exploded against the bottom of the aircraft. The bombs really saved
our lives, stopping most of the flak which just bounced off them. If they'd
been ordinary bombs they would have exploded and we'd have disappeared
in a puff of smoke.

'I told the rear gunner to get rid of half his guns and ammunition to help
lighten the aircraft. I heard: "Wheeeeeh!" and said: "What's up, Jim?" He
replied: "The string of ammunition is like confetti going out." At least he
was enjoying himself.

'Larry Guthrie came up with his parachute clipped to his chest and yelled:
"Are we baling out, Skipper?"

'I yelled back: "You're not."

'"What d'you mean?"

'"Your parachute's got a bloody big hole in it."

'Shrapnel had smashed into his 'chute. Larry hadn't seen the damage in
the dim interior when he put it on. The wireless operator didn't say a word,
he just ripped it off and flung it angrily down towards the rear of the
fuselage.'

Two engines were still working, luckily one on each side, but it was a long
way home and their problems had accumulated like bad debts. The rudder
and aileron trimmers had been shot away, throttles and rev controls severed,
all aerials were u/s, the wireless operator's radio set was dead, and so were
both air speed indicators. When Purvis levelled off the engine controls had
gone: no throttles, no pitch levers.

'They were all floppy and loose. I couldn't control the two engines that
were still working, nor alter their settings. They were running smoothly, but
it was impossible to put more or less boost into either of them and if one had
caught fire it could not be feathered. Both engines were pulling against each
other, but the one on the starboard side was pulling most strongly, trying to
drag us to the left. There was no help from the trimming tab and I had to put
all my weight on the rudder itself. It was so difficult to hold straight. After a
while my leg, stretched out solid, was screaming from the strain and I looked
for a bit of relief by trying to do it standing up, because there was no room
on the pedal for anyone to help me.'

When Purvis asked his navigator for a course home Stoddard slammed
his skipper's captain of aircraft's chart in front of him and growled: 'Here,
find your own bloody way home, I'm going on strike.'

Startled, Purvis said: 'What's wrong, Dave?'

'When I was at the back helping Sam we caught another packet from the flak. It's smashed a hole beside my position. Every one of my maps and charts has been sucked out.'

Purvis recalls the dicey situation: 'We were supposed to leave the target by the way we went in, but if anything happened I didn't want us to be over the sea. The wind was from the west that day, so I thought if I headed due north I was bound to hit England. That was all I was worrying about. No airfields were marked on my chart and I intended putting down at the first airfield we saw. Sam did what he could from the rest bed, advising me on transferring fuel to and from different tanks. I could just see the engineer's instruments and one of the others came forward to check them.'

Purvis suddenly felt another draught and looked back to see the rear door wide open. The rear gunner was standing there, not strapped in, calmly holding the Elsen which he slung out, watched it disappear and shut the door. He was on intercom and the pilot said:

'What the devil did you do that for, Jim?'

The gunner replied: 'Well, you told me to get rid of any surplus weight.'

'What happens if I want to use that?'

'You're not leaving that seat. Whatever you want to do you'll bloody well do it where you're sitting.'

The Lancaster was still at 1,500ft, to the east of Brest, when they crept over a hill which was marked on the pilot's map at 1,113ft. All the way across France they saw farm hands working on the land looking up, waving. Even if they did not know it was a Lancaster heading shakily towards England, after years of war French people easily recognised a British aircraft. RAF pilots were told to synchronise their engines so they sounded silky smooth. German aeroplane engines with their 'whoooh! whoooh! whoooh!' created a more sinister image.

The Lancaster crew did not know how far the Allies had got after D-Day and could never be sure when the ground below was still occupied. They managed to avoid towns and flak emplacements, but had they been attacked by a fighter the crippled aircraft would have been dead meat. It seemed the Germans had lost interest in attacking a bomber which appeared to be a goner from the moment it limped away from Bordeaux. They passed to the east of La Rochelle, feeling more confident, but ahead stretched a wide expanse of the English Channel.

They stared down at the water, crossing fingers as the two engines dragged them slowly homewards, listening for the tiniest hiccup which might interrupt their continuing roar, while Larry Guthrie wondered, bleakly, if he could survive dropping into the Channel without a parachute. He had heard that an aircraft coming down into the drink was not a soft landing.

The first bit of England the navigator identified was Start Point, to the east of Salcombe, Devon. The nearest airfield was Bolt Head, a coastal fighter base. Purvis hauled the bomber to port and when they were over the aerodrome Guthrie fired off two red Very cartridges. An answering green came from control and all other aircraft were instructed to keep their distance until the Lancaster had landed. It was about 6.15pm. Far to the north the first 550 Squadron bombers were dropping into their base beside the Humber.

The undercarriage had been pumped down manually by Scholefield. Purvis remembers the moment they turned in:

'It was a bit tricky. I went across the runway to set the compass direction, then did a long sweep over the sea, sticking the nose down gently, to lose height, which is bound to increase the air speed. I did a big circuit, trying to lose air speed and I was now down to sea level, practically touching the tops of the waves. Ahead was a 600ft cliff and we were heading for the bottom of it. At the last moment we pulled up and touched down at the end of the wire-mesh runway. It seemed to be a perfect landing and I told Ken, the bomb aimer, who was sitting beside me to knock the fuel switches off as we carried on down the runway. We had no brakes, the air pressure had gone. The others were in the crash position at the back. We overshot the runway and burst into a field. Luckily there was no fence or hedge because we were still going at a fair lick. There was one place where I could have turned, down a slight hill, but the wood at the end would have stopped us rather comprehensively.

'I had a feeling that at the far end of the field was a cliff face, with a long messy drop into the sea. I also saw a six-foot-high dry-stone wall which seemed the best option at the time and I turned towards it.

'We hit the wall square on with a loud crash and stopped, finely balanced, on top of it. The undercarriage was knocked back eighteen inches and we were stuck there like a monstrous seesaw. The wireless operator stood up when he heard the wheels running along the runway and his hand was hurt when we hit the wall. I had a dislocated bone in my lower back which was not discovered until years later.

'It was too high to leave by the rear door so I got out through the hatch above my seat and jumped on to a wing. By then an ambulance and fire tender were there. The ambulance backed under the wing and we slid down on to its roof.

'When I was on the ground someone said petrol was leaking from the engines so I quickly climbed back in and found that instead of switching off the fuel leading to the two good engines Ken had turned it on for the two which had been feathered. I'd never asked him to do this before and had been too busy to watch what he was doing. Petrol was pouring out of all four engines. I knocked all the switches off and thought I might as well get all our stuff out. I found the navigator's bag, then noticed the sponge rubber cushion which I kept in my aluminium bucket seat. There was a hole in the middle where a piece of shrapnel had almost come through after bursting through the floor. If it had travelled another half-inch with any impetus I'd have been speaking in a squeaky voice. I fished it out and kept it for years.

'I also picked up the first aid and escape kits and noticed the number on them. Outside I told Ken: "Do you realise this is the first time we haven't had No 13 and we got shot up?" No one had been superstitious in the crew, but they were after that.

'On a later operation when we went to get the kits the No 13s had all gone and the crew refused to fly. When the Wingco came round Ken got in his car and went to every aircraft until he found the No 13s and swapped. Thirteen has been my lucky number ever since.'

Bob Purvis was awarded an immediate DFC for his skill and coolness in getting them back. He tried in vain to get an award for Sam Leary, the flight engineer, who had given his skipper a steady flow of advice while in great pain as he lay on the rest bed. Leary was taken to hospital and never flew again with Purvis. Dave Stoddard, the navigator, was later decorated with a DFM.

Their aircraft was classified Category B, dismantled and taken away on three huge Queen Mary transporters to be repaired and the following February was being flown at a heavy conversion unit.

Although 550 Squadron was expanded to three flights by the end of 1944, it was operational less than two years. Sixty-one of its Lancasters had failed to return, 150 aircrew were killed and 189 posted missing. The airfield was closed in October 1945.

CHAPTER FOURTEEN

APPOINTMENT WITH DEATH

The Wellington was a thunderous sphincter-rupturing blur, bursting suddenly out of the haze, passing inches above them. They ducked instinctively as the great roar of the four engines from the two medium bombers briefly merged, then looked round, shocked and frightened, the moment gone, but the image of a near collision indelibly printed on their minds.

'Christ,' spluttered Ted Crabtree, the Australian pilot, peeling away, 'to hell with this, we're not getting killed. I'm going back.'

Minutes later they were on the ground at 14 OTU Cottesmore, Rutland, still seething, waiting to confront the crew of the offending aircraft. It was 7 July 1943.

Crabtree's wireless operator, Bob Dack, said: 'We'd been sent to practise bombing on a small range at Grimsthorpe park, Lincolnshire. It was a fine sunny day but there was a lot of haze and we could not see the target. We were flying at 6,000ft. Other aircraft were at different levels. I was leaning over Ted's shoulder trying to help locate the target when: "Whoooosh!" and the Wellington went over. It was absolutely terrifying. We learned the other aircraft had been flying at 7,000ft and they couldn't see the target either. They had an instructor who told the pilot: "Go down 1,000ft and try there." The pilot reminded him that another aircraft was 1,000ft below but the instructor shrugged and said: "The sky's a big place, we'll miss that."

'The other pilot was a friend of Ted's but our skipper didn't mince his words when they landed. We had some hairy times on OTU in those worn-out old Wellington ICs, including getting lost over Birmingham in 10/10ths cloud when barrage balloons were rising all round us like mushrooms. Once, coming in to land at Saltby, a satellite of Cottesmore, the port wing dropped and was pointing at the ground. It kept doing this but somehow Ted got the plane on the level to touch down. We found out later that only one flap had come down. It scared everyone.'

Twenty-two-year-old Flight Sergeant Ted Crabtree was a man with an awful secret which he one day confided to Sergeant Dack who, at thirty-three, was the crew's grandad. The pilot had sold women's underwear at a shop in Sydney, but was fearful about having his leg pulled and being given a cringing nickname.

They lost their first navigator, Flight Sergeant Ken McKenzie, an Australian, who was taken off flying immediately when he fainted in church one Sunday after running to get there on time.

The new man was Sergeant Alan Sales, not much over twenty, who had recently left university.

Sergeant Nelson Noble, a Canadian, the bomb aimer, was a self-contained young man, who spoke only when it was necessary and went his own way. He once forgot his parachute, a court-martial offence. He remembered it as they waited to take off on a five-hour trip.

The pilot growled: 'Where is it?'

Nelson replied: 'I may have left it in the crewroom, or somewhere.'

'My engines are running, I'm not stopping for anyone,' snapped Crabtree. 'You'll just have to hope you don't need to bloody bale out. If you do, you must walk home.'

Sergeant Dack was one of seven children living in the Lincolnshire village of Barholm, where their father, William, ran a farm. He also owned four blacksmith's shops. He was a hard man, who made his children leave school at fourteen to start earning a wage. Bob, who could have gone to grammar school, worked on the farm and gained experience in a smithy. He had saved hard from his frugal wages for flying lessons at Peterborough Flying Club because, more than anything, he wanted to fly. He was married to Anne.

Sergeant Vic Lander, the rear gunner, was a spiritualist, whose startling predictions made his crewmates uneasy, especially at night when he claimed to see dead friends or relations standing at their bedside. From Lancashire, an RAF regular, he was married, nearly as old as Dack.

Telling his crewmates they should not worry about going on bombing operations, he said: 'My spiritual guide has assured me we're going to be quite safe and will come out of it without any bother.'

The only injury Bob Dack suffered at a training camp was while they were stationed at 1661 HCU Winthorpe. They had finished the course and were waiting for a posting. Dack decided to go alone to the cinema in Newark after the rest of his crew had been confined to camp for returning late from leave.

He says: 'My right knee had been troubling me for a long time. I came out of the cinema and jumped on my bike. There was a terrible wrench in my knee and I fell on the pavement. It was in the blackout and I lay there moaning, writhing in agony as people stepped round me. I can still hear one woman's sneering voice: "Those drunken airmen."

'I got up with the aid of the bicycle, hopped on one leg up the hill out of Newark, and back to camp.

'Next morning Ted and someone else helped me to station sick quarters, where the medical officer thought I was swinging the lead.

'I said: "I can't bend my leg." He snapped: "Put it down, I've heard this one before."

'A big fellow, he grabbed my ankle and yanked. I yelled so loudly at the excruciating pain the senior medical officer came in from his office next door. He felt round my knee and said my cartilage had come out. I was taken to RAF Hospital Rauceby where the cartilage was removed.

'Ted and Alan came to see me. They'd been posted to Bardney, near Lincoln. I was worried about my position in the aircraft and said I hoped their new wireless operator was only temporary.

'Ted said: "We're very sorry, Bob, but you're out. They replaced you straightaway, there was nothing we could do about it."

'They said they were leaving for Hanover on their first op that night. They promised to return next day to tell me how they got on. They never did, and it wasn't until weeks later I heard they were all killed on that first trip.'

Dack was out of commission for months, catching pneumonia during convalescence, then being trapped in a bureaucratic limbo at Scampton with dozens of other spare bods who had all, for different reasons, lost their crews. Posted back to Winthorpe he was crewed up again.

His pilot was Flight Sergeant Tommy Hall, twenty-three, with whom Dack felt comfortable and secure in the air. From Wraysbury, on the Thames, Hall was cheerful and positive.

Flight Sergeant Ronnie Parker, a shy quiet Australian, was the navigator. The bomb aimer, Flight Sergeant Tom Gill, at thirty-two, was blunt and outspoken. He had been a range boss in Queensland and shared Dack's responsibilities as crew grandad.

Sergeant Cyril Beston, twenty-one, from Nuneaton, was short, energetic and quick thinking.

To 'Grandad' Dack, the two gunners were, at eighteen, little more than schoolboys. The mid-upper, Sergeant Tony Poole, came from Sleaford, Lincolnshire, where he had worked in a bank. Sergeant Jock Robertson, a sturdy well-educated youngster, whose home was in the Lake District, was the tail gunner.

Posted to 106 Squadron at Metheringham their formidable first operation was to Berlin on 24 March 1944, which became known throughout Bomber Command as The Night of the Strong Winds.

They took off at 6.50pm in Lancaster EB593 Y-Yorker. Dack says:

'One of my duties was to listen out for the winds. The Pathfinders in front were sending wind speeds back to base who relayed them on to the Main Stream. Our calculations had to be based on that wind speed to get us to the target at a certain time. The timing was imperative. We were told the winds at 20,000ft were 60mph coming from the north-north-west. We found out much later they were nearer 160mph.

'Our instructions were to bomb on the red flares which, when they hit the ground, would cover about half an acre. I peered out of the astro hatch as we drew nearer the target. It was terrifying, with endless rows of night fighter flares dropped on us and flak being pumped up continuously.

'The skipper said: "Righto Bomb Aimer, let's have your instructions."

'Gill replied. "There are no instructions yet, there are no bloody flares down there to bomb on. We shall have to go round again. I didn't come all the bloody way from Australia to drop my bombs anywhere."

'As we started a long wide circuit around Berlin we heard the Master Bomber shouting: "Come on, Pathfinders, get those bloody flares down, never mind what time it is."

'We saw the flares drop as we flew round the outskirts of Berlin. It was a bit bumpy, but they didn't pick us up on radar, we got back into the stream with the tail enders and bombed on the red marker.

'Tom Gill was satisfied. "Right on the dot," he said. Then there was that unhappy half minute flying straight and level to give your photoflash time to explode and the camera to take a picture.

'Our course was to fly south then turn west on the homeward run. But the high wind carried us much further south than we wanted to go. We ended up coming across the Ruhr Valley, the hottest place in Germany. There was a vast curtain of exploding shells as far as the eye could see, exploding around our height. We had to go through, there was no way we could dodge it.

'Then the bomb aimer said: "Hang on Tom, there's a gap over to starboard." I looked and sure enough there it was as if somebody had pulled the curtains back for a Lancaster to get through.

'Tommy whipped the aircraft round and flew straight for this gap. Showing our inexperience we were just congratulating ourselves when: "Wham!" A radar-directed blue-white searchlight slammed straight into us. It was joined by ten or so other lights and in no time we're in a blinding cone. They had waited for Joe Muggins to fly through that lovely gap. The mousetrap. A nice bit of cheese.

'The pilot did everything he could, short of turning the aircraft upside down. He weaved, darted, danced, slowed down, descended, climbed, and the flak came up in shovelfuls. We heard it bursting around us above the roar of our engines.'

The rear gunner cried: 'My guns have gone! my guns have gone!' Robertson did not elaborate and the others assumed he was sorting out his Brownings which had probably jammed.

The port engine caught fire, then flames were seen pouring from the starboard outer. The extinguishers did not work and the flak was undiminished.

The pilot yelled: 'That's it, chaps. Start baling out.'

Before anyone had time to move for his parachute the engineer cried: Hang on! Tommy. 'Hang on. We're not finished yet.'

The pilot said: 'I can't get out of it.'

Cyril Beston replied: 'Stick the nose straight down and dive down to 10,000ft. We might escape the searchlights.'

'I'll never be able to pull out with only two engines.'

Dack said: 'I'll come up and help you, Tommy.' The wireless operator squeezed behind Hall so he could reach over his shoulders.

Hall said: 'Don't touch anything, Bob, until I shout. Right, here we go.'

Dack recalls the gut-churning seconds as they plunged into a scorching dive:

'We were going at a terrible speed and spotting things on the ground which we shouldn't have been able to see, when we reached a point where he started to pull out. Tommy shouted: "Righto Bob, pull."

'We pulled with all our might and she came back ever so slowly out of that perpendicular dive, you thought she was never going to make it, until he cried: "All right, Bob, I've got her. We're out of it".

'The engineer shouted: "And we've put the bloody fires out." And we'd escaped the searchlights.'

They crept cautiously over the coast and the North Sea and were beginning to think of a welcome kip when Dack received an unwelcome message on his radio which he passed to the navigator.

It said Metheringham was covered by fog and they were told to land on the emergency airfield at 26 OTU Wing, Buckinghamshire.

Around this time Jock Robertson asked the skipper for permission to leave his rear turret which had been damaged by a shell over the Ruhr.

The pilot touched down light as a feather, afraid the tyres had been punctured by flak. After almost eight hours in the air they joined a long row of other diverted 106 Squadron aircraft.

Bob Dack says: 'None of us could sleep after that lot. Then, just as we became drowsy a horde of sparrows living in the roof of the Nissen hut we'd been allocated started up a loud twittering dawn chorus. Joining them was a booming voice over the Tannoy telling us to report to the flight office immediately for our return to base.

'We found a crowd of trainees around poor old Y-Yorker which was full of holes. Some probably considered remustering after seeing the damage. We got our stuff out and looked at the rear turret. A shell had gone right through it, missing the gunner by half-inches and destroying the gun mountings. The guns were pointing towards the ground. We hitched lifts on other aircraft and found a lovely sunny morning in Metheringham.'

On 26 March they took off at 7.45pm in JB566 C-Charlie, among 705 aircraft briefed to attack Essen. There was a problem with the boosters and halfway across the North Sea they had only managed to crawl to about 14,000ft.

It was too low but Dack believed he knew how the sluggish Lancaster could be persuaded to go higher.

He said: 'Would it help if you jettisoned the big one.' That was the 4,000lb Cookie.

Hall said: 'We're supposed to take a picture of the target. The photograph will show we've jettisoned.'

'I can get rid of the bomb without triggering the camera. No one will know.'

The navigator broke in: 'I believe he's right, I've heard something about this.'

Dack added: 'You need to open the bomb doors first.'

After a moment's thought the pilot said: 'Righto, bomb doors open, Bob, do your stuff.'

Dack says: 'Near my seat was a little slot in the floor, no wider than my finger. I'd been taught that in an emergency, with a hung-up Cookie, you could push an ordinary wooden ruler down there and release the bomb. We were still over the North Sea when I slid my ruler in the slot and felt around for the switch. I gave it a push, the bomb fell out and we started climbing. It was a sweet moment. We dropped our four 500lb armour-piercing bombs and canisters of incendiaries through 10/10ths cloud into Essen.'

Four nights later, again flying JB566, they set off for Nuremburg. Sixty-four Lancasters and thirty-one Halifaxes were lost, the worst night for Bomber Command in the entire war. The raid that should never have got off the ground was doomed to failure, due mainly to navigational difficulties after an incorrect wind forecast, and because night fighters were waiting for the bombers.

Dack recalls: 'The flight commander had told us we could go on a week's leave after this one and I'd written to Anne telling her to expect me. Our daughter, Sheelagh, was six. Valerie was a baby. I was looking forward to that leave.

'The moon period was too far advanced, no one thought we would go to Nuremburg and we waited for the telephone call to tell us it had been scrubbed. But the call was not made.

'We crossed Belgium and into Germany. There was flak here and there, not giving us much trouble, then the gunners started reporting a lot of bombers going down. They got the skipper a bit edgy and he told them to shut up, then started weaving because night fighters were in the stream. We were on a long leg which was taking us across central Germany and directly between two of Germany's biggest night fighter stations. I can't imagine which clots put us there.

'Shortly after the rear gunner reported we were leaving vapour trails from all four engines I heard an enormous thump. It was an Me-110 with Schräge Musik, attacking from the rear. Our gunners hadn't seen it. Just one burst: "Brrrrh!" and it was gone. I felt the whole aircraft shiver as if a giant had hit us with a club.

'I groped about on the floor, found my parachute and clipped it on. After Berlin I hadn't kept it on the rack. That's what saved my life. All the practising for baling out and following the drill I knew was useless because in an emergency you had no time. I switched on the intercom and heard a babble of voices. Tony Poole, the mid-upper shouted: "The whole ruddy port wing's on fire." I looked out and saw it blazing from root to tip, with a great flood of flames pouring out.

'Amidst the confusion I heard the skipper shouting: "Bale out, everybody! Bale out!" I unplugged some equipment, including the oxygen line. We were at 23,000ft. I knew we'd only got seconds without oxygen. Officially, I was supposed to walk down the fuselage, help out the rear gunner then jettison the rear door. But when I looked back the flames were coming up through the fuselage floor with the metal burning like a sheet of newspaper. At least one shell had gone through a canister of phosphorous incendiaries. Others had been within a few inches of cutting me in half. The whole fuselage to the rear was a solid wall of flame and in the middle of it I saw the silhouette of Tony Poole. My only way out was through the escape hatch in the bomb aimer's compartment.

'Worried about oxygen I turned to go. The navigator was standing beside me and I tapped him on the shoulder, pointing forward. But he hadn't got a parachute on and was in a complete daze. Still on intercom, I heard the skipper screaming: "Get out quick! I can't hold her, she's breaking up." At that moment the aircraft seemed to collapse as the wing broke off. Rolling over and over we hurtled towards the ground, the engines, still working, pulling us down at a tremendous speed. First the engines were roaring, then they screamed, then howled. The howling was almost too much. I'd been swept off my feet and was pinned with poor little Ronnie against the side by G-force. There was nothing we could do about it.

'The big bomb was supposed to go off on impact. I was worried about that Cookie, although it wouldn't have mattered if the bomb bay was empty. Hitting the ground would kill us all just as well. An eternity of time passed, although I knew that within seconds we would hit the ground. My mind was working furiously: how do I get out of this one? But I had no answers.'

Before the wing fell off Cyril Beston, the engineer, his parachute on, had dived down two steps to the escape hatch. To his surprise the hatch was open. He reached forward to pull himself out as the Lancaster began falling and, to his horror, was unable to move.

'Then,' says Dack, 'there was an almighty explosion and I was outside the aircraft, spinning rapidly over and over, but going up, not down, with my legs wobbling about. Then, as I was wondering what had happened, I started falling. I pulled the ripcord and remember the little pilot 'chute swishing up by my face. Later, I was swinging gently, as if I was playing on a child's swing. The moment my parachute opened, alone in the sky, I heard a voice and suddenly realised it was mine, shouting: "I'm sorry, Anne, I shan't be coming home on leave."

'I heard a mighty boom from below, the parachute flapped wildly above and there was the sound of things whistling through the air around me. My aircraft had struck the ground.'

Bob Dack drifted down, aware that he had lost his flying boots and socks. The immediate past, clinging to him like a bad dream, gave him no confidence for what he might meet on the ground. He landed gently, with the canopy catching in the topmost branches of a tall tree which stood in a big wood.

'After a time the old grey matter started to work and I thought: where am I now? And how did I get out of the aircraft? Then I heard a sound. A clink and a rustle, followed a moment later by a thump. I heard shuffling footsteps moving through the dead leaves. Oh my God, bloody Germans out looking for me already. But the footsteps disappeared.

'I started swinging until I found a sturdy branch for my feet. I thought that I couldn't fall now and if I pressed my quick release the upper branches would whip the parachute off me and I'd just drop forward and hold this branch. That's exactly what happened except the 'chute cords caught under my throat. For several seconds I hung there terrified, until I managed to dig my fingers inside the tightening cords and pulled them up and over my face, almost ripping off my nose.

'I slithered down the trunk to the ground and checked for injuries. I seemed to be unhurt although blood was trickling down my face. I reached inside my battledress and found my pipe, a pack of tobacco I had bought in the mess just before we took off, and a box of matches. It was a brand-new American Corncob pipe, light as a feather. I lit up and smoked that whole pipeful. Wonderful. When it went out I filled it up and smoked another one without moving, still sitting under the tree.

'I started wandering about, wondering where the aircraft had landed. I came to a narrow track in the wood and walked along it in my bare feet. It was cold and uncomfortable walking. I found the body of Tom, the bomb aimer, lying at a bend in the track. The moon was still out and I could see he was not wearing a parachute.

'I walked on then came back and sat with him for a time. I was a bit woozy but I talked to him until I felt it was time to go. I said: "It's no good, Tom, I shall have to leave you and find my way out of this wood".

'I found myself on the edge of the wood, looking over open heath land. Further on was an empty forester's lookout fixed on tall poles but after walking another twenty yards I passed out.

'I came to with a stick prodding me. It was brilliant sunshine with a white hoarfrost sparkling on the grass which fell away into a valley where there was a tiny village with red-roofed houses and a church in the centre. It was very picturesque, but my feet were like blocks of ice. The old bloke who'd been poking me suddenly raised his walking stick. He was thinking seriously about hitting me. Having thought I was dead I'd startled him by sitting up. He'd been told awful tales about what the terrible English do when they capture a German and he was threatening me and shouting to a group of men running towards us. Some were armed with shotguns.

'The villagers gathered round and babbled a bit. One prodded me in the chest with his shotgun and I carefully watched his trigger finger. He shouted: "Pistole!" I said: "I have no pistol. Look." He seemed disappointed.

'I was taken down this hard stone track. My poor feet didn't like it a bit. After a while I said: "I'm not having this any more" and sat down. "Do what you like with your bloody shotgun."

'When they threatened me I pointed to my cut and bleeding feet. They stood round me while I had another smoke. When I'd finished I got up and said: "Come on." And we moved off.

'Going down into the little village of Berghausen, which is north of Frankfurt, we were met by a throng of mothers, babies and children and we soon formed a considerable procession. I was an object of great curiosity, but no one showed me any hostility. We went to the Bürgermeister's office. A little fellow, he was jabbering away on the telephone. I looked round and there, sitting in the corner, was young Cyril, so battered I didn't recognise him at first. He'd also lost his boots, but had hung on to his socks. His face, like mine, was covered in blood. We were a wretchedly filthy pair.

'He jumped to his feet and cried: "Bob, how the hell did you get here?"'

They had plenty of time to talk about that terrible night when they were both incarcerated in Stalag Luft VI, at Heidekrug, on the Baltic.

It was Cyril Beston Dack had heard moving through the wood. The engineer had landed in a tree about fifty yards away from the wireless operator, but he had fallen fifteen feet, spraining both ankles.

They were the only survivors from C-Charlie. Tommy Hall, the pilot, was found with his hands still gripping the control column. The rear gunner was also in the wreckage. Dack believes the others were blown out of the Lancaster. None was wearing parachutes. Hall was awarded a posthumous DFM for his outstanding work on the Berlin sortie.

Tom Gill, the bomb aimer, had been desperately close to getting out. Virtually lying on the escape hatch in the nose he was in the ideal position. It was clearly Gill who had opened the hatch before hurrying a few feet for his parachute. It would have taken him seconds; too many seconds. He might even have had the 'chute in his hands, an eye blink away from clipping it on, when the wing fell off and he was cruelly trapped by G-force. No one can imagine the misery of a man so close to life being brutally hustled into an appointment with death.

In England Bob Dack's family received the news that he was missing with great distress. In the week before he was captured Dack's younger brother, Eddie, a soldier, was killed at the Anzio beachhead in Italy.

Beston arrived back in England three weeks before Dack who was flown home in a Lancaster from 106 Squadron.

'The bomber crew were all strangers to me,' says Dack. 'There was only one thing they were sorry about. They had arrived at Metheringham just before the war ended and hadn't had the chance to go on a bombing operation. I said: "You don't know how lucky you are." But I don't think they believed me.'

CHAPTER FIFTEEN

THE GOERING FACTOR

Tom Forrest and his family left Great Yarmouth on 17 October 1940, escaping the German bombers which occasionally made hit-and-run attacks on the town's naval base, scattering a few bombs inland and spraying bullets indiscriminately among the nervous population. Forrest liked to avoid trouble, but with the benefit of foresight he would not have accepted a new job in Coventry. On 14 November, the savage mauling of the West Midlands industrial city by the Luftwaffe began and the Forrests thought with increasing fondness of their former Norfolk home.

Jack Forrest, then seventeen, an apprentice carpenter and joiner, recalls ambling through Foleshill that night at around 7pm, looking for a shop selling cigarettes, when the sirens went:

'There had been raids before which were a nuisance and I thought: "Oh no, not again." I bought my fags and got home in Ransom Road where we assumed, as usual, the bombers wouldn't find us. Then it started getting heavy so we walked 200yd to the air raid shelters at Edgwick Primary School. They were full of people. We heard the loud thumping and banging of bombs all around us, but everyone was amazing: laughing, joking and telling stories.

'When we left the shelter the first thing I saw was an ambulance in a bomb crater. There was a series of craters all along the road with bits of vehicles in them and Christ knows what else. My mother got her key to open our front door but it had been blown out with all the windows. The house was a bit damaged, but we were among the lucky ones.'

During the raid, which lasted from 7.20pm until six the following morning, over 500 tons of high-explosive bombs and 30,000 incendiaries fell on Coventry, killing 568 people and seriously injuring 863. One third of the city's factories was wiped out and one in twelve homes destroyed or rendered uninhabitable.

Jack Forrest still had anger in his heart when, two years later, the slim six footer volunteered to join RAF aircrew and became a flight engineer with 619 Squadron.

His skipper, Pilot Officer Kimberley 'Kim' Roberts, a pipe-smoking

Australian, was three weeks older than Sergeant Forrest. His family ran Haywards department store in Bunbury, south of Perth. He had trained on Tiger Moths at Cunderdin and twin-engine Ansons at Geraldton. Chunkily built, he stood about 5ft 7in. A fearless, press-on type, he rarely got excited except in the mess where, after a few beers, the officers crowded round hooting as a pianist struck up and Roberts went into his gyrating impression of a woman stripteasing.

The Roberts family lived across the road from the Slees in Bunbury. Frank Slee had been a Royal Flying Corps pilot in the First World War. When young Roberts returned home to say goodbye before leaving for England he was invited over to the Slees for a drink. Frank Slee suddenly drew an Iron Cross from his pocket and hung it round the youngster's neck saying it had been given him by the German fighter pilot who shot him down after a dogfight over Belgium on 8 June 1917 during his first flight over enemy lines. The name 'Hermann Goering' was engraved on the back of the medal. Slee said Goering had landed his aircraft, shaken his hand and presented him with the medal in a remarkable gesture of aircrew camaraderie. He was the pilot's seventh victim. The German went on to destroy a further twenty British aircraft. Slee told Roberts to keep it as a mascot and shoot down some Germans while he was wearing it.

Roberts never removed the Iron Cross on the squadron, not even in the shower. It became the crew's mascot and the pilot often flourished it eagerly to urge on his crew during an operation.

As the crew progressed through their tour and became closer Roberts invited his engineer to join him in Western Australia after the war.

Forrest says: 'We had three Jacks in the crew and when Kim asked what I wanted to be called I mentioned my grandfather who had run away from home in Bury St Edmunds to join a circus. He was called Showman. Kim said: "We'll call you Young Showman".'

Warrant Officer Jack Lott, had already served with Transport Command in the Middle East. Aged twenty-four, from Chiswick, Middlesex, he had been a traveller with the boot polish company, Cherry Blossom. He had a sardonic sense of humour, and a prodigious memory, useful for a navigator.

The wireless operator, Flight Sergeant John Tucker, a happy-go-lucky married man from Aldershot, was Morse mad, muttering messages to himself in code anywhere on the airfield.

Flight Sergeant Reg De Viell, from Kingsbury, Middlesex, already losing his hair at twenty-nine, was known fondly as Curly. The bomb aimer was married with a son, and his wife, Vera, was expecting their second child.

Sergeant Johnny Williams, the mid-upper gunner, was a tall fair-haired youth of nineteen, from Gravesend, Kent. Lionel 'Lucky' Virgo, from Adelaide, their rear gunner, was, like many Australians, an assiduous poker player.

They enjoyed drinking together in a village pub and their skipper often borrowed an NCO's jacket so he could join his crew in the sergeants' mess. They regularly took their ground crew out for a mixed grill at a restaurant near Coningsby.

Two 619 Squadron crews were loaned out to squadrons based at East Kirkby on the night of 15 February 1944.

Forrest says: 'One crew flew with 57 Squadron, we went to 630 Squadron. We'd only been back off leave three days. The target was Berlin, not a happy prospect. It's a funny thing but before an op my mind went crackers thinking of what might happen to us, but once we were on our way I was fine, even though we saw so many people killed.

'The worst thing about our job was the closeness of the aircraft. A near miss in those days was something I never forgot. Our rear gunner once screamed: "Fucking dive!" Kim went straight down, we heard the engines of the other Lanc as it virtually scraped over our roof and I ducked, that's how close it was. The other bomber was being chased by a fighter which, luckily, ignored us.

'I saw two bombers collide over Frankfurt. There was a great explosion and they both disappeared. We were going over Munich on our bombing run when I looked through a perspex blister and saw a Lancaster with its bomb doors opening. The next minute it wasn't there, just a mighty flash. Some of the wreckage knocked bits off our mid-upper turret. We often saw a great flash on the ground and knew it was one of ours that had gone down. We used to think: "Thank God it's not us".

'We had a reasonable trip to Berlin. My main concern that night was filling in my log. We called up East Kirkby and were on the approach to the airfield through a bit of fog. I looked at our altimeter which said 700ft. I don't remember anything else until I woke up in the wreckage of the Lancaster with the trunk of a tree an inch or two away from my face. I learned later that we had struck the one hill in the area, at Old Bolingbroke, taking down several trees before grinding to a halt. Another ten yards and we would have smashed into a thick wood. It was 3.30am and we'd been in the air for 7hr 20min. Berlin had been more welcoming. We all had cuts and bruises, except the pilot who was strapped in. I was standing in the cockpit when we hit the ground at 120mph and was black and blue from head to foot. Lucky had the worst experience. We heard him calling for help.

'The rear turret had been torn off and he was caught in a tree. We lit a bonfire with dead branches and leaves to attract attention and it was not long before a meat wagon and fire engine arrived. It took some time to get Lucky down. Both his arms, a leg, seven ribs and his jaw were broken. He was in a hell of a state, but later returned to the squadron and completed his tour.

'The Lanc's nose was split in half and the rest of the kite shattered. Three engines were recovered but the fourth, the port outer, was never found even though chaps dug down 30ft into the boggy ground.

'The first thing you say when you crash is: "I'll never fly again". So did I. But after seven days' survivors' leave we went up for an air test. We flew over what was left of our old Lanc, but we were as right as rain.'

After Virgo was taken to hospital they had a succession of spare bod tail end Charlies. The pilot hung on to one of the replacements, Flight Sergeant Gill King, from Sydney. He had emigrated with his parents from Portsmouth when he was eighteen months old. Just over six feet tall, he was a reliable man to have in the rear turret.

On 15 March they took off from Coningsby in Lancaster LM378 J-Jig to attack Stuttgart.

About to start their bombing run over the target at 20,000ft, King yelled: 'Corkscrew port, go!'

Nearly thirty tons of Lancaster, packed with bombs, fuel and ammunition, fell towards the earth like a twirling stone barn, but they were too late to prevent a Junkers-88 fighter shooting them up.

Forrest again: 'Kim regained control, but we were badly damaged. The port tail fin and rudder were all raggedy and the guns out of action, except one Browning in the rear turret. Gill yelled: "The bastard's coming in again!"

'I stuck my head in the engineer's observation panel with my parachute tucked tightly between my legs, ready to bale out and saw the fighter coming in. It was seventy-five yards away when a little stream of tracer went out from our rear turret straight into his port engine and it blew up. Then the navigator shouted: "What about the bloody bombs?" Kim said: "I'll drop 'em." He opened the bomb doors, the bombs fell out and we staggered away.

'No one was hurt although ninety holes were counted later in the fuselage. It was a struggle to get home. The foot rudder controls were vastly different now because of the damage. The air flow keeps the aircraft going, so when you've got something out of kilter it makes things harder. I was lending my hands to Kim on the control column. After we got out of the target area it was a clean trip home, there was nothing wrong with the engines, although we reduced speed from 165mph to about 150. We were a bit later than the others getting back to base.

'We dropped height over the sea and Kim called up Coningsby to explain the situation. A fire tender and ambulance were waiting for us. When we landed we could hear the fin and rudder clanking along the runway behind, hanging on by the wires. We got out, looked at the aircraft and said: "Oh my God, did we get back in that?"'

After debriefing they went to breakfast. The pilot was bawled out in the officers' mess by the station commander.

He said: 'Roberts, you are improperly dressed.'

'Why, Sir?'

The group captain jabbed the pilot's chest. 'You should have a DFC ribbon up there.'

Roberts had been awarded an immediate DFC for getting them back. Gill King was decorated with a DFM for shooting down the fighter.

On 16 April they were transferred to Dunholme Lodge, an airfield they shared with 44 (Rhodesia) Squadron.

Forrest missed the comfort of Coningsby.

'It was terrible at Dunholme. The runways went up a hill and down the other side. All the billets looked as if they had been taken up in aeroplanes and dropped by parachutes, landing anywhere. It evolved into a satellite of Scampton.

'Facilities were pretty basic, but the food was good. I always felt ashamed when I came home on leave because rationing was strict and my mother, like everyone else's mother, struggled to get a decent meal on the table. We were each given two bars of chocolate before an operation. I drew fourteen bars and often gave my share to my sister, Gladys, who worked at the Dunlop tyre factory in Coventry.'

Many crews were superstitious, performing little rituals before takeoff encouraging the gods to protect them on sorties. The ritual of one Coningsby wireless operator had evolved into an extravagant performance. He danced on the wing waving a multi-coloured umbrella before clambering into his Lancaster clutching the magic brolly. The capering spell did not save him the night his aircraft was shot down.

On 3 May, sent to attack a German military camp near the French village of Mailly-Le-Camp, in their regular aircraft, LM378, a cannon shell ripped through a fuel tank in the starboard wing after they had bombed. They smelled petrol but, incredibly, there was no fire. The fuel was quickly transferred to the other tanks, although 200 gallons leaked into the sky.

On the morning of D-Day they were again in LM378 hitting gun emplacements at La Pernelle on the Cherbourg peninsular. This was Gill King's thirtieth and last operation, even though he pleaded to be allowed one more trip. The Australian government insisted that its young fliers were sent home immediately after completing their first tour, so King was on his way. Roberts had one more op before he was due to follow him.

They were sent up again late on D-Day night as Allied soldiers pushing in from the Normandy coast were checked by the German defenders of Caen. Their job was to bomb bridges outside the French river port. It was, according to Jack Forrest, a day of great excitement. They were part of a massive armada of 1,065 aircraft whose crews had been briefed to bomb lines of communication in or near French towns behind the battle area. Six of the ten Lancasters lost were from the 5 Group raid on Caen where aircraft waited impatiently for the targets to be properly marked before flying over heavy concentrations of German guns at bombing heights below 3,000ft. One Halifax was also lost.

Kim Roberts, now a flight lieutenant, on his last trip, had a new rear gunner, Flying Officer Guy Wyand, who was at the beginning of his second tour.

Forrest, on his twenty-ninth op, says: 'I only saw him when he joined us at dispersal and there was no time to say hello. We took off in Kim's favourite aircraft, LL783 C-Charlie, at about midnight and the sky was full of aeroplanes. The weather was not good, heavy rain with a low cloud base, which meant everyone was flying under it in a narrow band. We hit a lot of other aircraft's slipstreams which made life a bit unpleasant at 2,000ft, but once over the sea we got sorted out and conditions improved.

'Charlie was known as Cinders of the Clouds. Painted on the port side was a nymph-like creature with long flowing hair.

'We skirted the Channel Islands, flew across Normandy towards Caen and seemed to have more room to ourselves. We had expected to have a good view of the fighting at the French coast, but apart from the odd flash of gunfire or searchlight things seemed fairly quiet. We reached Caen and bombed the target.

'We headed for home at 1,800ft, just beneath the cloud, unusual for us as we normally flew much higher. I didn't like it because there was little room for manoeuvre if we got into trouble. When we were twenty miles inside France, heading for the Cherbourg Peninsular, I was crouched down looking at my instruments, writing the details up in my log. I heard John Tucker, the wireless operator, say to the rear gunner: "Can you see an enemy fighter behind us?"

'Wyand replied: "All I can see is Lancasters."

'John was clearly worried and said: "I'm sure there's a fighter nearby. I can see it on Fishpond."

'Both gunners said they couldn't see any Germans and the skipper told them to keep a sharp lookout. John Tucker was not a man who would imagine trouble and he repeated his claim that he was certain a night fighter was in the vicinity. The rear gunner again said he could not see it.

'Within seconds there was a tremendous bang and crash, the aircraft shuddered, Kim took immediate evasive action, started to corkscrew, and I heard a scream from the rear gunner as we were attacked again by the Ju-88. I saw a stream of tracer rush past and hit both starboard engines which immediately caught fire.

'Kim called up everyone in turn. There was nothing from John Tucker, or either gunner. I think they had all got clobbered, although I don't know if they'd been killed. It all happened so quickly. I activated the fire extinguishers and we were feathering the propellors and stopping the engines when the fighter came in again, guns and cannons blazing, and the inner port engine caught fire.

'Kim immediately snapped: "Abandon aircraft, chaps," adding: "Where's my parachute, Showman?"

'The pilot's 'chute was passed over and clipped on and there was time only to glimpse the flames streaking back forty feet from three Merlin engines and Kim struggling to keep the bomber level. Reg De Viell, the bomb aimer, pulled up the escape hatch, but didn't drop it out. He put it in the nose. He was a tidy chap and didn't want to waste it. He looked back at us before dropping out then I felt the toe of the navigator, Jack Lott, up my bum. I heard him shout: "Go on, Showman, get mobile."

'We were no higher than 1,700ft when I went out. The noise of the Lancaster disappeared, the silence was awesome, my parachute opened and quite soon I was down. The approved manner of landing by parachute is to roll over on to one shoulder to break the fall. This I did only to find myself up to my neck in water. I'd landed in a marsh.

'After releasing my 'chute and scrambling on to dry land I heard someone splashing around. It was Reg who'd lost his flying boots. We couldn't see or hear any of the others. We had a good look round when the sky began lightening, finding an orchard surrounded by thick hedges and deep scrubland. As the sun rose we hung our saturated clothes on bushes to dry. We saw a lot of our fighters with white stripes painted under their wings, identification marks for Allied ground troops to recognise.'

They spent the whole day in the orchard, near the town of Carentan, sustained by Horlicks tablets and cigarettes. As night descended they slipped away, heading north-east under a bright moon, nervous of flickering shadows which they imagined were Germans pursuing them. Their spirits were raised by the sound of RAF bombers passing overhead and, later, seeing the sky turned red by a blazing target.

They skirted two villages where there were too many barking dogs for comfort, finding shelter at dawn in a thick hedge. At night the Germans came to life. Forrest and De Viell heard the coughs of tank and truck engines being started up and the rumble of convoys moving along roads under cover of darkness. As more Germans arrived the airmen's progress became slow and frustrating.

Parched, the pair decided to move on in daylight, searching for water. They were feeling desperate when they found a watering hole used by cattle. Filling their little water bags they added purifying tablets and watched a squirrel darting through the branches of a tree, while waiting twenty minutes before they could take their first sip.

The two airmen were creeping along a thick hedge which ran beside a road when two German soldiers on bicycles stopped for a smoke. They hardly dared move an eyeball as the Germans chatted, argued and laughed before the creak of their bicycles signalled their departure. That night the Britons crawled beneath undergrowth which had accumulated in a dried-up ditch, sleeping fitfully during showers of rain before continuing their long walk towards the Allied lines.

On the afternoon of 10 June, weak from hunger and thirst, moving stealthily beside a long hedge they disturbed a German soldier urinating. He covered the men with a rifle and marched them towards a group of a dozen paratroopers laying mines. The Germans, who had served in North Africa, stole De Viell's watch and Forrest's cigarette lighter. Forrest later resisted the attempt by a German to take his watch.

Marched to a farmhouse they were locked in a cowshed, given water and a hunk of black bread. De Viell was pleased to accept a pair of decent boots which he drew, sighing, on to his sore feet. Ordered on a lorry with German soldiers they drove through Carentan, which had been bombed or shelled. The lorry ground its way through columns of enemy soldiers to Périers, pulling up outside a small chateau being used as a dressing station.

Forrest recalls being marched to a slit trench outside the entrance to the chateau:

'A German colonel was sitting in the trench. He looked up and said, in beautiful English: "Good evening, gentlemen. I am sorry to see you in this predicament." He told us he'd been partly educated at Cambridge. He was very civilised, we had a glass of wine with him and a polite conversation about the war. He told us our Second Front would not last long because the Fuehrer had many secret weapons. Three days later the first V1s were fired on Britain.

'We were moved into the house with five American doctors, three medical orderlies, and five wounded men, all captured paratroopers. The medics were tending wounded Huns who were brought in from the front. Some had limbs missing and internal injuries, a sobering sight. They were patched up then sent to a proper hospital further inland.

'We were given food and wine and Reg and I had our first wash since leaving Dunholme, with cold water and gritty soap, but it felt good. We slept well on the hard floor, not waking until ten next morning.

'We had to bury a big young German soldier who had been hit by shell splinters and bled to death. We wrapped him in a bloody blanket and left him under four feet of soil. A day later we wakened to the sound of bombs being dropped by American B-26s and later P-47 Thunderbolt fighters circled over our heads until they found some trucks to play with.'

It was with some relief that they were moved from Périers to start the long grim journey into Germany, via Paris: first to Dulag Luft for interrogation near Frankfurt, then to Stalag Luft VII, Bankau, in Silesia, by truck, train and coach, running a savage gauntlet of British and American aircraft who shot at anything moving in enemy-held territory.

It was not until they returned to England after the war that Jack Forrest and Reg De Viell found out they were the only survivors from C-Charlie. The Lancaster had crashed in a farmer's field at Baupte, near Auvers in Normandy. A fifteen-year-old boy saw the blazing bomber at roof height with the pilot, still at the controls, desperately attempting to avoid buildings and land safely. The Lancaster broke up as it smashed into the ground. Years later the boy, now a farmer, told researchers that the main body of the aircraft burst into flames. The cockpit, with Kim Roberts still inside, became an inferno, and he saw the pilot being consumed by fire. There was nothing left to put into a coffin. Two bodies were found in the wrecked tail.

Two other men had baled out and died. A farmer going to milk his cows that morning found one body at Hameau Drieu. A German soldier told the farmer and his neighbour to keep away then looted the body. The second man was lying in a field about 200yd behind a castle. The four airmen were buried by Resistance fighters and farmers in the cemetery at Auvers. They were later transferred to military cemeteries: three at Bayeux, the other at Tilly-sur-Seulles.

In 1992 Forrest and De Viell made an emotional visit to the field, near the Carentan-Cherbourg railway line, where their Lancaster had crashed. They met the farmer, Roger Montmellien, who showed them bits of the mangled aircraft he had collected.

Not expecting to find any further remains of C-Charlie the two veterans of Bomber Command picked up several mementoes of rusty air frame and engine, including components which had been made in Coventry. Other relics of the wreck are in Normandy museums. They were taken to see the graves of their four crewmates where they stood, heads bowed, weeping, reliving that awful night in June 1944.

Forrest says: 'We were treated royally, with a civic reception, and shown much love and kindness as we visited many poignant and important places.'

Jack Forrest is now seventy-eight, but not a day passes without him thinking of the night when five of his mates died:

'Every day I feel guilty because I survived and they did not. One minute we were seven happy-go-lucky young chaps and the next minute there were only two. The navigator was right behind me and I wonder why he didn't make it. As I left the aircraft I hoped Kim would somehow bale out, although there wasn't much height.'

The life of the pilot's mother, Ethel Roberts, was turned upside-down by the war. Her husband, Fred, a World War One veteran, had died in 1940. A second son, also Fred, was a prisoner of war in Germany, and his brother, Newton, was embroiled in the Pacific war, manning a gun on the battleship, *Australia*. Their sister, Moya, was in the Women's Royal Australian Navy and Ethel's eldest son, George, had returned from service overseas to run the family store.

Kim Roberts' family have often wondered, had his body been spared by the flames, what the Germans would have made of an Allied bomber pilot wearing an Iron Cross, which had been awarded to Hermann Goering, Hitler's head of the Luftwaffe.

A memorial to Kim Roberts – a man with no grave – paid for by the people of Auvers and his family, unveiled in 1996 in the presence of the two crash survivors, stands at a site near where their Lancaster ended its last flight.

CHAPTER SIXTEEN

THE WRONG AIRFIELD

The bomber pilot peered anxiously into the sky. The weather was fine, warm, a wafting breeze, without a cloud to be seen. Good flying weather. Flight Sergeant Norman Marsh was a handsome man, a broad six foot two inches, with powerful shoulders and huge hands, tough as anvils, yet they rested as lightly as a cat's paws on the controls. It was too easy to relax after leaving the target and he had relentlessly hammered into his crew how crucial it was for everyone to remain alert at all times for the sly split-second appearance of German night fighters spitting death. There was never a moment to relax until they were safely round a table in the debriefing room at Ludford Magna.

The attack came, as he knew it would, from the rear. Only there were six bastards this time, each one determined to nail him. Marsh's evasive tactics were swift as they swooped in line astern, quickly fanning out, guns and cannons blazing, the enemy pilots hunched gleefully over their controls, eager for the kill. But Marsh had the edge, wrenching open the throttles and plunging into a breathless disappearing corkscrew, clinging to the juddering controls. Faster! faster! faster!

The fighters, their hawking fire power silenced, flew in dismayed disarray as the bomber hurtled out of sight. One by one the fighters peeled off, landing in a tight group, their pilots panting.

One yelled: 'Jammy bastard! We'll get you next time.'

Another grumbled: 'We'll never catch the bugger, he's bigger, stronger and madder than any of us.'

Norman Marsh, wildly whooping, appeared at full speed from behind a bush and charged recklessly towards them, braking at the last minute, the old bicycle skidding to a halt, throwing up a shower of dirt at the bottom of the large disused quarry.

With twinkling eyes the Australian regarded his crew for a moment, that huge grin embracing them with the sort of warm affection only a bomber man would understand, knowing that each of the six men would, if necessary, sacrifice himself for a crewmate.

'All right, you useless bastards,' he growled cheerfully, thrusting a hand through his thick dark wavy hair. 'I guess that's enough fighter affiliation for today. I hope the bloody krauts are as flatfooted as you lot on our next op. Come on, I'll race you to the pub. Last one buys the beer.'

Marsh led the way at a rush out of the quarry, his massive thighs pumping, pedals whirling, rapidly accelerating, easily drawing away from the others who struggled wearily up the steep bumpy incline on their sit-up-and-beg bicycles, having run out of energy making loud machine gun and cannon noises. He was a supercharged Maserati to their wheezing Austin Sevens. Marsh never had to buy the beers after one of his extraordinary fighter affiliation exercises on their camp bicycles.

They had found the quarry when cycling in search of a village pub along a narrow lane near Ludford Magna, Lincolnshire, where they were stationed with 101 Squadron. Probably the toughest and fittest man on the squadron, Marsh enjoyed these merry romps, which had a serious purpose: concentrating the chaps' minds. They were more fun, safer too than the real thing had been in training: charging about in a Lancaster over the North Sea against nimble single-seater aircraft armed with cameras instead of guns sent up to attack them by Fighter Command.

One of the fighter bicyclists was Marsh's navigator, Flight Sergeant Charlie Kaye, who recalls the pilot:

'We often went to the quarry to play fighter pursuit on bikes. Norman pretended to be the bomber and we were the fighters trying to intercept him. We never did. He was quicker than any of us. He was a very easy-going fellow to fly with and a fine pilot. But he didn't talk much about himself, none of us did. We had an important job to do and lived for the present.'

Marsh came from Geraldton, a seaport north of Perth, Western Australia, where he was a good tennis player, cricketer and swimmer. He worked for Western Australian Railways as a draughtsman before joining the RAAF at eighteen, graduating as a pilot at 5 Service Flying Training School, Geraldton, in 1942. While training he often brought home on weekend leave part of his flying gear for younger brothers Allan and Fred to try on.

Fred Marsh recalls: 'Norm was very family orientated. One of his favourite big-brother acts was to kneel on a bed with either of us on his back and go for a pretend motor bike ride. He even sent money home for Christmas presents in 1943, which included new bikes for Allan and me.'

Norman Marsh was phlegmatic, self-assured, good humoured, blunt, but fiercely steadfast to his crew. He may have been marginally more fond of the LACW telephonist he met on their nights off, carrying under his arm a rolled blanket taken from his bed in the billet. It was likely that Marsh had spotted the potential of thick cosy bushes in a grassy corner of the quarry. After returning from his passionate tryst he often joined his crewmates in the pub.

Although he could be noisy and brash Marsh had an unexpected gentle and sensitive side to his stormy character. His crew were astounded one night at a village pub, when the pilot quietly took his bitter with its splash of lime, sat in front of the battered piano, ran his great fingers softly over the keys and played, quite beautifully, *The Rustle of Spring*.

Charlie Kaye was brought up in Anfield where, in 1940, much time was spent at night sitting in the Anderson shelter at the bottom of the garden in Yelverton Road as German bombers attacked Liverpool. It was a crush for the parents and their six children, scary too. Kaye says:

'One night an ammunition train was hit on a railway siding half-a-mile from our house which was badly shaken. It was like being in the middle of an awesome thunderstorm. The screaming bombs coming down was the most frightening part. It was almost a relief when they exploded because you were still there. Looking out next morning there was a sort of cotton wool all over the garden, which we thought was the beginning of biological warfare and my father told us not to touch it. Next day we learned it was gun cotton from the shells and swept it up.'

Kaye did not start his schooling until he was seven, leaving at fourteen, regretting that he had not been selected for a grammar school. In May 1941 he left his job as a joiner, making air raid shelters and shadow factories which were sited on spoof airfields, and went into the RAF. He soon regarded his new employer as the University of the Air, hungrily soaking up knowledge at the numerous lectures he attended, gaining confidence when finding he could keep up with young men from public and grammar schools.

He says: 'The great thing about Ludford was that the airfield stood on either side of the village, which had two pubs. It was like having a couple of pubs on the airfield. When we moved in our hut was surrounded by a field of potatoes. We cooked them on the big coke stove in the billet to supplement our diet. The older women in the village were kind, inviting us into their homes for afternoon tea and home-made cakes.

'We shared the hut with another crew with whom we enjoyed a bit of skylarking. Then they were shot down. All their gear was cleared away and we saw their stripped beds in the morning. It was very depressing and happened more than once.

'I had a reputation for being slow. After briefing I always hung about the met man's office for the latest forecast winds. I wanted every scrap of information that I could take with me on the op. I was usually last on the crew bus.

'I became keen on astro-navigation. I think I was one of the few navigators who got a good astro fix over enemy territory, plotted it and used it for the wind change. That was when we were in difficulties out of Gee range. With astro fixes you take three shots and get three position lines. If they give you a small cocked hat, a small triangle, where they cross, you've got a good fix. If it's a big cocked hat it could be way out.'

Marsh's wireless operator was Sergeant Don Ince, a Londoner. He was quiet, self-possessed, steadier than his crewmates, never panicking in tight situations, always willing to try and locate a direction-finding position for Kaye.

Once, during a bombing operation, Ince reported mildly: 'Skipper, I think it's raining and we've got a leak. The rain is coming into my position.'

'It's not bloody raining,' exclaimed the pilot, stifling a chuckle. 'I've just used my piss pot.'

The wireless operator went quiet as, after a fearful shudder, he tried to mop himself down.

Kaye says: 'Some skippers handed over the controls to the engineer before nipping down to the Elsen for a slash, but Norman never did, he liked to be in front, in control. He preferred to use his can, an old fruit tin, which he kept somewhere handy near his feet. He got it from the kitchen and never went on an op without it. Unfortunately, it didn't have a lid. Poor old Don happened to be in the way when it was knocked over.'

The pilot lost his bomb aimer and flight engineer who went LMF after three operations.

Kaye recalls: 'We were all waiting at dispersal after pissing on the tail wheel. Although they'd both been to briefing they did not appear at the aircraft and we didn't go on the trip. The bomb aimer, a pilot officer, had brought his wife to live in rented accommodation near the station, which was a mistake. The two men were very friendly and the engineer, a sergeant, spent a lot of time talking at his home. They were got rid of pretty quickly. Next day there was no sign that they had ever been on the station.'

Their new bomb aimer was Flying Officer Middleton who was tall, well built and good looking.

Flight Sergeant François De Brock, a Belgian, replaced the departed flight engineer. His crewmates called him Bill. He was garrulous, arrogant and determined, with an exaggerated swagger and a singular hatred of the Germans.

Kaye says: 'He regarded himself as one of the most important members of the crew, which no doubt he was. Trouble was, he let everybody know this. But that was his style. We got on quite well. Bill was a bit opinionated, but Norman dealt with that quietly by telling him: "Well, if you think so, you might be right, but I'm the skipper".'

Mid-upper gunner Flight Sergeant 'Glen' Glendinning, from the Glasgow area, was aggressive, positive and single minded, giving the impression that he had been brought up in a tough environment. Sergeant Geoff 'Titch' Watson, the rear gunner, who stood about 5ft 3in, was from Golders Green, London. Black haired, cheeky, good company, he came from a theatrical family, had appeared in small parts on stage and, spontaneously, sang songs from West End shows.

Their first operation was a gardening trip, dropping mines off La Rochelle, France, on 27 June, which Kaye recalls:

'We felt it wasn't a proper operation because it was only dropping mines. We thought we'd just have to fly over and drop the mines in the water. But there was a bit more to it than that. We didn't see any fighters but there was a heck of a lot of flak from the ground and from flak ships which knocked us about more than we'd expected.'

From the autumn of 1943, 101 was the only squadron in Bomber Command to fly Lancasters which were equipped with Airborne Cigar, or ABC as it became known. In addition to its bomb loads the aircraft carried this sophisticated equipment which was used by additional specially-trained wireless operators who had a knowledge of German. As the Lancasters filtered into the attacking stream ABC picked up transmissions from German fighter controllers. The operators then transmitted warbling tones or noises from the engines which drowned out the controller's instructions to the fighters.

Kaye again: 'ABC aircraft had to take part in every operation. Consequently, 101 bombers tended to fly more often than other squadrons. We also had to be spaced out in any raid because we were protecting the other squadrons with the ABC. We were given separate takeoff times. The ABC equipment protruded quite a bit out into the fuselage and the operator sat just behind the mid-upper turret. He normally came in, checked his equipment then had to get out of the way while the rest of us climbed in and got to our positions. Our special wireless operator could be a different fellow on each op.'

Norman Marsh and his crew first attacked Berlin on 23 August. They would fly six more times to the German capital. On each occasion it was never less than a chilling prospect. It was on Christmas Eve 1943, the target again Berlin, when Charlie Kaye admits to feeling disturbed.

'This was the first time I had an uneasy conscience. I had seen the extensive damage in Liverpool where a lot of children had been killed. As we were running into the target over Berlin I looked down into the flames and thought: "How many kids down there are not going to see Christmas Day?" That made me feel just a bit uneasy. The only way I could reassure myself that we were doing the right thing was by thinking of what had happened to Liverpool and, of course, this was all-out war.'

Bomber Command's Christmas present to Adolf Hitler left 178 people dead on the ground. Sixteen Lancasters were lost.

Kaye's twenty-ninth operation was also to Berlin on 29 January 1944. It was their sixth trip to the German capital.

Several diversionary raids were despatched to Germany to confuse the fighter controller, including six Mosquitoes which bombed Berlin before the main attack. Another eighteen Mosquitoes attacked night fighter airfields at Deelen, Leeuwarden and Venlo, while Pathfinder aircraft – four Halifaxes – helped a mine-laying operation for the first time when sixty-three Stirlings went gardening in Kiel Bay, five hours before 677 aircraft were scheduled to hit Berlin.

The German controller kept a cool head, critically analysed a confusing situation and made the right decision by concentrating his fighters over Berlin. Twenty-six Halifaxes and twenty Lancasters were lost that night, 6.8 per cent of the force. Many people were killed and about 180,000 bombed out of their homes. Numerous public buildings were damaged, including the new Chancellery, five embassies and six hospitals.

Middleton released the bombs from Lancaster V-Vic at 20,000ft through broken cloud and they moved purposefully away from the target area.

Kaye again: 'I had given the skipper a course between north-west and north to steer out of Berlin and we were on our way when there was a shout from Glen in the mid-upper turret. A fighter was attacking on the port quarter. He gave Norman instructions to take avoiding action which he did immediately.

"'Corkscrewing port!" Norman yelled, and as we dived for safety I heard Glen's Browning machine guns opening up. There were a lot of bangs on our fuselage as the Messerschmitt 110 came after us and I waited for something to explode but nothing did. There was a loud cry of triumph as Glen said he had hit the fighter and it was going down. Our kite was dropping so quickly, then the skipper said, perfectly calmly: "Hang on, hang on, I think I've got her. Do you know where your parachute is, Charlie?"'

Kaye was among those who had been in the grip of G-force, struggling to move but restricted by a terrible unseen but irresistible power as he tried to find the parachute which he had dropped beneath the navigator's table before takeoff. There was a moment of frozen terror when he thought the 'chute had disappeared. Scrabbling hopelessly around on the floor in ever-widening circles from the table, with the Lancaster plunging out of the sky, he could not find it. The odds against survival were astronomical for anyone caught in a stricken wartime bomber without a parachute. Men did fall to earth without one and lived to tell their staggering tales, but they were a tiny lucky minority. And such luck was distributed indiscriminately by the fickleness of fate.

Kaye's flapping hands eventually slapped against his parachute. He was trying to clip it on when the corkscrewing became less agitated and the pilot came on the intercom:

'Hold everything! Hold everything. We're okay, chaps.'

They were not as okay as they had been before the savage attack by the German fighter but the bomber was under control. The mid-upper gunner reported extensive damage to the tail, half of which had been shot away. A shell had smashed through the port tail fin, bits of which were falling off or flapping about uselessly. Fortunately the starboard tail fin was undamaged but the pilot's job had been made more difficult. Rear gunner Geoff Watson, untouched a short distance from the devastation, was badly shaken but unharmed. Cringing in his turret he had seen the fighter's shots slam into the Lancaster. It was over in seconds. There was only time to think of his escape after Glendinning had shot down the Messerschmitt, when the grim awareness of what might have happened crawled over Watson like an army of heavy-booted cockroaches.

No one had been injured and the pilot set about the difficult task of getting them home. Icy draughts screamed in to claw spitefully at them through scores of holes in the battered fuselage. None of the holes was much bigger than a man's fist, but the aircraft now seemed vulnerable and less able to carry them home without more problems developing. The good news was that all four engines were turning over sweetly.

'I was crawling about on the mucky bottom of the fuselage, hanging on to my parachute,' says Kaye. 'Later when we got word from the skipper that we were okay and had more or less levelled out at 12,000ft, in a fairly unsteady flight, I began looking for my equipment which had shot off the table when we went down.

'I had a very small masked light on the navigation table, although it didn't shed any light underneath and I had to feel my way around, but I found what I wanted and could carry on navigating. The chart was still there, pinned to the bolted-on table. I also found my sextant and that was a good thing because I realised we were north of track and I wanted a position. It was too far for Gee which we always lost more or less as soon as we crossed the enemy coast by German jamming which obscured all the signals. I decided to take a sextant shot and got an astro fix. I calculated a new wind and course for base, carefully avoiding a couple of heavily defended areas and gave it to Norman.

'We were going down steadily at first but gradually Norman was able to maintain height. He tried to get higher but was afraid to do too much climbing in case he exacerbated the damage to the tail. The damage meant he had to use the starboard rudder a lot to help with the steering. It was a struggle for him. Bill De Brock, the engineer, helped a great deal, handling the throttles, slowing down the engines' speed for part of the time and keeping a sharp check on petrol consumption. We didn't know whether the fighter had hit a petrol tank.

'We crossed the enemy coast at around 6,000ft and I remember thinking that the North Sea is quite a lot of water and we were losing altitude the whole time. I wondered if we might have to ditch and thought about all that dinghy drill we'd had.

'I only once thought we might have to bale out when we flew over an armed British trawler. It fired at us until we were out of range. We weren't hit but it was an awkward moment. These trawlers were probably more dangerous than anything else because you didn't expect them. We fired off the colours of the day, which they should have known and stopped shooting, but the shells continued coming up. It only lasts a short time when that happens, then you're away from it, but it's a bit alarming because they clearly meant to hit us. You couldn't blame them really. Anything coming from the German or Dutch coasts could be threatening and they weren't taking any chances.

'Norman kept reassuring us in his slow lazy Australian drawl: "Don't worry fellers, we'll get back." His words were very comforting, but he was that kind of chap. When he was confident he was quietly confident, he didn't shout or bluster. And, of course, he did know the situation we were in better than any of us.

'The engines were still perfectly okay, but we were maintaining course with difficulty. As soon as we got within r/t range the skipper explained our situation. He let Ludford know we were damaged and could he have priority landing, which he got. Most of the others were already down.

'We crossed the Lincolnshire coast at 500ft. Visibility was not good. We were within Gee range and I was homing on to Ludford with the Gee co-ordinates. Right next door to Ludford was another Lancaster airfield,

Kelstern. It was so close you could see both sets of perimeter lights which, from the air, appeared to be touching. Although we got over Ludford Magna the skipper – and we were all a bit shaky – got on to the wrong set of lights. Pilots followed the perimeter lights until they saw a funnel of yellow lights. The funnel, of course, leads you on to the runway in use. Norman took this, thinking it was our airfield, and he went into land, making a pretty good approach considering the difficulty of handling the controls. He was helped by the engineer who was controlling the revs to get the landing speed correct.'

Sighing with relief as the aircraft sank towards the runway, the rear gunner shattered the calm, suddenly shouting: 'My God, there's another aeroplane. Get out of the way, Skipper.'

'Okay Geoff, don't worry,' the pilot replied, laconically.

Then, a cry from the mid-upper gunner: 'It's a Lanc coming in right above us.'

It was their closest shave of the war. Fortunately, they had been spotted. The other Lancaster, a great thundering heart-stopping sinister mass, its engines bellowing, scraped by no more than a few slender feet across them. Its vigilant pilot desperately called on every single horse power of his Merlins to heave it clear of the intruding aircraft, overshoot the runway and make another approach, saving sixteen lives.

Kaye says: 'It was a lucky escape. We had no idea until after we landed that we were at the wrong airfield. We were being controlled by Ludford Magna who thought we were landing at Ludford. The runways of the two airfields must have been more or less pointing in the same direction. The Kelstern Lanc was directed to land on the same runway that we were aiming for. Fortunately its pilot's eyes and experience made him realise what was happening pretty quickly. Approaching us from the rear he probably saw our damaged tail. He opened up, overshot and allowed us to land safely. And were we glad he did. Considering the dicey situation our skipper did a pretty good landing. We were taxiing round when we realised what had happened.

'We never met the other Lancaster crew, I wish we had. I expected that we would all be hauled up before the CO and get a good ripping off. Strangely, nothing was said about it. I think due allowances were made for the fact that we'd had a bit of a shaky do and we had brought the aeroplane back. Shortly afterwards we were recommended for gallantry awards. I thought the Lanc could have been patched up but we were told the damage was too severe. It was left at Kelstern and scrapped. We got the crew bus back to Ludford and were debriefed there. I heard later that an unexploded German cannon shell had lodged in our main spar. It had passed within a couple of feet of me on the left-hand side.

'Bill De Brock was very upset. He snapped: "I brought this aircraft back, I wanted to show my flight engineers at Ludford what it was like".'

They flew twice more together, an unspectacular op to Berlin and finally to Leipzig. Most of the crew were decorated at the end of their tour. Marsh, De Brock, Middleton and Glendinning each received a DFC. After collecting his DFM Kaye was commissioned, posted to RAF Shawbury, Shropshire, on an advanced navigation course and, following a spell instructing, joined pilot Flight Lieutenant Joe Brogan, from Wigan, who had had a hairy first tour.

Brogan was based at Malta when it was a prime target for the Luftwaffe. While waiting on the island runway in his Wellington, as second pilot, to take off the Germans came over dropping bombs. The aircraft was hit and three of the five crew, including his pilot, were killed. After Brogan left hospital he was given his own worn-out Wimpy.

Kaye – now a flight lieutenant – and Brogan flew Halifax IIIs with 171 Squadron – in 100 Group – which had been formed in September 1944 for RCM (radio counter measures) and was based at North Creake, Norfolk, until the end of the war, by which time the navigator had flown on fifty-seven ops.

After surviving thirty bombing operations Bill De Brock, now a pilot officer, had enjoyed himself on 101 Squadron and was keen to carry straight on with a second tour. The others wanted a break from bombing and turned down the offer to continue flying as a complete crew. De Brock, however, was determined and wangled himself on to a Pathfinders' squadron. The engineer was only there a short time before he was shot down and killed.

Norman Marsh, also commissioned, wanted to remain in England and was posted after a spell of leave to a heavy conversion unit as an instructor. On 20 November 1944 he went up on a stormy night for a routine air test, when his pupil pilot reported an oil leak in the port inner engine. They landed at a wet bleak Yorkshire airfield and left the Halifax with the engines still ticking over. Marsh, a punctilious man, strolled over to the droning engine with the trainee pilot and looked intently for the leak. For some reason, as they talked, perhaps losing his balance in the strong wind, Marsh stumbled and the tip of the spinning propellor smashed into his head. He died from his terrible injuries in Harrogate Infirmary two days later. He was twenty-two.

CHAPTER SEVENTEEN

TAFFY'S WAR

Few young men were less adequately equipped to deal with the rigours of fighting a war than Bill Thomas. Timid, painfully shy, fearfully nervous of any kind of authority, he had not ventured more than twenty miles from his home before March 1943 when his mother saw him off on a train at Clarbeston Road, for the long journey to London, and the beginning of his great adventure in the vast world outside Pembrokeshire. He was eighteen.

Despite his diffidence and apparent lack of self-confidence, Thomas had set himself a daunting task at the beginning of the war: to join the RAF and be a wireless operator in a bomber.

His inner strength was nurtured at an early age by quiet and respectful observation of his mother, whose resilience and determination proved that by overcoming the shock of her farmer husband, Trevor, walking out in 1928 anything was possible. Lottie Thomas worked all hours cleaning other people's houses and doing jobs on farms to feed and clothe herself and four children, although they were always desperately poor.

Bill Thomas can only remember his mother once losing her composure. He was twelve. He recalls:

'Mum left us in bed early one morning when she went across to a neighbour to borrow a drop of milk for breakfast. While she was there I heard this loud hissing noise, then a mighty explosion, the whole house vibrated, the roof was blown completely off at the back and there was a huge hole at the front. My mother ran back, screaming. She thought she'd lost us, but we were all right. The Primus stove had exploded in the kitchen.'

They lived in a two-bedroom cottage at the village of Clarbeston Road. Bill Thomas, a bright boy, outstanding at arithmetic, passed the examinations to go to the grammar school at Haverfordwest, six miles away. Lottie Thomas, determined he should have every chance, scraped up enough money for a school uniform and railway season ticket, but soon realised it was impossible to pay for all the books he needed. No one was prepared to help and, crushed, she was forced to withdraw her son from the grammar. He returned, cheerfully enough, to the village school.

At fourteen Thomas worked as office boy and clerk for James Williams brewery in the nearby small town of Narberth where he had lodgings. He joined the ATC, mixing with young men who had similar ambitions. His confidence grew, he was called up and posted abroad. He came top of his course at 70 OTU Shandur, Egypt where he galloped ahead in Morse, which he found easy, achieving twenty-five words a minute.

Posted to Italy, he was the only Welshman on 25 (SAAF) Squadron. His vastly experienced skipper was twenty-eight-year-old Lieutenant Dick Richards, a former trainee veterinary surgeon from Johannesburg. Richards had a bushier dark moustache than film star Clark Gable, but similar bewitching eyes, and pretty girls clamoured for his attention. Witty, charming, well educated, Richards had all the attributes which less attractive and accomplished men were unable to tolerate and the pilot made several enemies at Campo Marino.

He was never forgiven for returning from an aborted raid and landing at 160mph, carrying the bomb load instead of jettisoning it, as ordered, over the Adriatic island of Jabouka. The crew were grounded ten days for this oversight. Richards also incurred the everlasting enmity of the squadron adjutant, a veteran of the First World War, after relieving the older man in the mess of the company of an attractive young woman singer from a visiting concert party.

The second pilot was Second Lieutenant 'Mac' MacIntosh, a quiet man, who read the Bible and prompted the skipper's mild observation: 'Don't worry, Taff, we'll all survive because Mac's religious.'

Richards' words were severely tested one day when he gave MacIntosh his first opportunity to land their twin-engine Martin Marauder bomber. Thomas still trembles at what happened next:

'Mac was not very experienced. He got us into a stall and we fell sideways, straight down. Through my little window I could see the sea galloping up towards us and thought that was the end of it. Then I saw the skipper grab the controls. The aircraft made a terrible revving noise and he managed to pull it out less than 100ft from the sea. We climbed back to 1,500ft and landed. The skipper, badly shaken, said: "We nearly had it today, Taff, but Mac's buying all the drinks tonight." He did, too. The officers came into the sergeants' mess to celebrate that we were still alive, but Mac was never given his own crew.'

The American-built Marauder was given several unfriendly nicknames after entering service with the USAAF in 1941, including Flying Torpedo, Flying Prostitute and, more chillingly, the Widow Maker, although after modifications, its pilots recovered their sense of humour. The medium bomber was powered by 2,000hp Pratt and Whitney R-2800-43 engines, and huge propellors lifted it to a service ceiling of over 20,000ft. Thomas remembers its comfortable quarters but even more, the extremely high approach speed of 140mph required to land a Marauder and the long run needed to take off fully laden.

'On one sortie we were No 11 aircraft, but failed to take off into the wind on the first attempt, and pulled to one side at the end of the runway to allow

No 12 to get airborne. Anxious not to miss this mission we were given permission from the control tower to take off down wind. We sped away with a 4,000lb bomb load, failed to get off twice and just made it the third time, only 100yd from the end of the runway, just as I thought we'd bought it. We caught up with the rest of the formation halfway across the Adriatic.'

Round faced and squarely built, navigator and bomb aimer Lieutenant Cedric Askew, preferred to be known as Pete. Depending on his mood, he regarded the crew's three NCOs with an aloofness which they ignored.

Tough Tanganyikan Sergeant Jock Rudd, the barrel-chested mid-upper gunner, was afraid of nobody, always ready for a fight, but unswervingly loyal to his crew. If anyone had squared up to a crewmate, Rudd would probably have tossed him into the sea, which lapped at the end of the airfield's single runway.

Few rear gunners were as old as Sergeant Tommy Allen, who dropped his age by several years for the chance to have a go at the Germans, whom he loathed after they bombed Plymouth, flattening his house in Howe Street. Allen, a former postman, was forty-one in the summer of 1944, the same age as Flight Sergeant Thomas's absconding parent. He became a good friend of the young Welshman, falling naturally into the role of substitute father, but his solicitousness was not always based on orthodox principles.

During a twelve-day leave in Rome, when Allen and Thomas visited the Vatican, the gunner took out a penknife, told Thomas, white faced and scared, to keep cavey, and coolly prised four small pieces of mosaic out of a wall which they shared as souvenirs.

Married, with an invalid daughter, Allen had already served in the Army and Royal Navy and suddenly decided he wanted to fly. He wrote in chalk 'A present from Plymouth' on all their bombs before leaving on a raid.

The middle-aged gunner did not flinch from telling off his pilot if anything went wrong. When Allen found Richards throwing up at dispersal beside the aircraft before takeoff one morning after a heavy session in the mess the previous night he administered a stern lecture which finished with the cutting words: 'You should be ashamed of yourself.'

Thomas again: 'Tommy could not stand idiots. We had an American fighter escort on a raid when the Yankee pilots amused themselves by roaring up through the formation and shooting past our tail plane, which annoyed Tommy who told the skipper over the intercom: "If they do that again I'm going to shoot the buggers down."

'The fighters returned, still messing about, and Tommy waggled his .5in Colt-Browning machine guns at one. Next thing they'd disappeared. We never saw them again. Tommy had put the shits up them. Some Yanks pretended to dive bomb Marauders, turning away at the last second, not very bright.'

On one sortie, two minutes from the target, an explosion rippled through their aircraft. No damage was found and they assumed their port tyre had burst. Thomas again:

'With this in mind the skipper deliberately landed on the starboard and nose wheels, easing down on the port side after reducing speed. The pilot was immediately reported by the control tower for making a poor landing, but the squadron commander, Lieutenant-Colonel Bosch, accepted the skipper's explanation. Only later we discovered that the explosion had been a sighter burst just underneath us which had been put up by the German ack-ack to gauge the height of the attacking bombers. It was a close call.'

They had crewed up at Shandur, where in August 1944, they survived their first hairy moment. Richards' Marauder was one of three bombers flying in formation at 4,000ft. Thomas recalls what began as a normal local exercise:

'We were flying as Number Two on the lead aircraft's starboard side, not quite wing tip to wing tip. The third Marauder was in a similar position on the port side, slightly below us. I was in my wireless compartment when the aircraft gave a terrible shudder which was followed by an awesome creaking noise as if someone was opening a huge old barn door. From my position I could see the skipper who turned round with tears streaming down his face. He shouted: "Send the emergency signal, Taff".'

As Thomas began rapidly tapping out 'OOO' in Morse to Shandur, the Number One Marauder was spiralling helplessly towards the ground.

Just after the three bombers emerged from a bank of cloud the leader and Dick Richards' aircraft had touched. The four-bladed airscrew of Richards' port engine smashed into the other Marauder, chopping off its huge fin and rudder, known as the policeman's helmet, sending the aeroplane into an uncontrollable spin. The six-man South African crew, experienced officers with at least two operational tours behind them, were all killed.

The four blades of Richards' port airscrew were badly buckled at the bottom, bent round like hockey sticks, scraping the cowling as they rotated, but the pilot made a near-perfect landing and, badly shaken, they returned to the crew room.

'There was talk straightaway about sending Dick back to South Africa, which would have meant the end of his war,' says Thomas. 'But a senior South African pilot with the rank of major, suddenly burst into the crew room, grabbed our skipper by the shoulder and snapped: "Come on, straight back up." We waited anxiously as Dick went up for about half an hour to make sure his nerve hadn't gone and I was given a bollocking for sending an emergency signal instead of an SOS. Next day we went up again with the major who occupied the second pilot's seat for three or four trips. Thankfully, Dick recovered well and I remained in his crew throughout my forty-three sorties with 25 Squadron.'

There was one survivor from the midair collision, an RAF wireless operator, Flying Officer Cooper DFM, a Londoner, well into his thirties, who had only gone along for the ride. He had been standing near the astro hatch and was flung out as the aircraft fell out of control. Luckily, his parachute was clipped on. He landed heavily, breaking a collar bone and ankle. That night Cooper heard from his wife in England that he had just become a father.

The aircrews lived in tents at Campo Marino pitched on a field near the aerodrome on the shores of the Adriatic, beside the Bay of Termoli. Inside their tents, 300ft above the airfield, they felt the vibrations as each aircraft took off and landed on the hard sand of the beach, which had been reinforced by pierced steel planking. Thomas recalls the hair-raising journey in three-ton trucks to the airfield which some pilots feared more than going on a sortie.

'We climbed 400yd up a road before plunging down a cart track beside an almost vertical escarpment with a sheer drop of 200ft on one side and a ninety-degree turn half way down. The drivers were black men from the African National Corps, who sometimes caused pandemonium when they missed the gear while trying to change down as we hurtled towards the sharp bend.

'When we arrived at the camp we had three days' incessant torrential rain, no fun when our accommodation was in a large marquee, about thirty of us sleeping head to toe. I'd never drunk anything in my life stronger than orange squash, but I got so cold that Dick persuaded me to drink two small brandies. I didn't notice the cold for the rest of that night. I was carried through the rain to the marquee where I was put to bed. We were later moved to smaller tents and I shared one with our two gunners. The officers, also in tents, were no better off. My bed was a piece of solid wood from the top of an old desk balanced on four ten-gallon drums with a ground sheet, one blanket and my greatcoat.

'That November the weather was so atrocious we only got one sortie off the ground. Most of the time was spent on familiarisation and practise bombing on Jabouka island until the weather improved. It was bitterly cold at nights, with no heating in the tents. Local newspapers said that winter was the coldest in Italy for seventy-two years. We had frequent blizzards and the camp was turned into a quagmire after the snow melted. Gales ripped away tents and blew roofs off briefing rooms and messes.

'The food was terrible, mostly dehydrated tinned stuff and boiled rice. I would have given anything for a fresh potato. At teatime they put on the table a 14lb tin of margarine, which was rock solid. You needed a hammer and chisel to get it out.

'Stinking communal toilets, or shitters as they were known, were in a big tent about thirty yards from our tent. Inside was a massive deep square pit with ten or so seats on each side. You left your dignity outside when you went in there, carrying your own toilet paper.

'There was no real social life. When I wasn't flying I just hung around the camp. The town of Termoli was five miles up the road, but I never went there, it had a bit of a reputation with bad girls and whatnot.'

Although the allure of pretty shapely girls with flashing dark eyes and sexy accents, who were available a short distance away was irresistible to some hot-blooded airmen, the innocent young Welshman's fear of devious young women was greater than his curiosity about what they might have to offer.

Also based at Campo Marino was the RAF's 39 Squadron, equipped with Marauders, and two Italian squadrons flying Martin Baltimore medium bombers. The Italians had little interest in fighting a war in which they might get hurt and were often seen breaking formation and returning to base when they saw the flak spewing up from the target.

Targets were mainly over Yugoslavia: German garrisons, marshalling yards, gun positions, bridges, oil and ammunition dumps, troop and transport concentrations, even single-track railways snaking through the countryside. Partisans had liberated Belgrade in October 1944, but the Germans remained in strength in Yugoslavia until the end of the war.

On 1 April 1945, just after lunch, they were sent to bomb a target in Yugoslavia, flying in two boxes of six Marauders. It took less than an hour to reach the Yugoslavian coast. They were at about 8,000ft, preparing to start climbing over the Dinaric Alps when a pilot in Dick Richards' group contacted his box leader to report an overheating engine they feared was about to catch fire. He was told to return to base with Richards' bomber as escort. Bill Thomas recalls what happened:

'Quite soon afterwards it was clear they were unable to maintain height and we saw them bale out and drop into the Adriatic. We began circling them and the skipper said: "Taff, send off an SOS, Pete'll pass you the position." I sent it and got a "Message received and understood from base." Within seconds they came back with "IMI" which means "repeat message". I repeated the exact position which the navigator had given me, thinking I must have sent it wrong the first time.

'When they came back with a second IMI I got on the intercom to Pete, our navigator. He said: "Oh, bloody hell, Taff, I've boobed." He gave me the correct position which I sent to base and it was passed to a Catalina on its way from southern Italy. His first position had put the crew somewhere inside Yugoslavia. Luckily, I had already told Campo Marino that the crew which needed rescuing were in the drink.

'Their Marauder had flown a decent way before it went out of control. I saw it hit the water and explode in a red flash before disappearing. I imagined us in that bomber, unable to escape, and have been afraid of fire ever since.

We kept the other crew in sight for one-and-a-half hours. I was at the Morse key all that time sending an almost constant stream of messages about what was happening, and receiving a whole lot back. They were bobbing about in their orange mae wests, pretty pleased that we were there. They didn't have a dinghy and Tommy dropped a life raft, but the slipstream caught it and it didn't get anywhere near them.

'We buzzed over the water no higher than ten or twenty feet. Round and round and round. It seemed to take the Catalina an age to arrive. I saw the big flying boat land on the sea and start picking them up. We waved and set off for base with a minimum of fuel in the tanks. One chap later gave me a piece of the parachute which had carried him safely into the Adriatic.

'I was quite pleased that I hadn't made a single error in my signalling during the whole operation and was congratulated by the CO back at the airfield.

'When I looked to see if Lieutenant Richards was on the flying list for next day he wasn't among the twelve crews scheduled to go up. That night the skipper, the navigator and second pilot came into the sergeants' mess singing "Blue-eyed Taff" and told me I was down to fly with Captain Benson, the squadron leader. I knew Dick and other people didn't like him and said, rather bluntly: "I'm not flying with that bastard."

'The skipper told Benson that I wanted to stay with my own crew and I heard no more about it. I was later told that Benson was a decent fellow and firmly believe that my decision ended any hope of promotion and a medal.'

One of Bill Thomas's duties on the Marauder was to man the two waist guns shortly before they flew over the target. The Brownings were fired through a hatch on either side of the fuselage to protect the aircraft's belly from attacking fighters. Before opening the hatches he strapped on a safety harness to avoid being sucked out of the aeroplane by the slipstream.

'Getting aft,' says Thomas, 'was a tricky manoeuvre which involved me taking my parachute pack on a hazardous walk along a six-inch wide girder, the central catwalk. I turned sideways to negotiate the bomb racks which were on either side, then tapped on the mid-upper gunner's feet so he could rotate his turret and allow me to crawl through a narrow space underneath to get to the guns which were beyond a small bulkhead door. It was impossible to get across the catwalk carrying the parachute. I had to keep leaning down, placing my parachute ahead of me, then shuffle towards it, pick it up, put it down again and continue shuffling. It was difficult and slow.

'On one occasion, Pete Askew, the navigator, was late telling me that we were approaching the target. I was creeping along the catwalk when suddenly there was an almighty clatter as the bomb doors burst open and we were over the bloody target. I hadn't expected that and could see the ground passing ever so slowly beneath from a height of around 10,000ft. There was only yawning space on each side of the catwalk. It was a fairly unhealthy position to be in. There was flak coming up, too, although I didn't see any of it as my thoughts turned quickly to self-preservation.

'I only had the bomb racks to cling on to. I didn't dare move. If I had missed grabbing the racks I might have fallen out without my parachute. Or I might somehow have managed to dive the three feet to the bulkhead door. I didn't get to the guns. I heard the bombs go and, at last, the pilot closed the bomb doors.

'I grabbed my parachute and, dragging it behind me, retreated. I hadn't been frightened, but was quite pleased to get back to my seat. I sometimes thought that the skipper and navigator did it on purpose because they were full of devilment. I laughed it off and told Pete: 'You bugger, you didn't tell me in time.'

Another day the navigator's call came even later and there was no time for Thomas to start walking the plank aft. Instead, he remained at his position over the target before stepping up into the cockpit to witness an unusually savage and accurate flak attack.

'First came the red flash, then smoke, turning into the shape of a giant cauliflower, then the horrible smell of cordite. In the midst of it all I heard the skipper's calm voice over the intercom: "Those bastards have got their first team out today."

'On that raid all our formation suffered slight damage and it was only after returning to dispersal we found out from our ground crew that the navigation light on the port wing tip had been completely shot away'.

Delayed messages were not restricted to those spoken over the intercom. On another sortie Dick Richards' formation received a message from base: 'Do not bomb. Partisans have captured.' The signal arrived thirty seconds after the bombs had been released.

On 4 May 1945, four days after Adolf Hitler had committed suicide in his bunker deep below the beseiged Chancellery in Berlin, 25 Squadron set off for its last raid of the war. That day high-ranking German officers signed an unconditional surrender on Lüneburg Heath. Perhaps news of such a momentous event had not yet penetrated to air force chiefs at Campo Marino for 25 and 39 Squadrons left, as planned, to attack a bridge over the railway line between Dugo Selo and Popovaca, just east of Zagreb in Yugoslavia, part of the Germans' east-west line of retreat. They were told, at briefing, to expect little or no flak. Intelligence officers had clearly misjudged the aggressive mood of the German defenders.

That morning wireless operator Warrant Officer J. N. Thirion, a new arrival at 25 Squadron, had been going round the crews in his flying kit trying to beg a ride on a Marauder, desperate to get at least one bombing raid in before the war ended. The South African was rejected by the pilots who did not want to risk ending their run of good luck by carrying an extra bod.

They rumbled pleasantly over the Adriatic, Dick Richards' Marauder flying as No 5, formating on No 4, HD667, which was piloted by Lieutenant 'Mac' Van Rooyen, a popular and amiable South African farmer, who had a warm smile and vast handlebar moustache, which had been caricatured in *Old Stooge*, the squadron newsletter. They were known as The Farmer's Crew. The gunners in Van Rooyen's aircraft, both sergeants, were pals of Bill Thomas. The Welshman had been chatting the previous night to the mid-upper, Butch Neale, from Leamington Spa, sitting round the stove in the mess. John Cox, the tail-end Charlie, came from the Kent village of South Darenth. It was difficult to grasp that the end of the long war was in sight, at last they could all make plans which six months ago would have seemed to be ludicrous dreams.

Since October the tactics had been to make only one attack run on a target to preserve the element of surprise. But today a quick one-two was preferred because of difficulties experienced with the new T1 bombsight and the new manoeuvre of bombing at right angles to the target.

The twelve bombers from 39 Squadron went in first, bombing without opposition, but the situation had changed when 25 Squadron were poised to attack. Although no anti-aircraft guns had been reported near the bridge they were there today in strength. Over the target the Marauders, led by Lieutenant-Colonel Bosch, were caught in a box barrage of flak. The Germans, beaten on all fronts, were making a stubborn last stand, several of the dozen Marauders were damaged and after the bombs fell away Thomas heard his pilot gasp: 'What the bloody hell is Mac up to?'

Richards did not realise that Van Rooyen's aircraft had sustained a direct hit from the flak before his bomb doors had closed. HD667's port wing suddenly lifted in an agonised gesture of despair and Richards, with a flurry of hands at the controls, took violent evasive action as the other Marauder almost dropped on top of them. Aghast, he watched his friend's aircraft flip over on to its back and slide into a deadly spin. Van Rooyen was seen desperately attempting to crash land, but the bomber made a slow turn to starboard, smashed into the ground and blew up. There were no survivors.

Three other Marauders were hit, including Bosch's lead aircraft in which thirty-four holes were counted after he landed at base.

Later that day a puzzled South African was seen wandering around Campo Marino looking for his friend, Warrant Officer Thirion. The entire airfield was searched and men looked for him in Termoli, but he was never found.

It was not until some time after the war that the mystery was solved. Villagers in Yugoslavia showed Allied officials where they had buried Van Rooyen and his crew in May 1945, but instead of six graves there were seven. In one they uncovered a body which was identified as Thirion. The kind-hearted Van Rooyen had taken pity on Thirion who had, after all, been up for his first – and last – sortie.

CHAPTER EIGHTEEN

BOMBING HITLER

Few wartime airfields were at their best just after 2am. RAF Strubby, set with its black sprawl of Nissen huts amidst the flat fertile fields of east Lincolnshire, where broad beans and cabbages flourished more heartily than young airmen, had little to offer anyone during the dead hours of night. Almost within spitting distance of the North Sea, cruelly windswept in the winter, Strubby was said to be nearer occupied Europe than any other air base in the county.

Dawn was hours away on 25 April 1945, when thirteen crews of 619 Squadron were dragged roughly from their beds and sent wobbling on bicycles in the unyielding dark towards the mess with the pungent taste of last night's beer lingering in their mouths, not quite ready to welcome a ridiculously-early fry up of bacon and eggs. They were briefed to attack Hitler's Austrian mountain-top retreat at Berchtesgaden, and the local SS barracks.

The war was nearly over, Germany was on its knees. The enemy were still displaying remarkably obdurate resistance defending their shattered country, but the young men of Bomber Command were at last able to make real plans, including the biggest end-of-term piss-up the world had ever seen.

This was the earliest Canadian pilot Flying Officer Wilf De Marco and his crew had been called for an op. As they sat rubbing their hands and yawning in the cold truck, bumping across the dark desolate airfield to their Lancaster dozing at dispersal, most could reflect on the twenty-seven operations from which they had returned safely. Twenty-five-year-old Sergeant Gordon Walker, from Toronto, had missed three ops when he was laid up in March with influenza. To save Walker from the ordeal of being a veteran rear gunner lumbered with the dubious role of a spare bod, his six crewmates readily agreed to fly the extra sorties with him until he had completed his tour.

It seemed longer than five months ago when, as sprogs, they were briefed for their first sortie. Since then they had aged five years. Some people would call it maturity. Veteran aircrews might describe them as suffering from the abject weariness of battle.

Full of apprehension and excitement they had taken off for that first op at 4.04pm on 22 November 1944, in Lancaster III LM756 F-Freddy, to attack the submarine pens at Trondheim, the medieval capital of Norway, a city and seaport, lying on the mouth of the river Nid, on Trondheim Fjord, 250 gruelling miles north of Oslo. One Lancaster had been left behind at Strubby when its embarrassed crew found that it had not been filled with fuel.

They flew at low level with another 170 Lancasters and seven Mosquitoes up the North Sea, gaining height as they drew near to the target, which they found obliterated by a smoke screen, and the Master Bomber ordered the operation to be abandoned. It was a miserable anticlimax. The aircraft turned back and jettisoned their bombs halfway home. The weather had closed in at Strubby and De Marco, short of fuel, was diverted to Thornaby, Yorkshire, which had an emergency runway.

De Marco's wireless operator, Sergeant Jack Speers, another Canadian, says: 'They told us we would be landing on FIDO. As we approached the runway in dense fog we saw a red glow ahead, which turned into two lines of fire and we landed safely in the middle of the runway. We had been airborne for 11hr 10min and, it seemed, for nothing. One lad joked: "If this is ops I want my mother".'

The engines were switched off and, crouched with weariness, they climbed down from the Lancaster. De Marco was twenty-four. A broad muscular boisterous six footer, of Italian descent, he came from Timmins, Ontario. Owner of an old banger, and never short of money, he often ventured alone to Grimsby where his crew thought he was hiding a secret girlfriend. When challenged to demonstrate his raw strength he picked up any two of his crew, tucking one yelping under each arm. An outstanding ice hockey player he spent his leaves playing and coaching at a rink in Liverpool.

De Marco's flight engineer, Freddy Cole, said: 'Wilf was a brilliant pilot. His sharp reactions got us out of trouble several times. He also had a terrific sense of humour. We had all done a bit on the Link trainer but he used to tell me to take over, sitting in his seat while he wandered casually aft, terrifying the crew by pretending no one was at the controls.'

After a boring exercise De Marco had been known to fly at zero feet over the sea off Skegness, dropping the tail, almost tickling the tops of the waves, listening to the roars of fury from the tail gunner who was not enjoying his unexpected cold shower. 'What the fucking hell are you doing, you stupid bastard?' yelled Walker. 'I'm half fucking drowned back here.' The rest of the crew hooted with laughter as the grinning De Marco climbed over the coast and pointed them towards Strubby. The crews from any ships in the area would be telling an extraordinary story years later about the day they had seen a Lancaster bomber make a perfect takeoff from the sea.

A thin, shy and unassuming man, Sergeant Cole had been an apprentice machine tool fitter in Civvy Street. From Exhall, near Coventry, his hatred of the Germans was intensified in November 1940 when the city was pulverised over several nights by waves of enemy bombers.

He says: 'They were arrogant shits who needed to be dealt with ruthlessly. I just wanted to kill the bastards and was determined to get into the RAF. I didn't have good enough eyesight to be a pilot, but the RAF thought I was best suited to being an engineer. I spent several months at St Athan, Cardiff, where the training was brilliant and I learned everything there was to know about the Merlin engines. The comradeship was special and, of course, there was the flying.'

The navigator, Warrant Officer Norman Johnston, twenty-one, was tall, slim, quiet and studious, always with his nose inside a book, with a growing interest in photography. He was engaged to be married to a girl in Calgary, Alberta, where his father was an undertaker.

Johnston and Cole became pals and the Canadian occasionally spent his leave at the engineer's home, visiting the flattened areas of Coventry, which refuelled their hatred for the Germans. It was here at the Wheatsheaf pub where the quiet man was roused to boiling anger, standing shoulder to shoulder with Cole, fighting off American GIs who had made the mistake of calling the navigator 'a Canadian bum'.

Flight Sergeant Arthur Sharman, twenty-six, a furniture designer, from Streatham, south London, before joining up, was the bomb aimer. Cole described him as 'shit hot' at his job, often recording the best aiming point of the squadron.

Jack Speers, twenty-four, an aircraft fitter, from Barrie, Ontario, and Gordon Walker were great pals, sharing the same reckless high spirits. They developed a taste for British beer and a couple of times finished up cheerfully sozzled in deep Lincolnshire dykes, having gone off the road on their stolen bikes.

Cole remembers going with the crew to a dance one night at Alford village hall when a stationary steamroller was spotted parked at the top of a long incline.

Walker shouted: 'I bet you can't drive that, Jack.'

'Who can't?' replied Speers, gleefully climbing aboard and releasing the brake. The steamroller began rumbling down the hill, gathering speed, with Speers desperately clinging on, crying out with excitement, trying unsuccessfully to steer the steel monster to safety as the others galloped, yelling, in pursuit. The steamroller, out of control, smashed into a wall near the village hall and they scattered as Alford thought a bomb had fallen. Cole says a local newspaper carried a report about the runaway with quotes from the police who had mounted a wide search for the culprits. They were never caught.

Mid-upper gunner Sergeant Ted Norman, only nineteen, spent most of his spare time at home in the nearby market town of Boston.

'As our tour progressed we were very lucky,' says Speers. 'We sustained minor damage and had several landings short of base because of diminishing fuel and bad weather. In training at Market Harborough, Leicestershire, a motor caught fire in our Wellington as we took off. We turned for an emergency landing, came down hard and wrote it off. Luckily, we were unhurt.

'Besides Berchtesgaden, two other trips stand out in my mind. We flew to Munich three times. The first occasion, on our second operation, was on a night with a glittering full silver moon. It was like daylight in the Alps and we flew lower than the peaks to avoid radar.

'Switzerland was a beautiful sight, with no blackout, all lit up. We were briefed to bomb at 5.10am after the moon had disappeared, just before daybreak to give us total darkness. The target was identified by smoke and fires to the south of the town, and by red and green TIs. We bombed from 16,000ft and flew back into the mountains when dawn was breaking. We didn't encounter any problems, but this was a spectacular flight. The glow from the fires could still be seen when we were 100 miles away.

'We had a narrow escape on the night of 21 December 1944 when we attacked Pölitz, near Stettin.'

Flying LM630, their target was a synthetic oil factory.

Speers again: 'We took off at 4.54pm, having been briefed to fly over Denmark and Sweden. Although Sweden, like Switzerland, was neutral there were a lot of German fighters present. Routed directly over Stockholm a heavy flak barrage came up as we approached. As we arrived with the whole stream the flak stopped and when we had cleared the area a huge "V-for-Victory" was blasted up in tracer fire behind us.'

The target was obscured by smoke, but they dropped their bombs at 10.08pm and were turning off the target when the engineer spotted an aircraft heading towards them on a collision course and screamed: 'Dive, Skipper! Dive!'

Everything hit the ceiling and when Speers tried to use the radio they found that the aerial fixed to the mast behind the astrodome to the twin fins on the tail had been ripped off by the other aircraft.

Drawing near to England and told that Strubby was again consumed by fog, they were directed north to land at Lossiemouth. They touched down at 3.17am, another marathon trip.

They attacked Dresden on 13 February 1945 and, homeward bound, could see the leaping fires 150 miles behind. The crews were told they were hitting large concentrations of German troops, but pacifists still rise up in a great swell of anger over fifty years later because of the number of civilians killed. As many as 50,000 are believed to have died during two raids by the RAF and another by American aircraft, dropping a total of over 2,570 tons of bombs.

'For us,' said Cole, 'it was an uneventful trip, just another raid, and we were doing what we had been told to do.'

On 23 March they bombed Wesel to support the Allied troops crossing the Rhine and Field Marshal Montgomery was so pleased by the accuracy of their bombs he wrote a letter of congratulations to 619 Squadron.

Before the war the small town of Berchtesgaden, standing about 1,700ft up in the Bavarian Alps, was popular with tourists. Here mines of rock salt had been worked for 800 years and the townsfolk were known for their skills as toy makers.

To the War Cabinet in London the only tourists likely to be visiting Hitler's mountain retreat, apart from RAF bombers, were Nazis and if any of them perished in this raid it would be a day for rejoicing. Bomber Command sent 359 Lancasters and sixteen Mosquitoes to flatten Hitler's so-called Eagle's Nest and each excited crew, buoyed up by the knowledge of their task, was fervently hoping that he was in residence. In fact Hitler was hiding like a rat in his bunker, deep beneath the Chancellery in Berlin.

A total 857 sorties were made that day, with other aircraft attacking coastal batteries on the Frisian island of Wangerooge and an oil refinery at Tonsberg in southern Norway.

De Marco was at the controls of Lancaster III LM756 F-Freddy which took off at 4.19am. Freddy was their regular aircraft, one they had already flown on operations fourteen times. They were comfortable in it and were always pleased to see it waiting for them at dispersal. Five other Lancasters from 619 Squadron flew to Berchtesgaden. The raid was supported by three groups of American fighters.

Cole says: 'One of the Yanks flew under us early on in the flight, showing off, going from one side to the other. I was glad to see the back of him, although he hung around for a while then disappeared. I didn't see any flak or German fighters on the way. It looked as if it was going to be a milk run. But that soon changed.'

Speers recalls: 'We were among the six wind-finding crews which meant we led the stream, dropped bales of Window to block radar sightings from the ack-ack guns, and broadcast wind direction and velocity back to Bomber Command as we did a run over the target. This information was collated then sent back from Command to the whole stream for bomb sight settings.

'The target was very hard to find in the mountains, and this was made worse by a mist, and snow lying on the ground.'

Eight Oboe Mosquitoes, here to help with the marking, were frustrated by their signals from a ground station being blocked by the mountains, even though they were flying at 39,000ft.

'Our job was to bomb the SS barracks,' says Speers, 'and we had to fly very slowly to spot them as they were long lines of buildings with every other section camouflaged to make it all resemble a small village. Others were to bomb the power station or the Eagle's Nest.

'As we had killed time on the approach to the target the first wave was close behind us and by the time we had done an orbit and come in on our own bombing run they had bombed and gone and we six came low over the target, almost like stragglers. By now, the Window was too low, the flak was heavy and the guns in the mountains had us in a crossfire. We sustained little damage on the bombing run and I heard Art Sharman call: "Spot on, Skipper", after releasing the bombs.

'We held a steady course for the camera run, but were caught in a heavy crossfire and took several hits. Seconds later we were hit from all directions and I ended up under the wireless set. The intercom was u/s and we couldn't communicate with each other.'

Arthur Sharman, the bomb aimer, says: 'I was in the nose lying on my belly having just released the bombs from about 12,000ft. I had watched the bombs fall and was pleased to see one land in the middle of the square and another hit the SS barracks. The photoflash had just gone off when our aircraft was hit. There was a big explosion and the intercom went dead. I couldn't see the pilot, but it was clear we only had a short time to get the hell out of it.'

He did not bother checking with the pilot to see if it was all right to leave. Sharman had done his job, there was no point hanging around. He clipped on his parachute, dragged open the escape hatch and was first out. He landed in the top of a tall fir tree and slid down to the ground, breaking a leg. He recalls the moment:

'I was lying on the ground in agony, with no chance of getting away, when the Germans arrived. They must have seen us coming down. They forced me to walk on my broken leg, kicking me down the mountainside and once, when they levelled their guns at me, I thought I was going to be shot. They took me to the SS barracks which we had just bombed. I didn't receive any treatment to my leg until I was returned to England three weeks later.'

Just before Sharman released the bombs navigator Norman Johnston, unable to suppress his eagerness, asked the pilot if he could come into the astrodome to look outside as he had never before peered down at a target they were attacking. The request could be equated to signing his own death warrant. Johnston stood briefly beside Cole, on the spot usually occupied by the engineer, and gazed down, transfixed by the bombs falling from his aircraft and the explosions far below.

When, seconds later, their Lancaster was riddled by gunfire, shrapnel burst in through the windscreen and struck the wide-eyed navigator. Johnston recoiled and fell, his face a mask of horror and pain, flinging out a despairing hand, grabbing the D-ring of Cole's parachute which lay on the engineer's tip-up seat. The 'chute opened and yards of silk spilled into the cockpit as Johnston lay dying. Cole, his life saved by the insatiable curiosity of his friend, believes Johnston was killed by a sliver of metal ripped off one of the propellors by a bursting shell.

The port inner and starboard inner engines were on fire. Cole feathered them, but the extinguishers didn't work and he heard the skipper yell: 'Get out! get out!'. The aircraft was also on fire at the back and he saw Speers, injured by shrapnel, limping forward silhouetted against a great wall of flame, and he had a moment to think about the scattered silk of his parachute.

The navigator was clearly dead. Even if he had been badly injured there was little anyone could do. Unlike soldiers under fire with a trench to fall into and gather their senses it was now a case of every man for himself to avoid oblivion.

Speers again: 'I was supposed to leave the aircraft by the rear door with the gunners. There was a thin bulkhead door aft of the main spar which I tried to open, but the floor of the bomb bay had been blown up and it would not budge. The main cock which balanced the wing tanks had been cut and the fuel was burning furiously. The gunners could not survive in the inferno that rushed through the rear of the fuselage.

'I headed towards the front of the aircraft and found the body of Norm Johnston. There was no response from Wilf when I hit his knee, which was the drill as you evacuate the aircraft. The front of the cockpit had been blown away, he could not have survived. Part of the instrument panel had gone. Art Sharman had opened the escape hatch and was gone. Freddy was there ready to jump, but his 'chute was in a bit of a pickle after being accidentally pulled.'

Speers clipped the parachute on to the engineer and gave him the thumb's up. Cole carefully drew the silk into a big bundle and sat anxiously with it beside the hatch. Speers gave him a push and was relieved to see the engineer disappear safely into space without the exposed parachute snagging on the hatch.

Cole, whirling helplessly through the sky, passed out for a moment and, coming round, saw their blazing Lancaster blunder into a mountain and explode. It contained the mangled bodies of the pilot, navigator and both gunners. It was a cruelly incongruous sight as Cole drifted down serenely that fresh spring morning, trying, with little success, to accept that the six men whose lives he had shared for several months, and who were all robustly alive fifteen minutes ago, had been suddenly reduced by four. Four good pals he would never see again. Four lives brutally ended. Four futures tossed into a dustbin and four families devastated. So lucky not to be one of them, he was unhappy to be shorn forever of their company. But the warm memories of his lost companions would remain intact for ever.

Three meadows lay far below and luckily he landed unhurt in one of them, otherwise he would have struck the side of a mountain. A second Lancaster was lost on this operation.

Freddy Cole was picked up quickly and taken by truck to the SS barracks in Saltzburg. He says:

'Soon after I arrived American planes came over and bombed Saltzburg and I was taken by two SS guards to an air-raid shelter beneath a castle. They weren't very friendly. I was later moved to a cell in Saltzburg police station which I shared with two French men and two prostitutes. It was not a happy experience.'

Jack Speers dived through the escape hatch and was struck by the awesome silence after his ears had been assailed by four roaring engines for several hours.

'I saw the 'chute above me and thought that at this time the ground looked so far away I decided to have a sleep. As I landed my foot struck a shrub, adding to my severe pain. I remembered that we had been instructed to bomb at 9.00am and a larger stream was due over the target at 9.20. I was in an open field and soon saw people approaching from every direction. There was no way of telling how they would treat me. Then the warning sirens sounded for another wave of bombers and they all ran away to the salt mines, which were used for air-raid shelters. Shrapnel had torn right through the joint of my left leg and left hand and wrist. I couldn't walk and just had to wait.

'I saw the incoming aircraft open their bomb doors and release their bombs. It was very noisy and the ground shook all around me. The all-clear sounded and the Germans again started coming towards me across the field.

'I hadn't known that we'd been provided with fighter cover and suddenly several American Mustangs appeared, firing rockets. The sirens sounded again and I was once more left alone.'

After the last Allied aircraft had disappeared the Germans picked up Speers on a ladder thoughtfully padded with hay and took him to a farmyard.

'I was transferred to a farm cart filled with hay, and an old grey horse was hitched up to it. Then more fighters swooped in shooting the place up with rockets and I was again on my own. I heard water running and saw a pipe going into a trough. My mouth and throat were dry. I crawled off the cart and had a long drink of the best water I had ever tasted. I dunked my head in the water and began thinking more clearly.

'As I was hauled up the mountain more people joined us, including shrieking women who tried to jab me with pitchforks. If it had not been for the soldiers guarding me I think the women would have killed me.

'I was taken to a building where Freddy and Art were being held, but the Germans would not let them see me. Eventually I was moved to the town of Hallein, 12km from Saltzburg. I was put into an old school house with other prisoners, mostly amputees who had been suffering from frostbite. I was kept in a little chamber off a room which contained about sixty other men. I didn't know the nationalities of the other prisoners, but they all had something missing: hands, feet, ears, noses, legs or arms. I was there over two weeks.

'I was put into a body cast as they had no bandages. They used paper which hardened with the plaster. I was soon afraid to move otherwise the fleas would go into a route march up and down my back.

'One fellow in the big room had an accordion and he played *Lily Marlene* and *The Beer Barrel Polka* from morning to night.

'I was interrogated many times by the SS who did not believe we could fly all the way to Berchtesgaden from England. They insisted that we must have taken off from one of the Allied airfields in Italy. By this time my leg was badly infected and I thought I might end up like all those other poor sods.

'When Hallein was attacked by a French tank division they got into Hitler's wine cellar and were soon so drunk the Americans had to drive them out before they could take the town.

'Everyone was running around saying: "Hitler kaput" and the Americans were here, so I hoped the war had ended, but no information came my way. Next day I could hear Americans talking outside under a little window, but none came into the building.

'There was a curfew on and no one would go outside. But I did get one old fellow to find me a piece of paper and a pencil. I wrote a note and put it in a piss bottle the Germans had given me and threw it through a window above my bunk, but still no one came.

'I was found about 5pm next day. They apologised for not finding me earlier and brought me cigarettes, wine and chocolate bars. I was carried down to a nice clean room and after receiving the benefit of a few cans of delousing powder and, more interestingly, some bottles of wine, I had the best sleep I could ever remember.

'I was later taken to a field hospital at Saltzburg, where the present airport stands. After a couple of days I was flown back to England with other injured airmen and spent the next three months at the 17th Canadian General Field Hospital in Woking, Surrey. I arrived home on 29 August 1945 on the hospital ship *Lady Nelson*.'

In December 1945 Arthur Sharman married Nancy Swift, the pretty nineteen-year-old WAAF cook he met when she was working in the airmens' mess at Strubby, a romance he had kept secret from the rest of his crew after meeting her at a dance.

Many years later Jack Speers and his wife, Barbara, flew from Canada to Austria and drove by car to Klagenfurt where his four former crewmates are buried. A parish priest had defied the Germans by giving them Christian burials in Hallein. Their remains were later removed and reburied by the Americans.

Speers says: 'I shall never forget the loss of those boys whom I look back on as brothers. I had a good cry when I saw each of their graves.'

CHAPTER NINETEEN

DUTCH COURAGE

One night in 1940, at the height of the London Blitz, German bombers rumbled over the capital leaving another tumultuous trail of destruction and death. A stick of incendiaries was dropped across west Kensington, where fires began burning fiercely.

One incendiary plunged through the flat roof of a foreign diplomat's four-storey Edwardian residence in Pembroke Gardens. No one was at home, but the family next door had spotted the danger. Bob Haye, a tall thin youth of seventeen, climbed on to the roof with a stirrup pump, put the end of a hose through the hole and, lying on his stomach, directed it at the incendiary's threatening glow. His stepfather, Dr Walter Stein, a lecturer in philosophy, pumped, while Haye's mother, Johanna and his nineteen-year-old stepsister, Clarissa, rushed to and from their upper bathroom, carrying buckets of water. Both houses were saved and young Haye climbed down, flushed with excitement, knowing that lads, not much older than himself, were up there in fighters beating off the German invaders. The following March he began training as an RAF pilot.

Bob Haye had an unusual background for the RAF. Born Jan Bernard Marinus Haye in Java, of Dutch parents, who were divorced in 1929, he went to school at Hilversum, then The Hague, coming to England on holidays after his mother remarried in 1938. From birth his family always called him Bob. His ambition to become a pilot was fuelled by watching aeroplanes taking off and landing at Soesterberg airfield, near his industrialist great-grandfather Jan Blooker's large estate, where he had lived for six months. From 1939 he attended English schools and quite soon felt more British than Dutch.

He was at 11 OTU, Steeple Morden, Cambridgeshire, when he took off on his first sortie. The 1,000-bomber raids were on and to make up the numbers trainee crews were thrown into battle. Haye's aircraft was a clapped-out Wellington I and, not surprisingly, as the Wimpey struggled to gain height over the North Sea, he was forced back to base when both engines overheated, within sight of German searchlights guarding the Dutch coast.

Haye got his wings on 7 December 1941, the day the Japanese attacked Pearl Harbor, drawing the USA into the war. Afterwards, his proud mother took him to see a show starring Frances Day in the West End. It led to one of his more embarrassing moments, as Haye explains:

'Part of the show involved performers coming into the audience and as I was sitting in my sergeant's uniform at the side one of the chorus girls picked me out. I was supposed to carry her on to the stage. Unfortunately, she was so heavy I couldn't lift her.'

Haye flew with 57 Squadron, which was based at Scampton, a comfortable purpose-built peace-time airfield near Lincoln.

A good-looking brown-eyed auburn-haired gangling six-footer Haye was, in the early days, the only Dutchman serving in Bomber Command. Always known as 'Dutchie', he would later become a naturalised Briton. His straight talking occasionally got him into trouble with higher authority, but he was a good pilot, and particularly enjoyed practising takeoffs and landings. At Scampton, he once touched down and lifted off a Lancaster fourteen times during a night flying exercise. Repetition of an important task other skippers hated paid off when, later in the war, he safely brought down a Stirling after the starboard tyre burst on takeoff, earning a green endorsement in his logbook.

They shared the airfield at Scampton with 617 Squadron who put up with considerable teasing in the mess about spending so much time training without going on a single sortie. From March to May 1943, 617 Squadron crews practised low-level flying without knowing that on May 16/17 they would be sent to attack the great German dams.

Haye, then a pilot officer, says: 'There was a lot of camaraderic, friendly rivalry and riotous games in the mess. I remember my old flight commander Dinghy Young having his trousers set on fire. Guy Gibson was cheerfully using a poker to work the trousers into the flames.'

High jinks sometimes led to a bewildering loss of memory. Haye says:

'I remember waking up on two mornings holding my shoes outside one of the former married quarters which was used for WAAFs. I don't know much more about it than that.'

On 8 March 1943 Haye lifted off the grass runway at Scampton in his regular Lancaster I ED306 W-Willie, of 57 Squadron, to attack Nuremburg with 334 other aircraft. They lost their way, arriving ten minutes after the raid had finished. Bombing was widespread, straying outside the city boundaries. Damage to factories and homes was considerable and around 300 people were dead. The full fury of the Germans could be expected to focus venemously upon any British bomber which was foolish enough that night to wander alone above their savaged city.

The solitary aircraft was caught on the bombing run in an awesome cone by two large groups of searchlights. After dropping his bombs Haye escaped by executing an Immelman turn, which was named after a German First World War pilot.

He recalls the gut-churning moment at 12,500ft, on the bombing run, when the Lancaster heaved itself upside-down.

'We were thrown into a loop, half rolled on top of it and turned into the opposite direction from which we were coming. I did the loop by accident, blinded by the searchlights as I saw the speedometer running back. I looked up through the canopy and saw Nuremburg burning, which was a little unnerving. The crew were thrown about, the flight engineer's seat collapsed and the portable Elsen toilet turned over. Upright, we dropped the bombs and got the hell out of it. The rudder was damaged, the aircraft shuddering and we were relieved to get back for a priority landing at Scampton.'

The rudder was replaced, but ED306 never performed satisfactorily after that night and Haye's polite request for another aircraft was abruptly rejected by his squadron commander, Wing Commander 'Hoppy' Hopcroft.

Haye was in the cockpit of W-Willy in a stationary queue of Lancasters on the perimeter track on the night of 15 March, waiting for the order to take off, when a warning of thick fog rolling over Lincolnshire by morning came through and the operation was cancelled. Crews disembarked and made urgent tracks for their messes, leaving the Lancasters, bombed up, until morning when, indeed, Scampton was fog bound. Ground crews were unloading the bombs when a corporal from the photographic section removed the photo flare from ED306 – and dropped it.

The flare burst into flames and W-Willy exploded, hurling blazing incendiaries on to the two aircraft next to it which also blew up. Some courageous pilots went out and tried to taxi some of the threatened aircraft away, but the inferno spread to another three Lancasters.

Amazingly, only one man was injured after falling from a fire engine, but 57 Squadron, with six bombers destroyed, without a German in sight, was declared non-operational.

Haye says: 'We were re-equipped with Lancaster IIIs, but for some time the story went around that I had taken drastic measures to get rid of a Lancaster I didn't want.'

Haye was given ED667, retaining the call sign W-Willy, and was at its controls on 13 May when he took off shortly before dusk in a force of 156 Lancasters and twelve Halifaxes to attack the Skoda armaments factory of Pilsen in Czechoslovakia.

At twenty-four, Flight Sergeant J. A. Redgrave, the navigator, from Enfield, Middlesex, was the oldest member of Haye's crew. Fair haired, with a small moustache, he was quiet and thoughtful.

Sergeant Stan Allison, the Canadian wireless operator was about nineteen, but looked younger. The bomb aimer, Sergeant C. F. Saville, whose home was in Kentish Town, north London, was regarded as the crew's sceptic.

Sergeant Roy Betteridge, of Gosport, Hampshire, taller than his skipper and as thin, was flight engineer. Sergeant F. L. R. Gilliver, of Harrow, Middlesex, the mid-upper gunner, had a shock of dark hair and Haye remembers his big ears. The rear gunner, Sergeant Curly Williams, rarely seen with a serious face, was a bit of a joker.

It was dark when they crossed the Dutch coast. As usual, Haye was weaving.

He says: 'When I joined 57 Squadron, which was then based at Methwold, Suffolk, we flew Wellington IIIs and I was second pilot to Sergeant Ronnie Croston when we attacked Frankfurt. I learned a great deal from him because this was my first real operation over enemy territory. He weaved all the time, from left to right and back again. He told me that if an enemy fighter sees you weaving he thinks you've spotted him. From that night onwards I always weaved.'

They were attacked by a German fighter over the Zuider Zee, but Haye took evasive action and slipped away. In moonlight, approaching the German border, the navigator asked his skipper if he would fly straight and level so he could check the compasses. Reluctantly, Haye did so at around 19,000ft, but on this, his twenty-third operation, he felt vulnerable, stripped of the one trick which he was convinced had helped keep them alive by fooling the German pilots. Redgrave was still busy when a Messerschmitt Bf-110 attacked unseen from the rear, guns and cannons blazing, ripping through the Lancaster's unprotected belly from tail to nose. Haye instinctively turned into a dive to port.

He says: 'While I was diving my rudder went, so all I could do was use the ailerons to turn slowly round 180 degrees. We were beginning to burn, I opened the bomb doors and asked Saville to jettison everything, which he did. I closed the doors and kept slowly turning as we were drifting down.

'I guessed the worst damage had been done near the tail unit because of the damage to the rudder and particularly that I had to use my big trimmer to help keep the stick right back. Almost from the moment we were hit I knew we were badly on fire, and would go down.

'I struggled with the controls, putting my feet against the dashboard and pulling back on the stick because I had no rudder. There was tremendous pressure on the control column which wanted to go forward all the time. Immediately after I told the crew to abandon the aircraft the intercom went dead. My flight engineer straightaway brought my parachute and put it on my lap. He, or it may have been the navigator, or both, were trying to shout something in my ear, but I couldn't understand what was being said.'

Haye also recalls the blurred figure of Gilliver, standing nearby, and he noticed the mid-upper gunner was not wearing a parachute and hoped it had not been lost in the confusion.

Haye again: 'I shouted to anyone who could hear me: "For God's sake get out! Get out!" I held her as long as I could and managed to keep her up otherwise she would have gone straight down. Then suddenly I felt I had no aircraft, no controls, they were not responding. I couldn't hold her, she just seemed to snap. I was now probably down to 10,000ft. The aeroplane was going down, turning slowly. Nobody else was in the cockpit, although I didn't see them all go, I was too busy.'

The Bf-110, which was fitted with Schräge Musik cannons, only made the one attack on Haye's Lancaster. The German pilot, Hauptmann Herbert

Lütje was a man in a hurry. Based with 8 Nachtjagdgeschwader at Twenthe, Lütje shot down six of the nine RAF bombers lost that night.

Alone in the cockpit of a burning falling aeroplane, an eerie experience, Haye clipped the parachute on to his harness which he found 'bloody difficult'. Knowing he had to get out quickly to avoid ending up as a puddle on the ground he scrambled through the dark to the escape hatch in the nose and jumped out head first. It was midnight. He recalls the moment:

'As I came out something hit me under the jaw and I somersaulted. But I remained conscious and thought: "Don't pull the 'chute for a while, get clear of the aircraft first." I saw the Lancaster as a fireball plunging past me and watched it burning on the ground as I came down.

'It was so peaceful in the sky and I was unaware of any other aeroplanes, but I was terribly worried about my gunners. Had they got out? I was most anxious about Gilliver. Why was he standing beside me in the cockpit? Did he have time to collect his parachute and get to the rear escape hatch? It occurred to me that his 'chute might have been burned. You begin to ask why these things would happen. I felt that had I known, would I have gone out with him clinging on to my parachute? If I had I would probably have lost him to the jerk of the canopy opening. I just thought I could have done it had I known. Would I have done it? I wondered.'

Haye landed south-east of Albergen near a fence in a cornfield a few yards from the Zonderman family's farmhouse. At the time the pilot believed he might have dropped into Germany and hid his parachute, mae west and flying clothes in a field. He emerged from the field in the civilian white shirt which he always wore on ops, and cautiously approached the house.

Haye again: 'I heard whispering inside the house, I was that close, but I couldn't make out the language. I did not recognise the dialect and didn't think it was Dutch, so I started walking. I couldn't find my compass until later that morning so I walked west by the Pole Star. I saw in the distance the glow of the burning Lancaster and gave it a wide berth because the Germans were probably already there.'

Redgrave came down north of Albergen and began walking towards the wrecked aircraft, hoping he might find his friends. Nobody was there. He hid in a wood but next day was caught by the Germans who showed him the crumpled Lancaster before taking him away.

Saville evaded the Germans for some time until they pounced in Paris. Allison came down in a tree between the towns of Baasdan and De Haar. He blundered into a poacher, Gerard van Derwal, who paused in his nightly hunt for snared rabbits to show him a cosy haystack inside a shed. Allison settled wearily on the hay which belonged to the Wennegr family who looked after the wireless operator for three days before passing him on to Resistance worker Bernard Evers from the little village of Hezinge. Allison was later captured by the Germans.

Betteridge found a haystack but next morning told the farmer he should warn the police so he could surrender. The engineer was arrested by Wachmeester Loohuis and taken to the police station at Borne.

Their aeroplane had smashed into three pieces. The rear turret was found some distance from the rest of the Lancaster in the Almelo-Noordhom canal, with the lifeless body of Curly Williams inside it. Haye believes the gunner was killed by the first shots from the Bf-110. Another part of the tail came down south of Albergen.

The main body of the aircraft, its engines still bellowing, struck the ground, careered across a field and crunched into a wall behind the Leemhuis farmhouse. Ruptured fuel tanks exploded and sent a fireball hurtling with a loud roar high into the air. The farmer and his family were badly shaken but unhurt. When the fire was out Gilliver's body was found in the twisted wreckage.

After nearly sixty years Haye still wonders what prevented his mid-upper gunner from escaping. Where could he have been when the pilot baled out? Is it conceivable that Gilliver's parachute had been lost during the corkscrew and he was rooting around for it in blind terror through the long fuselage? Did he become trapped by the spreading flames?

Forty-one years after being shot down Bob Haye was invited back to the site where the main wreckage of the Lancaster crashed. When he and some journalists reached the spot he scuffed around in the ground with his shoes and, to his amazement, found a few pieces of perspex which had survived from the burned-out bomber. When he looks at them today he is still astonished and moved that he has such small but tangible reminders of that terrible night in 1943.

Weary and hungry after walking for hours on paths and through cultivated fields, Haye found another farmhouse, but no one answered his hopeful knock. Soon afterwards he found a haystack, dug himself in and tried to rest.

When he later approached the farmworkers they were frightened and he continued walking, trying to put as much distance between himself and the place where he had landed to avoid the net put out by the Germans.

He says: 'Later that morning I came to a river with a ferry across it. I waited until the ferryman was alone then told him I was an RAF pilot and he took me across for nothing.

'While walking along a country lane a young boy came up on a bike and told me to follow him. He took me to a farm where they gave me food, a pair of trousers and a bicycle. I cycled for the rest of the day – avoiding the town of Almelo – and the next two days, probably covering 100 miles. I asked somebody the way, but my Dutch had an English accent, they didn't trust me and sent me in the wrong direction. I cycled through two groups of marching German soldiers on a main road. It was crazy, but they didn't take any notice of me.

'After several days I got near Amsterdam where I abandoned the bicycle and went for a drink in Warmoes Straat, the red light district. A woman at a bar told me to get away because people there were not friendly towards the British. I left straightaway, saw a German vehicle stop outside the bar and went into a cinema to calm down.

'At the railway station I bought a ticket for The Hague, because I had once lived there, but got on the wrong train, ending up at Zandvoort. I got another train to The Hague and as I came out of the station I saw someone I knew, Karel Eckhart, one of my young teachers at school, not much older than myself.

'I walked up beside him and said: "Hello, Karel."'

'He looked at me in astonishment and said: "Good God, Bob! You're supposed to be in England".'

Eckhart took Haye home and through a contact got in touch with Tonny Schrader who, at only twenty-six, was Holland's Deputy Minister of Food. Schrader told the pilot he would try to get him back to England. He controlled the boats which were involved in the distribution of food throughout Holland. He was also in the Resistance.

Haye moved in with Schrader where he met another evader, Alfred Hagan, a bomb aimer who had been shot down in a Halifax on his first sortie. One day the airmen were playing cards with two Dutchmen at Schrader's when the young woman from the house next door came in, carrying food for them. The beautiful petite twenty-two-year-old Elly De Jong was a courier for Schrader's Underground organisation and involved in espionage with another group, carrying pistols in her satchel when she went to play in hockey matches. A Holland 'B' hockey international, she spoke English and took escaping RAF aircrews by train to the south of Holland, passing them on to the next link in the Resistance chain. The work was dangerous and De Jong risked execution if she was caught.

Haye recalls the following days which might almost have been taken from the pages of a wartime novel written by Nevil Shute.

'I learned afterwards that Elly went home and told her mother that she had just met the man she was going to marry. We got to know each other, went for walks, visited the swimming pool, fell in love and became engaged. Elly, who was training to be a physiotherapist, promised she would not continue with her Resistance work and agreed to meet me as soon as possible after the war.'

The young couple had an emotional parting on the night of 26 July when a truck drew up outside Schrader's house and collected Haye, Hagan, and eight Dutchmen who were keen to join the Dutch forces in England. The truck drove to the Biesbos, near the river port of Dordrecht, which stands on an island in the Maas, where a twenty-five-foot open boat was waiting. They had supplies of food and water and expected to get across the North Sea within thirty-six hours. Everyone was excited, but apprehensive. The Germans constantly patrolled the Dutch coast and anyone found fleeing to England was not treated gently.

The captain of the boat, Dolph Mantel, started the inboard engine and slowly steered the boat through Hollandsch Diep, a wide passage between the islands towards the open sea. Once a searchlight, playing chillingly over the sea, sent them turning abruptly to hide behind one of innumerable sandbanks.

Next morning they awoke to find themselves drifting off the Dutch coast.

The inboard engine had failed and when they tried to start the outboard motor it was dead. No amount of tweaking and cursing by Mantel brought either back to life and they picked up the boat's four oars.

At this point they voted on whether they should turn back or continue. Hagan was among those who wanted to return to Holland, but Haye was one of the men who voted six to four to carry on. They immediately began rationing their modest supplies and water.

Haye remembers how difficult it was to make progress in a boat which was low in the water, not built for speed:

'We had four rowing, four baling or resting, and two resting. We rowed all day. The sea was calm, flat as a table top and, with the sun beating down, it was hot. We once saw something yellow which we turned off course to get to. We thought it might have been a ditched aircrew's dinghy, but it was a dead dolphin, upside-down.

'When we could no longer see Holland we took turns swimming around the boat to keep cool. It was scorching hot and some of us began peeling. It was a very queer feeling to swim and not see land round you.

'On the third night the weather began to deteriorate. It was not rough because we wouldn't have survived, but it was no longer like the previous days. That night was so cold we almost gave up, but we were still there in the morning.'

Time seemed stuck in a deep watery rut as the day splish-splashed by. Haye does not recall seeing any aircraft or boats as they dragged on the oars, wondering how far they were from England. Spirits were low and cheerful chatter had long since died, although the absence of life jackets was a mild talking point. Those who had wanted to turn back grumbled, criticising those who had voted to keep going. Leaking energy, they did not expect to survive much longer as the cold ate into their bones and the blisters on their hands began to scream. What at first seemed like a great adventure had turned into an appalling nightmare. That night, dispirited, they stopped rowing. They had not entirely given up, but hope had become a little blurred.

Next morning they were rescued. All gripes and groans were forgotten as they spotted a convoy of steaming ships. They shouted, waved shirts and heaved like demons on the oars as ships drifted past, apparently ignoring them. The last ship in the line, HMS *Garth*, a destroyer, hove to and grinning sailors hung over the side yelling encouragement. They were hauled aboard, exhausted but elated, then watched the seamen put ropes round their boat to bring it on deck. Their relief briefly died as the boat which had carried them from Holland suddenly broke in half and floated away. Taken quietly to the wardroom for hot drinks, they marvelled that the flimsy waterlogged craft had not tossed them into a watery grave in an empty sea.

They disembarked at Sheerness. Back in England after eighty days Haye rang his mother. Until that moment she had not known he was still alive. Haye and Hagan, separated from the others, were interrogated at the Air Ministry where the pilot revealed to a horrified Army officer, Captain Liddle, that his RAF-issue rubber water bottle, which he had abandoned in

Holland, had been stamped with the words 'Made in England'. Liddle assured him the bottles would be replaced.

Hagan received an immediate DFC, returned to ops and was killed.

The Air Ministry sent Haye on a lecture tour in which he shared his experiences with airmen who applauded his happy ending. He did 100 lectures in sixty days at airfields all round the country.

After a spell as a test pilot at Farnborough and instructing at Swinderby, Haye returned to operational duty to start a second tour with 83 Pathfinders Squadron, which was based at Coningsby.

Elly De Jong was too deeply involved with the Dutch Resistance groups to keep her promise to Bob Haye and, with her mother, Adrie, was sheltering a Jew at their home when they were betrayed to the Gestapo towards the end of 1943 and sent for trial. Adrie's death sentence was commuted to a life sentence. Elly was sentenced to death on four counts for helping Allied airmen, espionage, carrying arms and hiding the Jew.

Taken to Ravensbrück she was given thin clothing, on the back of which was stamped 'NN', Nacht und Nebel, meaning Night and Fog, the dreaded symbol worn by everyone awaiting execution. She was interrogated, kept in solitary confinement for several months, then forced to clean the gas chambers after they had been used.

Later, seriously ill with typhus, this physically frail, but unbroken young woman was helped and shielded by her fellow prisoners who struggled from their unheated accommodation hut on to the parade ground for the daily roll call at 6am, often without shoes, even in the frozen depths of winter.

Many people who worked in Elly's Resistance groups were liquidated by the Germans. She believes she only escaped the gas chamber because her interrogators always thought they might extract more useful information than the little they had so far forced out of her. When released from the concentration camp she weighed under six stone.

Adrie recovered from her ordeal and lived to be ninety-one. Holland decorated Bob Haye with a Distinguished Flying Cross. He and Elly were married in England on 28 November 1945. They have two daughters.

CHAPTER TWENTY

THE SURVIVOR

Flying Officer Duncan Moodie was at the controls of Lancaster I W4268 Q-Queenie as she ploughed belligerently through the night sky over Germany on 27 March 1943. From 44 (Rhodesia) Squadron, based at Waddington, Lincolnshire, Queenie was among 396 bomber crews who had been briefed to attack Berlin.

An earnest slightly-built young man of twenty-seven, Moodie had been born in Hong Kong. Returning with his parents to a new home in Edinburgh he contrived to stop off in North America to sign up in the Royal Canadian Air Force.

Known on the squadron as a pilot who did everything by the book, he was very thorough on safety and security, not much of a drinker, not someone to take chances or step out of line. But at 20,000ft all was not well aboard Q-Queenie. One by one the seven men aboard slumped unconscious in their positions until the bomber, with no firm hand on the controls, slipped like a monstrous braying ghost down through the rumbling layers of Lancasters, Halifaxes and Stirlings. If the crews of other aircraft saw her slipping eerily out of the bomber stream there was nothing they could do, except keep their distance.

At around 10,000ft Moodie stirred uneasily in his seat, opened his eyes and immediately realised what had happened, glancing at his altimeter as he grabbed the controls. He anxiously called up his crew and slowly, one by one, they responded.

In the nose, bomb aimer Norman Clausen was flopped out, his nose pressed uncomfortably against the floor, just behind the bomb sight. He recalls:

'I came to with the pilot's voice in my ears calling everybody up at once. There was quite a bit of panic for, at first, we didn't realise there was an oxygen problem. We didn't need oxygen below 10,000ft but had no intention of bombing Berlin that low so we jettisoned the bombs, aborting the trip. At Waddington they found a fractured oxygen pipe.

Clausen, tall, slim and blond, was born in Newcastle upon Tyne. He had an English mother, Evelyn, and a Danish father, Einar, who came from a fishing family in Svenborg. Einar's parents, members of the Resistance, were never seen again after being picked up by the Gestapo.

By the outbreak of war the family had moved to Dyce, near Aberdeen, where Clausen became an apprentice carpenter and joiner. His war nearly ended abruptly on the troop ship, *Otranto*, which was battered by ferocious Atlantic gales in January 1942. He and his companions, on their way to be trained as observers in South Africa, spent much of the turbulent voyage, shepherded by destroyers in a convoy to Durban, vomiting below or over the side where they twice saw German torpedoes streaking past within a few feet of their ship.

Moodie's wireless operator was Flight Sergeant Tom 'Geordie' Stamp, small, shy and quiet, who came from a small village near Newcastle upon Tyne.

The navigator, Flight Sergeant Jimmy Bundle, from Portsmouth, who had just left university, was very bright, but thoughtlessly scruffy, with an untidy mop of dark hair.

Flight Sergeant Len Drummond came from Burton-on-Trent, where his parents ran a pub. The mid-upper gunner was engaged to be married.

The motto of Flight Sergeant Arthur Hughes, the rear gunner, was 'love 'em and leave 'em' in his cheerful pursuit of young women. At nineteen he was the baby of the crew. The oldest, at thirty-one, was the flight engineer, Sergeant Les Melbourne.

The squadron was moved on 31 May 1943 to Dunholme Lodge, north of Lincoln, so concrete runways could be laid at Waddington.

The fate of Moodie and his crew was decided, in a convoluted way, when they were selected to be among sixty Lancasters to attack the small Zeppelin factory, now making Würzburg radar sets, in Friedrichshafen, deep into southern Germany, on 20 June 1943.

Clausen says: 'We were to try out a new system of a timed run across Lake Constance on a course to get us over the target. We lost our week's aircrew leave by spending ten days training on the coast near Mablethorpe and down the Wash, doing a lot of timed runs from various points. During this period we were confined to camp and I had special permission to marry my fiancée, Joan Hepworth, at Lincoln register office two days before the raid. Len Drummond was my best man, but the others were not allowed to be there.

'It was a long trip to Friedrichshafen because, instead of flying back over France in daylight, we had to go on to land at an American base in North Africa.

'We flew over Switzerland, bombed the target from 10,000ft then went across Italy and landed at Maison Blanc, Algiers, after a trip lasting ten hours.

'This was the first time we'd had a meal with our pilot. American officers and men ate and slept together. We were allocated a tent as a crew to sleep in. We had our tropical kit which did not display any ranks, but this didn't bother Duncan. He took us for a meal in Maison Blanc, but afterwards four of the lads went to look round Algiers to see if they could get their legs over.

'Geordie Stamp and Les Melbourne returned later, having lost Jimmy Bundle and Arthur Hughes. All of us, except Duncan, went out in a search party. Drawn to pathetic moans coming from a ditch we found them, so drunk they couldn't climb out. We carried them back to camp. We were all young and mad in those days. Life was hectic, men were being routinely killed, we needed to have some fun.

'Four days later we flew along the coast to RAF Blida. From there the other Lancasters flew back to England, bombing La Spezia, Italy, on the way, but we had an engine problem. We'd been going up on a flying test when the engine failed at 70mph on the sand runway and we went screaming round the airfield without taking off. It was a bit dicey and we might easily have turned over. On 26 June, after repairs, we took 2hr 30min to fly to Gibraltar, taking off later that day for another 8hr 40min trip home.

'After arriving at Dunholme Lodge, at around 7am, our squadron commander, Wing Commander John Nettleton, told us we were on operations again that night.

'Our skipper said: "No we're not. We're due for the leave we lost a fortnight ago."

'Nettleton replied, somewhat huffily: "In that case, you're posted. When you return off your week's leave you're going to Pathfinders."

'It's true they were short of Pathfinder crews at this time, but we hadn't volunteered to join them, we'd been press-ganged. We'd done eighteen operations with 44 Squadron. Now we were off to 97 Squadron, which was based at Bourn, Cambridgeshire.'

Nettleton had been awarded the Victoria Cross for his leadership of the raid against Augsburg on 17 April 1942, after returning in a badly damaged bomber. The pilot's Lancaster was shot down over the Channel after an attack on Turin on 13 July 1943. His body was never found.

Clausen again: 'All the operations were difficult. Some raids on Berlin were very bad because you flew through a terrifying corridor of flares that German fighters dropped from above. Usually, if you were picked up by a fighter in those conditions, you'd had it. The skipper always lowered his seat on the bomb aiming run so he could only see his instruments and was not distracted from what happened outside.

'For the first five trips on a Pathfinders' squadron you supported the markers. After four ops against Hamburg and one to Essen we became markers on the sortie to Nuremburg on 10 August 1943. We were backers-up, or recenterers of the original target indicator flares which had been dropped. Each flare only lasted three minutes so they were being dropped the whole time for the Main Force to bomb on.'

By now Norman Clausen had installed his wife, Joan, in a room at the Red Fox Inn on the Old North Road, three miles from the airfield. There were no ops on 17 October and the young couple slept at the pub, imagining how much more comfortable they would be at the end of the war. Early next morning he climbed on his bike, pedalled to the airfield and joined the crew on a flying test. That night they were briefed to attack Hanover.

'On a Pathfinder squadron you did forty-five operations as a double tour,' says Clausen. 'This was my fortieth, but as Len Drummond had missed four ops through illness we'd agreed to do extra trips so he could complete his tour with us instead of a strange crew. This was his first op back.'

It was still light when they took off from Bourn in Lancaster III JB220, carrying a 4,000lb Cookie, six 1,000lb bombs and five 250lb target indicators. They were part of a force of 360 Lancasters, eighteen of which would not return.

It was the first night that Clausen had sat all the way from England to near the target working the H2S set beside the navigator, identifying towns, keeping a check on their position.

'We came in towards Hanover from the north-east,' says Clausen. 'About fifteen minutes before the target we were on track and on time. I closed down the H2S, went to the front and the flight engineer had to move out of the way when I went down two steps through the hole in the metal floor to get to my position in the nose. I checked that all the bombs were on and everything was working.

'That night we were scheduled to be the first marker crew arriving over the target after the visual markers. We had to drop our greens on the centre of all the markers.'

The bombing run was going smoothly over cloud at about 21,000ft until the rear gunner said, cautiously: 'Skipper, can you do a bit of weaving? I think I've seen something.'

Moodie agreed, reluctantly, to a few seconds of gentle weaving, as they were nearing the target, to allow Arthur Hughes to peer beneath the Lancaster.

'Just as we levelled out there was a tremendous bang and the nose of the aircraft dropped straight down,' says Clausen. 'I was flung six feet to the back of my compartment where I hit the first step up into the fuselage. As I fell I looked up the steps and saw fire. The engineer had disappeared and the pilot's position was hidden from me, but I saw my parachute hanging on the starboard side. I seized it and passed out.

'When I came to I realised I was still alive, in the sky and dropping like a stone. There was a fire below, an aircraft burning. I grabbed for my parachute which was hanging above me from only one harness cord, pulled the D-ring, twisted once, then hit the ground, hurting my left ankle. I believe I was thrown out of the aircraft when it blew up at around 21,000ft. There hadn't been time to open the escape hatch. I had, with amazing luck, managed to clip one parachute cord to my harness before I blacked out, regaining consciousness no more than 300ft from the ground.'

Clausen landed in a field a mile from his burning Lancaster, about five miles from Belsen concentration camp. Another Lancaster, reduced to a blazing torso with its wings, nose and tail savagely ripped off, crashed near Clausen's aircraft. The bomb aimer's first thought was to get right away from the two burning wrecks.

He would not discover the truth about that grim night until after the war. The two Lancasters, one piloted by Duncan Moodie, the other, JB279, with Pilot Officer Len Hinton, an Australian, of 103 Squadron, from Elsham Wolds, at the controls, had collided above the countryside outside Hanover.

As Clausen was catapulted safely into the cold dark sky the tangled mass of the two bombers fell to earth. Of the other thirteen men aboard the aeroplanes, some were probably killed instantly by the massive impact of the collision. Others struggling to find their parachutes were held in the grip of the powerful G-force, unable to move, and waited to die. Some, in Hinton's aircraft, succeeded in baling out, although only Clausen from both bombers would live to tell the tale in England.

Three men from Hinton's aircraft baled out safely. The fate of two was mercilessly cruel, while the third suffered a miserable lingering death.

'Mr Stott, a wealthy builder, from Leeds, visited me after the war in Scarborough, where I was finishing my apprenticeship,' says Clausen. 'His only son, Tom, had been the wireless operator on Len Hinton's Lancaster. He asked if I knew anything about his son as he was one of three men who were not accounted for. He said Tom had the reputation of being a bit of a hot head and he was worried about what had happened to him. I said I couldn't help, except that I'd heard some shots after I'd hobbled about two miles through fields.

'The builder paid some people in Germany to investigate what had actually happened. They told him his son had been taken in by a young woman on the night of the collision after he'd baled out. He left her next day and joined some Poles who were on a prison working party. They gave him food and for some reason he followed them back into their camp where he helped organise an escape. But the Germans had been tipped off and were waiting when they got through the wire. He was beaten up and taken to hospital. He escaped from the hospital but the trail went cold until his father met two nurses who had met Tom on the Russian side, dying from tuberculosis. Mr Stott devoted his life to trying to find out what had happened to his son, but he never heard any more about him. No one even knew where the lad had been buried.'

The builder's inquiry agents also learned that Hinton's navigator and flight engineer, both sergeants, Tom Davies and Charlie Leach, baled out but were caught by Germans, shot dead and their bodies flung into one of the fiercely-burning wrecks.

These were the shots which Clausen had probably heard from a nearby lane as he climbed, shivering, into the top of a corn stack which stood invitingly in the middle of a turnip field. Clausen will never forget how close he came to joining the two dead airmen on their funeral pyre. A farmer and his daughter had been on the other side of a hedge, watching him drop out of the overcast sky. Another German in a signal box saw Clausen crossing railway lines. The farmer and the railway worker knew they should contact the authorities, but kept quiet. They did not want to be involved. And so, Clausen lived.

Len Hinton died with his bomb aimer, Ken Offer, and gunners Tom Bell and Vic Hawkins, all sergeants. Clausen's six crewmates were buried at Becklingen war cemetery, Soltau, together with Hinton and the three other men whose bodies were found.

Clausen had lost his flying boots when the Lancaster exploded, and his clothes were badly ripped. He had no food, drink, maps, or escape kit. He remained in the corn stack all that night and the following day. He heard traffic moving on the lane but no one came near.

When darkness fell he peered out, identified the North Star and started heading west. It was hard and painful walking across fields in stockinged feet. He thought of his wife in Cambridgeshire who would now be frantic with worry, and of his crewmates with whom he had shared so many hair-raising adventures. What had happened to them? As he walked through the long night frost sparkled in the moonlight and, almost more than anything, he wished for a pair of comfortable boots.

'I walked quietly through a hamlet with six or seven houses, resting up again next day in a wood. On the second morning, about 4am, I was going down a path at the side of a wood when I heard a horse and cart approaching. I scrambled over a hedge and ran down a valley. At the bottom there was a stream and high bank on the other side. I tried to jump the stream but rebounded off a barbed-wire fence and fell on my back into the water.

'When it was beginning to get light I found a clump of rhododendron bushes. I climbed inside them, sopping wet, wrung out my clothes and hung them on bushes to dry in the weak sun. That afternoon children were playing outside my hiding place, so I was either at the bottom of somebody's garden or near a school. No one saw me.

'My diet on the run didn't vary. I found turnips in fields, washed them in streams and ate them with corn from stacks I hid in.

'Early one morning I was walking along a track when I saw a horse and cart coming down from a farm at the top of a hill. There was a dog, barking. Concrete drainage pipes, about eighteen inches wide, and six feet long were stacked higgledy-piggledy at the side of the track. I crawled into one of the pipes and lay there, heart pounding. The cart rattled past and the dog began barking furiously at one end. I thought that was it, but the farmer, who must have seen me, just carried on. The dog left eventually and I stayed in the pipe for the rest of the day.'

Clausen spent one day buried in a hedge after almost walking into a sentry guarding a bridge over a river. Next night he crept away, walked several miles and found the river again. A few rowing boats were pulled up on some shale. Most were chained up and locked, but one was not, although it did not have any oars. He found a piece of loose timber, pushed the boat into the river, paddled across then pushed it back into the water and watched it float away without any feelings of guilt.

Clausen was a fit young man but after ten days existing on turnips and corn, and walking long distances without shoes, he had lost weight and stamina. He found a farmyard with about a dozen corn stacks, climbed up one and burrowed into the top. That night the countryside was covered by a thick fog. He found water, gnawed a turnip and returned to the stack. Without the North Star to guide him he could waste miles going in the wrong direction. He was there three nights.

He was found on 31 October, thirteen days after taking off from Bourn.

'It was about 4pm when I heard a lot of shouting and someone climbing up the stack, poking about with a hay fork. After the farm hand pulled the straw away from my head I climbed down a ladder and was confronted by about two dozen men, women and children. I was filthy, with a ginger beard and straw sticking out all over me, a bit of a sight. No one was holding any weapons, except the farm hand with the fork.

'I asked, with gestures, if I could have some water and something to eat. A woman fetched water, but no food, and twenty minutes later I was still standing there when three soldiers turned up on bicycles. They put me on the carrier of the second bike and I was given a lantern to hold. The soldier at the back and the one at the front were holding rifles. We went off with my lantern shining to the rear. In two miles we reached a little Army detachment and I was later transferred to a town jail near Diepholz, over fifty miles north-west of Hanover, about sixty miles from the Dutch border.

'I was moved by the Luftwaffe to a fighter airfield where I was given a pair of boots that actually fitted. That was a good feeling, although I was still wearing the old socks. Germans came to my cell to stare at me, the terrorflieger.

'I was taken to Frankfurt by a small stocky corporal in his forties, who was going on leave. He was friendly, but couldn't speak English, and carried a gun. The train had a corridor and the people who came into our compartment were muttering and glaring at me when the train went through the Ruhr and we could see the devastation caused by the bombing. The worst problem was in Frankfurt, getting the local train to Oberusel. We were packed tight and angry civilians, especially women, shouted and screamed, trying to hit me and the corporal waved his gun around to keep them off. At the station I ran the gauntlet of a crowd who were all trying to knock lumps off me, and several soldiers helped the corporal get me through the ticket barrier.

'At Dulag Luft I was given two blankets, a bit of soup and a piece of rye bread in my freezing cold cell. The boots were replaced by a pair of shoes, which had been given by the Red Cross.'

Clausen's first impression of Stalag IVb at Muhlberg was overwhelmingly depressing. The POW camp, between Dresden and Leipzig, was crammed with men for whom each day dragged miserably. He says:

'After being deloused I was put into a hut where 400 men lived, 200 on either side in three tiers of bunks. It was terrifying. Completely lost, I was given a bottom bunk. A wash block was in the middle of the hut, I recall four cold taps and one trough for washing. There were dim lights and sealed windows. Some chaps were on the floor brewing tea with what they called blowers, made from powdered milk tins in which they'd fitted little fans. You could boil up a dixie using a couple of little bits of wood and blowing it up like a blacksmith's forge. Black smoke was everywhere. Once a month you were allowed to go back through the de-louser, that meant you took off your clothes. These went through ovens to kill any lice, you had a shower and retrieved your clothes.

'Life was a bit rough. There were two stoves but fuel was short and it was cold at nights. But life was also interesting because, living so close together, you had to get on with everybody. They were not all aircrew. There were ground crews who'd been caught on the Greek islands, SAS, anybody who had a wing of some sort was classified by the Germans as aircrew.

'Prisoners in the Army compound elsewhere went out each day on working parties. They were in transit all the time. Considered dangerous, we were locked up in our compound at night.

'Russian prisoners were badly treated. Many died and their bodies were kept so the survivors could claim their rations. We thought we were badly off but outside our huts were brick-built rubbish dumps where we put our empty cans and potato peelings. The Russians sat in there eating our peelings and licking out our tins. They went to work every morning at the railway station three miles away. The first rank in the column had no legs below the knees. With leather pads over their stumps they set the speed of the Russian column. If they didn't march they were shot.

'When the camp was relieved the Russian prisoners caught the German guards in nearby woods and killed the lot. Then they set off killing the civilians and raping the women.

'One escape tunnel, dug from the outside toilet block, collapsed on the other side of the wire and was filled in with muck from the toilets. No one bothered with that again. The only RAF chap I knew who got out was a little Mosquito navigator. Caught at a local airfield trying to get on a Junkers-88, he celebrated there in the officers' mess where he was treated as a hero. He got boozed up and was sent back to us next day.

'In the next bunk to me was a New Zealand wireless operator who had escaped from a low-flying Douglas Boston bomber which hit some high-tension wires. The pilot and observer were both sliced up.

'Poles from the Warsaw Uprising came through Stalag IVb on their way to concentration camps, and after the Battle of Arnhem survivors arrived, singing, before being dispersed on working parties. We also saw Americans who had been captured in the Ardennes. Many were squashed into our hut. I'd never seen such a lot of demoralised people, worse than the Russians. They'd only been in the front line one night. They were sent to clear up the mess in Dresden after it was flattened by the bombing raids in February 1945.

'The Russians eventually took over the camp, but they couldn't feed us. We were told to help ourselves to whatever we could find outside and treat the Germans as they had treated us.

'One day, four of us, all RAF aircrew, decided to look for food. Most houses were empty, then we found a village where machine guns were going: "Brrrrh! brrrrh! brrrrh!" Russians were running into the front doors of houses and frightened German civilians came tearing out. They were grabbed and locked in the town hall. A Russian officer sent us round the back of a farmhouse where we found one of his soldiers with two great cast-iron cooking pots on fires. He set up a card table and four chairs, sat us down and fed us delicious stew and rice, as machine guns were still rattling around the village.

'We were eventually released from the camp, taken away in an American truck, and I was flown home by the end of May.'

Duncan Moodie never knew that on the day of his last sortie he was promoted to flight lieutenant, nor that he had been awarded a DFC for extricating them from a difficult situation when they were coned and hammered by flak over Hamburg on 27 July 1943. A posthumous DFM went to Jimmy Bundle. Clausen learned at Stalag IVb that he was to receive a DFM, but the former bomb aimer's most treasured possession is his Pathfinder's wings.

Clausen went to Edinburgh in 1945 to meet Elizabeth Moodie, his pilot's mother. She told him that she and her husband, John, had had three sons, but no daughters. A second son had joined the Army, the third had served in the Royal Navy. They were both killed.

Every year late on 18 October Norman Clausen and his second wife, Diane, raise their glasses to drink to the memory of the men who died on that terrible night in 1943.

GLOSSARY

ABC	Airborne cigar, a device for jamming German fighter controllers' transmissions
Appell	Roll call
Coning	A radar-operated master searchlight locks on to a bomber and is joined swiftly by other searchlights which hold the aircraft in a cone of light, exposing it to ack-ack and night fighters
Cookie	4,000lb high explosive bomb
D/R	Dead reckoning navigation
D-ring	Parachute ripcord
Dulag Luft	Interrogation centre at Oberusel, near Frankfurt-am-Main
Elsen	Chemical toilet
FIDO	Fog Investigation and Dispersal Operation (fog dispersal system)
Fishpond	An early-warning radar device
Gardening	Mine laying
Gee	Radio-based navigational aid
Groupie	Group captain
HCU	Heavy conversion unit
H2S	A radar device which could read through thick cloud and give a picture of the terrain below
ITW	Initial training wing
Kapo	Trusty
LACW	Leading aircraftwoman
LMF	Lack of moral fibre
Lord Haw-Haw	William Joyce, British traitor, who made wartime propaganda broadcasts from Germany. He was executed in 1946
Maquis	A member of one of the French underground resistance groups
Nachtjagdgeschwader	Night fighter squadron
Oboe	A precise radio bombing system using transmissions from two ground stations
OTU	Operational training unit

PFF	Pathfinders Force
Pundit	Indentification beacon
QDM	Magnetic course to steer for base, assuming zero wind
R/T	Radio telephone
Second dickey	A pilot going on his first operational flight with an experienced skipper
Schräge Musik	Jazz music – a pair of upward-firing machine guns or cannons mounted behind the cockpit of a German fighter. The RAF did not know of their existence until after the war.
Spare/Odd bods	Men without a regular crew
Sprogs	New recruits or inexperienced airmen
SPs, or Snowdrops	RAF service police
Terrorflieger	Terror flier
TIs	Target indicators
Vegetables	Mines
Wanganui flares	Sky marking by Pathfinders
Wimpy	Wellington
Window	Strips of aluminium foil dropped to confuse German radar
Wingco	Wing commander
Würzburg	German paraboloid radar for directing flak, searchlights and fighters
ZZ landing	Radio-controlled landing

BIBLIOGRAPHY

The Bomber Command War Diaries, an Operational Reference Book 1939-1945, Martin Middlebrook and Chris Everitt (Viking, 1985)
Jane's Fighting Aircraft of World War II (Studio Editions Ltd, 1992)
Combat Aircraft of World War Two, Elke C. Weal, John A. Weal and Richard F. Barker (Arms and Armour Press, 1977)
The Bombers, the Illustrated Story of Offensive Strategy and Tactics in the Twentieth Century, Robin Cross (Grub Street, 1987)
Famous Bombers of the Second World War, William Green (Macdonald, 1959)
Bomber Command, Max Hastings (Michael Joseph, 1979)
Avro Lancaster, The Definitive Record, Harry Holmes (Airlife, 1997)
Lincolnshire Airfields in the Second World War, Patrick Otter (Countryside Books, 1996)
Action Stations 1 Wartime military airfields of East Anglia 1939-1945, Michael J. F. Bowyer (Patrick Stephens Ltd, 1979)
Most Secret War, R. V. Jones (Wordsworth Editions, 1998)
The Night Blitz 1940-1941, John Ray (Arms and Armour, 1996)
The Other Battle, Peter Hinchliffe (Airlife, 1996)
Zij Kwamen Bij Dag En Bij Nacht (They Came By Night And They Came By Day), Martin Klaassen
Named For One Remembered Here, John D. Cox
Flypast magazine and Ken Delve

INDEX